UNIVERSITY OF NORTH CAROLINA AT CHAPEL HILL
DEPARTMENT OF ROMANCE LANGUAGES

NORTH CAROLINA STUDIES
IN THE ROMANCE LANGUAGES AND LITERATURES

Founder: URBAN TIGNER HOLMES
Editor: MARÍA A. SALGADO

Distributed by:

UNIVERSITY OF NORTH CAROLINA PRESS

CHAPEL HILL
North Carolina 27515-2288
U.S.A.

NORTH CAROLINA STUDIES IN THE
ROMANCE LANGUAGES AND LITERATURES
Number 241

THE NOBLE MERCHANT:
PROBLEMS OF GENRE AND LINEAGE
IN *HERVIS DE MES*

THE NOBLE MERCHANT:

PROBLEMS OF GENRE AND LINEAGE IN *HERVIS DE MES*

BY
CATHERINE M. JONES

CHAPEL HILL

NORTH CAROLINA STUDIES IN THE ROMANCE
LANGUAGES AND LITERATURES
U.N.C. DEPARTMENT OF ROMANCE LANGUAGES

1993

Library of Congress Cataloging-in-Publication Data

Jones, Catherine M.
　The noble merchant: problems of genre and lineage in Hervis de Mes / by Catherine M. Jones
　000 p. 00 cm. – (North Carolina studies in the Romance languages and literatures; no. 241)
　Includes bibliographical references and index.
　ISBN 0-8078-9245-9
　1. Hervis de Metz (Chanson de geste). 2. Hervis de Metz (Legendary character) – Romances – History and Criticism. 3. Epic poetry, French – History and criticism. 4. Chansons de geste. – History and criticism. 5. Businessmen in literature. 6. Literary form. I. Title. II. Series.
PQ1485.H33J66　　1993　　　　　　　　　　　　　　　　　　92-80590
841'.1–dc20　　　　　　　　　　　　　　　　　　　　　　　　　　　　CIP

© 1993. Department of Romance Languages. The University of North Carolina at Chapel Hill.

ISBN 0-8078-9245-9

DEPÓSITO LEGAL: V. 2.293 - 1993　　　I.S.B.N. 84-599-3316-4

ARTES GRÁFICAS SOLER, S. A. - LA OLIVERETA, 28 - 46018 VALENCIA - 1993

ACKNOWLEDGEMENTS

It is with sincere appreciation that I acknowledge those who helped bring this study to fruition. The initial research was made possible by the Newberry Library Exchange Fellowship to the Ecole des Chartes and a grant from the University of Wisconsin; a summer research grant from the University of Georgia provided funding for the remainder of the project. I wish to express genuine gratitude to Douglas Kelly, whose exemplary teaching and scholarship provided me with both inspiration and guidance. M. Jacques Monfrin, who first introduced me to the Loherains, also receives the expression of my profound thanks. For their invaluable comments on the early stages of this study, I thank Yvonne Ozzello, Christopher Kleinhenz, Peter Schofer, and Francis Gentry. I am indebted also to William W. Kibler and Norris J. Lacy for their perceptive comments and suggestions. For their unwavering confidence and support, I wish to thank my parents, Ronald and Mary Beth Jones; their contributions to my academic and personal growth are truly incalculable. Finally, I extend my deepest gratitude to my husband, Richard Neupert, whose advice, encouragement, and love were indispensable to the completion of this book.

for Richard and Sophie

TABLE OF CONTENTS

	Page
INTRODUCTION	13
PART ONE: *LA TRESSE*	31
Chapter 1: The Narrative Repertory	33
Chapter 2: Narrative Structure and the Poetics of Lineage	68
PART TWO: *LA CHANSON*	95
Chapter 1: Laisse Structure and Formulaic Style	97
Chapter 2: Narration and Performance	135
CONCLUSION	160
APPENDIX A	162
APPENDIX B	168
APPENDIX C	172
WORKS CONSULTED	174

INTRODUCTION

After long periods of relative neglect, the monumental *geste des Loherains* has begun to regain its place in the corpus of Old French epic production. Recent critical editions, essays, and modern translations attest to a veritable renaissance of the cycle among both scholarly and general audiences.[1] This renewed interest coincides with an important trend in the study of *chansons de geste*: later epic poems, long denounced as degraded forms of eleventh and twelfth-century "masterpieces," have become objects of serious scholarly consideration over the last twenty years. Since the bulk of the Loherain cycle dates from the thirteenth century, this body of texts offers valuable insight into the expansion and diversification of a prominent medieval genre.

Like the celebrated *geste* of Guillaume d'Orange, the *geste des Loherains* formed around a primary, "nuclear" song. *Garin le Loherain* appears to have been composed in the late twelfth century; it

---

[1] Jean-Charles Herbin completed a new edition of *Hervis de Mes*, under the direction of Gabriel Bianciotto, for his *thèse de doctorat* in 1989. The Presses universitaires de Nancy have published three modern French translations to date: Philippe Walter, trans., *Hervis de Metz: Roman du moyen âge* (Nancy: Presses universitaires de Nancy; Metz: Editions serpenoise, 1984); Bernard Guidot, trans., *Garin le Lorrain: Chanson de geste du XIIe siècle* (Nancy: Presses universitaires de Nancy, Editions serpenoise, 1986); Bernard Guidot, trans., *Gerbert: Chanson de geste du XIIIe siècle* (Nancy: Presses universitaires de Nancy, 1988). Recent articles include: Bernard Guidot, "Continuité et rupture: l'univers épique de *Garin le Lorrain* et *Gerbert*," *Olifant* 13 (1988): 123-140 and "La partialité du trouvère est-elle discrètement infléchie dans *Garin le Loherain*?" in *Au carrefour des routes d'Europe: la chanson de geste*, Actes du Xe Congrès International Rencesvals, Vol. 1 (Aix-en-Provence: CUERMA, 1987) 601-27; Catherine M. Jones, "Dispersed Parallelism in *Hervis de Mes*," *Olifant* 13 (1988): 29-40 and "Recasting *Raoul de Cambrai*: The Loherain Version," *Olifant* 14 (1989): 1-18; Philippe Walter, "Géographie et géopolitique dans la légende d'*Hervis de Metz*," *Olifant* 13 (1988): 141-63 and "*Hervis de Metz*: Le griffon et la fée," *Vox romanica* 45 (1986): 157-67.

is this tremendously successful narrative that provided the lineal and thematic superstructure of subsequent branches.² Set in the reign of Pépin le Bref, the story relates the bitter rivalry between two feudal houses: the worthy Loherains, led by Garin and his brother Bégon, engage in perpetual struggle with the treacherous Bordelais, led by Fromont de Lens and Bernart de Naisil. Succeeding branches prolong the conflict, extending the feud to the children of Garin and Bégon (*Gerbert de Mez*) as well as their children's children (*Anseÿs de Mes, La Venjance Fromondin*).³ The conclusion of the last branch assures us that the irreconcilable hatred exceeds the boundaries of its textual record:

> De toz les livres que on vos a chanté
> N'ot mort tant home ne tant estor finé
> Con de Fromont dont je vos ai conté
> Et de Begon et de lor parenté.
> Car la haine dure ancor, par verté,
> Et duera toz jors en ireté.⁴

Indeed, the murderous rivalry, which appears to have no basis in historical fact, attained such proportions that the popular expression "comme les guerres al Loherain Garin" was coined to describe chronic or long-lasting misfortunes.⁵

---

² Josephine E. Vallerie, ed., *Garin le Loheren, according to manuscript A, with Text, Introduction, and Linguistic Study* (Ann Arbor: Edwards Bros., 1947). An earlier, composite edition was published by Paulin Paris: *Li romans de Garin le Loherain, publié pour la première fois et précédé de l'examen du système de M. Fauriel sur les romans carlovingiens*, Romans des douze pairs de France 2 & 3 (Paris: Techener, 1833-35).

³ Pauline Taylor, ed., *Gerbert de Mez: Chanson de geste du XIIe siècle*, Bibliothèque de la Faculté de Philosophie et de Lettres de Namur 11 (Namur, Lille, Louvain: Nauwelaerts, 1952). The final branch survives in two different versions: Herman J. Green, ed., *Anseÿs de Mes According to Ms. N (Bibliothèque de l'Arsenal 3143): Text, published for the first time in its entirety, with an Introduction* (Paris: Les Presses modernes, 1939); Simon R. Mitchneck, ed., *Yon or La Venjance Fromondin: A Thirteenth-Century Chanson de Geste of the Lorraine Cycle* (New York: Publications of the Institute of French Studies, Columbia University, 1935).

⁴ *Anseÿs de Mes* vv. 14, 527-33.

⁵ Anne Iker Gittleman, *Le style épique dans Garin le Loherain*, Publications romanes et françaises 94 (Geneva: Droz, 1967) 17. On the medieval "cult" of Garin, see Léon Germain, "Le culte de Garin le Loherain," *Journal de la société archéologique du Musée Lorrain*, 42-43: 275-78. On the historical dimension of *Garin le Loherain*, see especially Ferdinand Lot, "L'élément historique de *Garin le Loherain*," *Etudes d'histoire du moyen âge dédiées à Gabriel Monod* (Paris: Cerf, 1896) 201-20.

While most of the Loherain continuations focus on the duration of this notorious conflict, one branch effects a return to lineal origins. In accordance with a general process of cyclic formation in the Old French epic, the *geste* also extends by reverse chronology, telling tales of the heroes' forebears in an attempt to render the totality of an illustrious lineage. *Hervis de Mes*, composed in the first half of the thirteenth century, relates the early adventures and exploits of Garin's father, all of which precede the great Loherain-Bordelais feud.[6] In this respect, *Hervis* represents a significant departure from the rest of the cycle. Nevertheless, the protagonist was not unknown to medieval audiences before the appearance of the massive poem devoted to his adolescence and early manhood. Indeed, the first thousand lines of *Garin le Loherain* recount the story of Duke Hervis, right-hand man of Charles Martel in a series of wars against the "Wandres" and other "Saracen" invaders. Although this material may have its roots in a legend originally distinct from Garin's story, it is clear that the later *Hervis de Mes* was conceived as a "spin-off" of *Garin le Loherain*. Projecting the *geste* into an increasingly mythical past, *Hervis* represents "l'oeuvre tardive qui est venue coiffer le cycle pour expliquer l'origine du lignage."[7]

In fact, this belated preamble *re*invents the lineal origins of the Loherains. Unlike the core of the cycle, *Hervis de Mes* depicts the heroic ancestor as a product of mixed lineage.[8] Born of a noble-

---

[6] Edmund Stengel, *Hervis von Metz: Vorgedicht der Lothringer Geste nach allen Handschriften zum erstenmal vollständig herausgegeben*, Gesellschaft für romanische Literatur 1 (Dresden: Niemeyer, 1903). On the dating of *Hervis de Mes*, see Pauline Taylor, Introduction, *Gerbert de Mez* XIII and Philippe Walter, "Le griffon" 158.

[7] Daniel Poirion, Préface, *Hervis de Metz, roman du moyen âge adapté par Philippe Walter* 6. There is some controversy concerning the respective sources of *Hervis de Mes* and the Hervis material in *Garin le Loherain*. Some scholars believe that the first thousand lines of *Garin* represent the incorporation of an originally separate legend. Still others feel that *Hervis de Mes*, too, stems from this older version. The latter view has been successfully refuted by Joël Grisward in "Essai sur *Garin le Loherain*: Structure et sens du prologue," *Romania* 88 (1967): 289-322. See also August Rhode, "Die Beziehungen zwischen des Chansons de geste *Hervis de Mes* und *Garin le Loherain*," *Ausgaben und Abhandlungen* 3 (1881): 134.

[8] It is true that Hervis is once called "Li dux de Mes, fils au villain Hervi" in three manuscripts of *Garin le Loherain*. As August Rhode points out, however, this reading is probably faulty ("Die Beziehungen" 127-28). The error is likely due to the confusion arising from a second Hervis in *Garin le Loherain*, the worthy Hervis le villain. However, a passage from *Gerbert de Mez* is more problematic: when

woman and the rich bourgeois she was obliged to marry, the young Hervis must overcome numerous obstacles before attaining the lofty status he possesses in *Garin le Loherain*. In its portrayal of the hero as a "noble merchant," *Hervis de Mes* participates in an intertextual system that exceeds the limits of the *geste des Loherains* and even of the *chanson de geste*. The interplay of social identities is common to a number of epic and romance figures of the thirteenth century: real or imagined crises of lineage also plague such characters as Vivien, Fergus, and Florent.

Indeed, much to the chagrin of earlier scholars, *Hervis* shares a number of traits with the romances of its day. As a result, the work's modern reputation has suffered from a long-standing critical bias exemplified by the studies of Léon Gautier and W. P. Ker. The latter deplores the "decline" of epic in the thirteenth and fourteenth centuries and attributes this "degradation" to "dilution" or "contamination" by a competing genre.[9] Similarly, Léon Gautier blames in part the regrettable influence of romance for "la médiocrité profonde des poètes du treizième et du quatorzième siècles."[10] References to *Hervis de Mes* manifest the same preconceptions of generic decay: while *Garin le Loherain* is seen as a product of the "genuine" epic tradition, *Hervis* is said to have deformed the elements of *Garin*'s prologue to create an implausible adventure story: "*Hervis de Mez*. . . met en oeuvre quelques éléments trouvés dans le prologue de *Garin*, mais en les noyant dans un flot d'aventures romanesques, sans respect pour leur caractère épique original."[11]

Medieval audiences did not share this bias. On the contrary, *Hervis de Mes* enjoyed considerable favor throughout and beyond the Middle Ages. Philippe Ménard, for example, demonstrates quite convincingly that Villon's *Testament* commemorates two feminine figures in *Hervis*, i.e. the hero's wife and mother:

Fromont asserts that Garin was the son of a bourgeois, Gerbert denies the charge, boasting "Et fu ses pere li riches dus Herviz" (vv. 4864-4881). It is not clear whether the suggestion of mixed lineage reflects an existing tradition or a mere ploy on Fromont's part. For a discussion of this problem, see Gittleman 211-212 n. 47 bis.

[9] W. P. Ker, *Epic and Romance: Essays on Medieval Literature* (1896; New York: Dover Publications, 1957). See especially pp. 51, 287, 312.

[10] Léon Gautier, *Les Epopées françaises: Etudes sur les origines et l'histoire de la littérature nationale*, 3 vols. (Paris: Victor Palmé, 1865-68) I: 442.

[11] Gittleman 14.

> Berte au grant pié, *Bietris, Alis,*
> Haremburgis qui tint le Maine,
> Et Jehanne la bonne Lorraine
> Qu'Englois brulerent a Rouan,
> Mais ou sont les neiges d'antan?[12]

The place of these characters beside the epico-historical celebrity Berte au grand pied (their supposed descendant) suggests that *Hervis de Mes* was widely known and appreciated by Villon and his contemporaries. Above all, however, it is the manuscript tradition that confirms the work's popularity among medieval audiences. Five manuscripts preserve all or part of *Hervis* in its original assonanced form, while a sixteenth-century prose translation of the "histoire de ancyenne rime et chansson de geste" survives in two manuscripts.[13] Philippe de Vigneulles, cloth merchant of Metz and author of the *mise en prose*, seems to have had a particular affinity for the story of Hervis, for he grants it a rather prominent place in his *Chronique de Metz*. The chronicle mentions Garin only in passing; it is Hervis who represents the illustrious ducal lineage, which Philippe traces back to Hector of Troy.[14]

It would seem, then, that modern scholarship has largely misrepresented a text that achieved rather wide success in the Middle Ages. Since the pioneering work of H. R. Jauss, it has become a commonplace to refute the "organic" conception of literary history which portrays the development of genres in terms of growth, flowering, and decay. Moreover, medieval vernacular genres clearly did not develop from a pregiven canon or set of norms, but tested out their possibilities through a process of variation and correction.[15]

---

[12] Philippe Ménard, "'Berte au grant pié, Bietris, Alis' ou la résurgence de la culture épique dans la 'Ballade des dames du temps jadis,'" *Romania* 102 (1981): 114-129. The quotation comes from *The Poems of François Villon*, ed. and trans. Galway Kinnell (Boston: Houghton Mifflin, 1977) vv. 347-52.

[13] See below, "Manuscripts." A prose Latin version was composed by Hugues de Toul: see Auguste Prost, *Etudes sur l'histoire de Metz: Les Légendes* (Metz: 1865) 499-505.

[14] *La Chronique de Philippe de Vigneulles*, ed. Charles Bruneau, vol. 1 (Metz: Société d'histoire et d'archéologie de la Lorraine, 1927) 162.

[15] Hans Robert Jauss, *Toward an Aesthetic of Reception*, trans. Timothy Bahti, Theory and History of Literature 2 (Minneapolis: University of Minnesota Press, 1982) 93-96. See also William Calin, "Textes médiévaux et tradition: la chanson de geste est-elle une épopée?" *Romance Epic: Essays on a Medieval Literary Genre*, ed. Hans-Erich Keller, Studies in Medieval Culture 24 (Kalamazoo: Medieval Institute Publications, 1987) 11-19.

As early as the twelfth century, but particularly in the thirteenth, the *chanson de geste* began to diversify by assimilating plots, characterizations, and narrative strategies which had previously been the domain of romance. Far from corrupting a previously "pure" genre, this readjustment assured the continued success of epic narratives. Accordingly, the Oxford *Roland*, the *Chanson de Guillaume*, and *Garin le Loherain* must not be considered more authentic *chansons de geste* than their successors; in fact, the corpus as a whole suggests that the incorporation of formal and thematic structures typically associated with romance is more characteristic than exceptional.

Such assertions might seem unnecessary in view of the significant body of scholarship refuting normative notions of genre.[16] Nonetheless, a recent book on the epic in Western literature demonstrates that the later *épopée* in general continues to be perceived and described in negative terms. Daniel Madelénat, in his analysis of structural transformations in the epic, persists in referring to the process as "décadence" and "dégénérescence éclectique."[17] Happily, most recent studies of the later *chanson de geste* attempt a more productive evaluation of generic functions. By examining evidence of both continuity and innovation, these studies distinguish the *constitutive* function of a dominant generic system (the *chanson de geste*) from the *dependent* functions of contingent generic structures (romance, hagiography, and folk tales, among others). Not content with a mere list of formal and thematic features, scholars such as Marguerite Rossi explore the aesthetic and ideological implications of different "hybrid" textual organizations.[18] With this kind of analysis, according to Jauss, "the so-called mixing of genres – which in the classical theory was the merely negative side-piece to the 'pure genres' – can be made into a methodologically productive category."[19]

---

[16] See especially Robert Francis Cook, "'Méchants romans' et Epopée française: pour une philologie profonde," *L'Esprit créateur* 23 (1983): 64-74.

[17] Daniel Madelénat, *L'Epopée*, Littératures modernes (Paris: PUF, 1986).

[18] Marguerite Rossi, *Huon de Bordeaux et l'évolution du genre épique au XIIIe siècle*, Nouvelle Bibliothèque du Moyen Age 2 (Paris: Champion, 1975). Other noteworthy studies are Bernard Guidot, *Recherches sur la chanson de geste au XIIIe siècle d'après certaines oeuvres du Cycle de Guillaume d'Orange*, 2 vols. (Aix-en-Provence: Université de Provence, 1986); Jean Subrénat, *Etude sur Gaydon, chanson de geste du 13e siècle* (Aix-en-Provence: Université de Provence, 1974); Ellen Rose Woods, *Aye d'Avignon: A Study of Genre and Society*, Histoire des idées et critique littéraire 172 (Geneva: Droz, 1978).

[19] Jauss 81.

If the Old French epic canon is to be revised in accordance with medieval tastes and standards, a descriptive study of *Hervis de Mes* must replace anachronistic, prescriptive judgments. Modern scholars have so often deprived the work of its generic "identity" that we have lost sight of its place within the medieval poetic tradition. Now, it is undeniable that *Hervis* exhibits a certain duality. Many formal properties anchor the text in the conventions of the *chanson de geste*: its assonanced decasyllabic lines, marked by 4/6 caesurae and grouped into laisses, reproduce the versification that characterizes most early Old French epics. Consistent with epic thematics is the struggle between the hero and Anseÿs of Cologne: like his successors, Hervis engages in feudal warfare to preserve his claim to Metz and Lorraine. At the same time, however, *Hervis de Mes* introduces and magnifies certain innovations found in many post-Oxford *Roland* texts. Modifications are apparent on the levels of form and content: the lyric function of the strophe, for example, is often superseded by lengthy narrative developments, thereby altering the "chant" aspect of the genre. Epic action, in which the hero is typically "a representative of the fate of his community," often gives way to romanesque adventures, i.e. incidents that *happen to* an exemplary hero who reacts to them in a unique way.[20] For this reason, many editors and critics continue to designate the text as a "roman."[21]

One modern alternative to the hallowed epic-romance dichotomy consists in distinguishing a subgroup of *chansons de geste* that display a very pronounced generic "mixture," a mixture made explicit by the use of intermediate terms (all modern) such as "épopée romanesque" or "chanson d'aventures."[22] These labels possess a certain heuristic value insofar as their grammatical signals differen-

---

[20] Jauss 85. It must be emphasized that Jauss's categories are descriptive (not prescriptive), and that they were devised in the context of twelfth-century French epics and romances.

[21] Edmund Stengel, in the Introduction to his edition, presents *Hervis* as "nichts anderes als ein für die Metzer Lokalgeschichte zurechtgemachter Abenteuerroman" (p. V). Joël Grisward refers to the work as a "roman" in his review of *Rückzug in epischer Parade* by Alfred Adler, *Cahiers de civilisation médiévale* 7.4 (1964): 502. In the recent series of Loherain translations, only *Hervis* is designated as a "roman du moyen âge"; both *Garin* and *Gerbert* are classified as "chansons de geste" in their subtitles.

[22] See William W. Kibler, "La 'chanson d'aventures,'" *Essor et fortune de la chanson de geste dans l'Europe et l'Orient latin*, Actes du IXe Congrès de la Société Internationale Rencesvals, vol. 2 (Modena: Mucchi, 1984): 509-15.

tiate the dominant and dependent genres. While some of the earlier distinctions between *chanson de geste* and *roman* became rather blurred during the thirteenth century, their divergent forms of poetic and metatextual discourse indicate that the two text-types were still perceived as discrete entities by medieval poets and audiences. This and other evidence suggests that verse epic and romance continued to fulfill different aesthetic and ideological functions throughout the Middle Ages.[23] It is therefore incumbent upon modern scholarship to recognize the secondary nature of romanesque traits in a genre that actually displays more continuity than has previously been thought.

The present study proceeds, then, from the assumption that *Hervis de Mes* inscribes itself primarily in the *chanson de geste* tradition. A short prologue orients the modern reader to the text's medieval mode of reception by revealing the traces of a performance, of a voice well-trained in the art of public recitation. Mediating between audience and material, the jongleur appeals to his listeners by evoking a *geste* well known to the community:

> Or *entendés* pour diu de maïsté!
> *Bone canchon* plast vos a *escouter?*
> Des *Loherens* vos voromes *chanter.*
> Si con Hervis le gentis et li ber,
> Cis qui fu *peres Garin* le redouté
> Et *le cuen Begue* qui tant ot de bontei.[24]

While one cannot infer from these lines that *Hervis* was the product of a purely oral tradition, the exordium deliberately links the work to an orally-conditioned textual model and an established heroic network. In that it also conforms to prosodic conventions of the Old French epic, *Hervis de Mes* clearly defines its own generic dominant.

Assigning a label does not, of course, account for the intricate blending of generic traits in this text. It is only by confronting

---

[23] The prologue, for example, remained an index of generic differentiation for a long time. See Emmanuèle Baumgartner, "Texte de prologue et statut du texte," *Essor et fortune de la chanson de geste dans l'Europe et l'Orient latin*, Vol. 2 (Modena: Mucchi, 1984) 465-73. Unlike many of the later epic texts examined by Baumgartener, the *Hervis* prologue does not evoke the presence of a "scripteur."

[24] Stengel edition, ms. E (as reconstructed from the variants) vv. 1-6. Subsequent quotations follow this pattern.

Hervis de Mes with its epic and romance antecedents and contemporaries that we shall understand its principles of combination, and these principles are vital to any theory of the work's function(s) and meaning(s) in the Middle Ages. Selecting from the rich variety of narrative and stylistic patterns to which the thirteenth-century *chanson de geste* was permeable, the *Hervis* poet(s) fashioned an engaging and instructive poem with profound social implications.

Not surprisingly, the text's ideological "message" has been as controversial as its generic identity. While it is clear that the narrative consistently opposes bourgeois and aristocratic values, there has been some debate as to the ultimate implications of the work. Auguste Prost and Joël Grisward maintain that *Hervis de Mes* reflects and legitimizes the rising influence of the bourgeoisie. Emphasizing the anomalous paternal factor, Grisward asserts that "la revendication majeure de tout le roman [*sic*], contrairement à l'opinion de M. Adler, ne concerne pas l'origine noble mais l'origine *bourgeoise* du jeune Hervis."[25] According to Alfred Adler and Philippe Walter, however, the triumph of the bourgeois value system is only apparent, for Hervis rejects the role of merchant's son and eventually emerges as the noble champion of Lorraine. Both Adler and Walter stress the fundamental role of matrilineal nobility in this process: as the essential transmitters of aristocratic birth, Aelis and Biatris guarantee the status of their male descendants.[26]

If the work is subject to such divergent critical interpretations, it is perhaps because previous studies do not sufficiently account for the *relationship* between genre and lineage in *Hervis de Mes*. The conjunction of genealogical and generic patterns in medieval narrative, well-documented by R. Howard Bloch, finds unique expression in this thirteenth-century composition.[27] To the hero born of mixed lineage corresponds a structurally heterogeneous text in which generic properties condition and complement the overall ideological framework. The present study will thus examine shifting poetic and narrative configurations in *Hervis de Mes* from two per-

---

[25] See Grisward's review of *Rückzug* 502. The author cites Auguste Prost, 380.

[26] Philippe Walter, postface to *Hervis de Metz* 197-201; Alfred Adler, "*Hervis de Mes* and the Matrilineal Nobility of Champagne," *Romanic Review* 37 (1946): 150-61.

[27] R. Howard Bloch, *Etymologies and Genealogies: A Literary Anthropology of the French Middle Ages* (Chicago and London: University of Chicago Press, 1983). See especially pages 93-108 and 177-78.

spectives: as indicators of generic stability and change, these patterns serve to readjust modern perceptions of the *chanson de geste*; as analogues of a socioeconomic conflict, the modulations of genre re-enact and illuminate the drama of competing world-views.

This sort of analysis requires at least two important qualifications. First of all, medievalists have always delighted in discovering the binary structures, both formal and thematic, that govern the composition of so many Old French texts. Indeed, how can one speak of the *Chanson de Roland* without evoking its two-part movement and the infamous opposition "Rollant est proz e Oliver est sage"? The latter example demonstrates, however, that we must not allow our perception of binary oppositions to lead to oversimplification. Robert F. Cook has demonstrated the extent to which modern scholars have misread "proz" and "sage" as mutually exclusive categories.[28] And Charles Altman reminds us that "a generation of computers has taught us that anything can be expressed through a series of dualities."[29] Accordingly, *Hervis de Mes* must not be envisaged as a mere checkerboard of epic/romance and noble/merchant oppositions; indeed, we shall see that its generic innovations do not always point to romance, which, of course, is a complex genre as well. Rather, I have attempted in these pages to identify dynamic structural *tendencies* that orient the interpretive process in certain directions.

Secondly, the relationship of literature to social "reality" remains a delicate and controversial problem. The majority of scholars who have taken an interest in *Hervis de Mes* have considered the text as a reflection of social reality in thirteenth-century Lorraine.[30] Paul Zumthor admonishes, however, that "l'idée d'une *mimesis* de la réalité quotidienne dans ses aspects socio-économiques est étrangère au moyen âge, peut-être même à la culture occidentale jusqu'au dix-neuvième siècle."[31] Although the text does contain traces of what was once its social and cultural function, the modern

---

[28] Robert Francis Cook, *The Sense of the Song of Roland* (Ithaca and London: Cornell University Press, 1987).

[29] Charles Altman, "Medieval Narrative vs. Modern Assumptions: Revising Inadequate Typology," *Diacritics* 4 (1974): 16.

[30] See especially Adler, "*Hervis de Mes*"; also Gijsbert Schilperoort, *Le commerçant dans la littérature française du moyen âge: Caractère, vie, position sociale* (Groningen, Den Haag, Batavia: J. B. Wolters, 1933).

[31] Paul Zumthor, *Essai de poétique médiévale* (Paris: Seuil, 1972) 115.

reader must supplement literal meaning with considerations of both historical and poetic context. Reading *Hervis de Mes* as both a product and an agent of changing horizons, we can hope to reactivate some of its signifying potential:

> Reste, parmi tant de risques, une certitude raisonnable: se replier sur ces messages mal déchiffrables où vibre pourtant encore, pour le lecteur attentif, l'intensité de ce qui fut un vouloir, une émotion sans doute, et la perception d'une beauté.[32]

SUMMARY OF *HERVIS DE MES*

Pierre, duke of Metz, has incurred numerous debts because of his extraordinary largess. He therefore arranges the marriage of his daughter Aelis to Thieri, the wealthy provost of Metz. Thieri acquits the duchy of its debts and temporarily assumes the functions of duke while Pierre makes a long-awaited pilgrimage to the Holy Land. Soon Aelis gives birth to a son, Hervis.

At the age of fifteen, the robust young Hervis wishes to be knighted. His father, however, fearing that the young man would waste too much money on knightly expeditions, decides instead to send his son to the fair at Provins, where he will be expected to make important purchases and to learn the value of money. Hervis reluctantly agrees to accompany three of his paternal uncles to the fair.

Once in Provins, however, Hervis refuses to remain with his uncles. Instead, he chooses his own lodging and lavishes vast sums of money on sumptuous meals. After failing to procure the items for which he was sent, Hervis begins his journey home, stopping along the way to buy a falcon and some hunting dogs with the remainder of his father's money. Upon his return, Hervis is severely chastised by the provost, but Aelis manages to make peace between them. Thieri decides to give his son a second chance and orders Hervis to accompany his uncles to the fair at Lagny.

Meanwhile, the elderly King of Spain has resolved to find a bride. He is advised that Biatris, daughter of Uistasse, King of Tyre, is the most beautiful and desirable woman in Christendom; it is also

---

[32] Zumthor 20.

known, however, that she would not consider marrying an infidel. The King of Spain becomes so enamored of Biatris (without ever having seen her) that he agrees to have himself and his people baptized. His ambassadors to the King of Tyre are successful in concluding a nuptial agreement: Biatris will marry the Spanish King after a period of two months if he keeps his promise to convert to Christianity. Biatris herself is disconsolate, for she does not wish to marry a heathen, and an elderly one at that.[33] However, she does not dare to challenge her father's decision.

King Uistasse and his wife plan a journey to Constantinople to inform their son Floire, King of Hungary, of Biatris's prospective marriage. During their absence, they entrust their daughter to the loyal Tyrian Baudri, who is nevertheless incapable of preventing a band of squires from kidnapping the fair Biatris.

It is just outside Lagny that Hervis encounters the squires, who have resolved to sell their captive; as soon as Hervis sets eyes on Biatris, he falls in love and resolves to buy her. It is agreed that Hervis will pay 15,000 gold marks for the lady, provided that she is a virgin. The squires swear to her chastity and willingly sell the unhappy Biatris, who refuses to reveal her true identity; Hervis nevertheless swears eternal fidelity and promises not to take advantage of her before they are married.

Unbeknownst to Hervis, three wicked young men have overheard the entire transaction and are plotting to kidnap Biatris from her new owner. Fortunately, Biatris has overheard their discussion and warns Hervis, who manages to kill two of the men and cause the third to flee.

Upon the couple's return to Metz, Thieri discovers that Hervis has again squandered large sums of money, and is convinced that his son has purchased a prostitute. The provost therefore bans Hervis and Biatris from the city and from any association with the people of Metz. Hervis's half-sister and her husband Baudri take pity on the couple and allow them to remain at their palace; but because of his father's ban, Hervis is able to marry Biatris only by forcing a canon to perform the ceremony. On their wedding night, Biatris conceives a son, Garin.

Only one thing now mars Hervis's happiness; he is forbidden to associate with his friends and is therefore avid for company. Hear-

---

[33] Biatris ignores the fact that the Spanish King has agreed to convert. This oversight will be discussed in the final chapter of the present study.

ing of a tournament at Senlis, he borrows money from Baudri and sets off to distinguish himself there. Although he has not yet been dubbed and chooses to remain anonymous, Hervis eclipses all the knights present by capturing the Count of Flanders for the Count of Bar, who is related to Aelis.

After devoting many months to the search for round tables and tournaments, Hervis returns to Metz; he has spent all the money given him by Baudri. Meanwhile, Biatris has given birth to a second son, Bégon. Hervis remains with his family just long enough to sire a daughter, and then sets out once again in search of adventure. At the end of six years, his enormous expenditures have ruined Baudri entirely. When Baudri has no choice but to ask Hervis and his family to leave, Biatris conceives an elaborate plot designed to solve their financial crisis and reimburse Baudri. She embroiders a beautiful silk cloth, wraps it carefully without showing it to anyone, and instructs Hervis to take the cloth to the fair at Tyre. He is to ask for lodging at the home of the Tyrian Baudri, where he is to spare no expense, and he is to sell the cloth for an exorbitant sum without revealing its true source.

Although he is skeptical of his wife's scheme, Hervis obediently follows her instructions and proceeds directly to Tyre. He stays at the home of the now-ruined and miserable Tyrian Baudri (to be distinguished from Hervis's brother-in-law), who has been stripped of his wealth since losing Biatris to the band of kidnappers. Hervis orders lavish meals and shows himself to be quite generous with his many guests. When Baudri discovers that his lodger cannot yet meet these expenses, he becomes frantic. However, Hervis reassures his host and sets off for the fair, where he unravels the silk cloth and puts it on display. The fabric is elaborately embroidered with portraits of Biatris, her father Uistasse, her mother the queen, and her brother Floire; the lettering on the cloth proves that it is Biatris's handiwork. Neither Floire, who happens to be visiting his parents in Tyre, nor Uistasse is able to wrest any information from the crafty Hervis, who pretends not to know Biatris. Faithfully following his wife's instructions, he sets a tremendous price for the cloth and doubles the figure every time it is refused. Finally, Uistasse is forced to pay 32,000 marks for his daughter's work, and Hervis is at last a rich man. When Baudri demands his share from the King, he receives instead all of the land and possessions that were taken from him following Biatris's kidnapping.

Hervis makes his departure with an escort to protect his newly-found wealth. He is followed closely by two of Floire's men, dressed as pilgrims, who must ascertain Biatris's whereabouts so that Floire might finally present her to the King of Spain. On the way to Metz, Hervis and his men encounter the giant Hinbaut and his evil bandits. Hervis slays Hinbaut, and, with the help of his men, succeeds in killing all of the bandits and in rescuing a group of clergymen kidnapped two days earlier by the outlaws. Among the grateful dignitaries are the bishop of Senlis and the abbots of St. Denis and St. Germain, both of whom are related to Hervis through his mother.

Hervis makes a triumphant entry into Metz, where he is greeted not only by his brother-in-law Baudri but also by Thieri, who has softened upon learning of Biatris's noble birth and Hervis's fortune. After a joyful reunion with Biatris, who begs him to make peace with his father, Hervis magnanimously forgives Thieri. The provost, who deeply regrets his past offenses, orders a belated wedding feast for his son and the noble Biatris. It is here that Hervis reluctantly reveals his past exploits at Senlis to the grateful Count of Bar. To make the celebration complete, Duke Pierre returns from the Holy Land, dubs Hervis and accords him the city of Metz as well as the entire duchy of Lorraine, for Pierre himself has decided to enter a monastery.

Shortly thereafter, however, Duke Pierre receives word that his brother, the Duke of Brabant, is dead. Although Pierre (and therefore Hervis) are the rightful heirs to the duchy, King Anseÿs of Cologne has besieged the land based on the spurious claim of his wife, Pierre's niece. Hervis hastens to assemble an army to assist the Brabançons, and he soon forces Anseÿs to retreat.

Meanwhile, however, Floire's spies have reported Biatris's whereabouts to her impatient brother, who fears the King of Spain's threats of retaliation. Floire comes to Metz disguised as a wealthy merchant and succeeds in kidnapping Biatris. When Hervis learns of this outrage, he immediately gathers five thousand young, able-bodied men and sets out to find his wife. While Biatris is being escorted to Spain to marry the King, Hervis re-captures her and accompanies her back to Metz. There he learns that King Anseÿs has renewed the siege of Brabant with the help of powerful kings and numerous soldiers; he leaves at once to fulfill his earlier mission.

The King of Spain, who is outraged at having lost Biatris a second time, besieges the city of Metz with the help of Uistasse and Floire during Hervis's absence. While Hervis and his army valiantly confront King Anseÿs and his allies, the people of Metz successfully defend their city against the Spanish army. Eventually, Hervis triumphs over Anseÿs, pursues the latter's fleeing army, and besieges the city of Cologne. Meanwhile, however, the plight of the Messins has grown worse: Hervis's young sons, Garin and Bégon, have distinguished themselves in battle, but both Bégon and the provost have been captured by the Spanish. Finally, just as Hervis receives word of his city's predicament, Bégon pleads with his grandfather Uistasse and his uncle Floire to take the side of their family. The two kings soften and desert the King of Spain, who is thus forced to give up the siege. The Spanish King agrees to make peace on the condition that he might lay eyes on Biatris just once; after seeing her, he vows to join a monastery and departs for Spain.

Meanwhile, King Anseÿs has been forced to surrender, and Hervis is on his way to save Metz from the Spanish. By the time he returns, the siege has been lifted and peace has returned to Metz.

Manuscripts[34]

E, BN fr. 19160 (formerly Saint Germain 1244); thirteenth century, Eastern French dialect. Folios 1-88 contain *Hervis de Mes* for a total of 10,530 lines; the poem is physically separated from *Garin le Loherain*. Although E is the most "incorrect" manuscript in terms of mechanical errors (omissions, senseless repetitions, negligent inflection, etc.), its presentation is the most concise and probably represents the oldest version.

---

[34] On the manuscript tradition of *Hervis de Mes*, see François Bonnardot, "Essai de classement des manuscrits des Loherains, suivi d'un nouveau fragment de *Girbert de Metz*," *Romania* 3 (1874): 195-262; Heinrich Hub, *La Chanson de Hervis de Metz* (Heilbronn, 1879); X. Pamfilova, "Fragments de manuscrits de chansons de geste," *Romania* 57 (1931): 504-46, especially 539-46; B. Schädel, "Bruchstück der Chanson de Hervis," *Jahrbuch für romanische und englische Sprache und Literatur*, ns 3, 15 (1876): 445-50; Wilhelm Vietor, *Die Handschriften der Geste des Loherains* (Halle: Niemeyer, 1876); and Philippe Walter, Bibliographie, *Hervis de Metz* 203. I extend my gratitude to Jean-Charles Herbin for his generous help in untangling the often contradictory sources.

N, Arsenal fr. 3143 (formerly Belles Lettres 181): fourteenth century, Francian dialect. This is the only manuscript containing assonanced versions of all four branches of the *geste*. *Hervis* is found in folios 1-43 plus one column from 44a, for a total of 13,144 lines; it is not separated from *Garin le Loherain*.

T, Turin L.II.14 (formerly G.II.13, formerly fr. 36), Cossentini inventory number R1639; early fourteenth century, Picard dialect. *Hervis* occupies folios 105-177 for a total of 12,928 lines; again, it is not distinct from *Garin*. **T** is considered to be the most technically "correct" version, although this manuscript shares with **N** several lengthy, romanesque additions to the **E** version. **N** and **T** also both attempt to amalgamate *Hervis* and *Garin* by removing certain contradictions on the level of narrative detail; however, these efforts lead only to further contradictions.[35]

Da, Darmstadt, Hessische Landes- und Hochschulebibliothek 3133; thirteenth century, Eastern French dialect. This is a fragment containing only 112 lines.

Em, Paris, Archives Nationales AB XIX 1734, dossier Moselle; late thirteenth century, Eastern French dialect. This too is a fragment, containing 278 lines.

v, Metz 847, formerly 97; prose translation by Philippe de Vigneulles of Metz, completed in 1515. Auguste Prost believed this manuscript to be Philippe's "brouillon autographe," but Edmund Stengel declared it a revised version of the manuscript Emmery.[36] The manuscript is in poor condition and was written in two different hands. *Hervis de Mes* occupies folios 1-59r.

Emmery: another version of Philippe's prose translation, more elegantly executed than Metz 847. The document was formerly in the possession of the Count of Hunolstein; however, Philippe Walter's recent inquiries have led him to declare this manuscript lost.[37]

---

[35] Rhode 134. A microfilm of T is available through the MLA collection at the Library of Congress (392). See Gittleman 327.

[36] See Georges Doutrepont, *Les mises en prose des épopées et des romans chevaleresques du XIVe au XVIe siècle* (1939; Geneva: Slatkine Reprints, 1969, 152-53.) A microfilm of this manuscript is available in the MLA collection at the Library of Congress (430F): see Gittleman 327.

[37] Walter, "Géographie" 142, n. 3. Excerpts may, however, be found in the partial edition of Le Comte Maurice de Pange, *La Chanson de geste de Garin le Loherain mise en prose par Philippe de Vigneulles de Metz: Table des chapitres avec les reproductions des miniatures d'après le manuscrit de la chanson appartenant à M. Le Comte d'Hunolstein* (Paris: Leclerc, 1901).

Although the manuscript tradition of the *geste des Loherains* is complex and rather controversial, it has been clearly established that the surviving verse manuscripts of *Hervis de Mes* belong to two separate families: **E, Da, Em** represent the "Lorraine" group, while **N, T** remain outside the "version commune" of the cycle as a whole.[38] Heinrich Hub believes that, at least for *Hervis*, the latter manuscripts were derived from a common intermediary source; given the nature of their additions, it seems clear that they are the work of more recent "remanieurs."[39] Edmund Stengel thus chose, for his 1903 edition, to implement the version of the story represented by **E**, but the less "barbaric" language of **T**; additions of **N** and **T** appear in the appendices. In the interest of textual unity, the present essay will focus largely on the older **E** version, supplying examples from other manuscripts when appropriate.

---

[38] Gittleman 12-14.
[39] Hub 74.

PART ONE

"LA TRESSE"

> La **tresse** suit de Hervi le membré.
> (*Hervis de Mes*, v. 4555)

> Tote la **tresse** vous en vorrai conter.
> (*Hervis de Mes*, v. 7)

Alarmed by the threats of the Spanish monarch, King Floire has Hervis pursued in the hope of finding the fair Biatris. For this mission, he selects two loyal polyglots ("Il n'est langages qu'il ne sacent parler," v. 3899) and orders them to cover "tout le cemin" (v. 3924). The first spy shrewdly follows the unsuspecting hero's "*tresse*," the "trace" or "trail" that will reveal the direction of his journey. Discovering the vestiges of a struggle ("Les ocis trueve, les mors et les navrés"), the informant correctly concludes: "'Ci a bataille et grans estours esté'" (vv. 4557-59). Eventually, the trail of dead and wounded bandits leads the two spies to Hervis and to the truth of Biatris's whereabouts. By virtue of their remarkable linguistic and topographical knowledge, the envoys are subsequently able to guide Floire directly to his lost sister.

Deceitful intentions aside, the role of the narrator in *Hervis de Mes* is not unlike that of Floire's informants. At the end of his prologue, the jongleur offers his listeners not only a "bone canchon," but also "tote la *tresse*" of the valiant Hervis. In the Lorraine dialect used by the scribe, *tresse* may constitute an alternate form of *trace*, the trail revealing the direction of a journey; *trace* may also designate a "suite" or continuation. The jongleur's function as storyteller thus consists in retracing the narrative and genealogical path lead-ing to the complete story of the heroic lineage.[1] Moreover, the "promise of *tote* la tresse" implies a more authoritative version of the story than that provided by the jongleur's predecessors or competitors. Ms. N is explicit on this point: "Mais tez en chante qui l'estoire n'en seit / Mais j'en dirai que bien l'ai *espiïé*" (vv. 9, 12). The reader or listener will therefore follow a narrative trace mediated by an expert informant. Those who are acquainted with the narrative may anticipate the pleasure of a familiar tale told now in its entirety; those encountering *Hervis* for the first time may look forward to learning the further exploits of a familiar *geste*. In either case, like Floire, the audience will undoubtedly discover hidden truths in the reported *tresse*.

It is precisely this level of represented action – the elements, composition, and implications of the *narrative* trajectory – that will concern us in Part One of this study. While the "told" cannot be divorced from its "telling" without an uncomfortable degree of abstraction, this temporary suspension of the epic's formal specificity will facilitate intergeneric comparison; Part Two will rejoin the *tresse* to its poetic and stylistic framework.

---

[1] As a metatextual term, the word "tresse" is a hapax in Old French narrative poetry. Godefroy translates "la tresse" of Ms. E's prologue as "la suite." This may be understood in the sense of "continuation," since the prologue does mention characters and events from *Garin le Loherain*. However, since *Hervis de Mes* is a continuation in reverse, Godefroy's "suite" should undoubtedly be understood as "what follows." Moreover, the word also means "action," "vestige," and "chemin," and the majority of examples from both Godefroy and Tobler-Lommatzsch correspond to these meanings. Mss. N and T replace "tresse" with "estoire."

CHAPTER ONE

THE NARRATIVE REPERTORY

Despite the absence of a normative generic code, the *chanson de geste* and the *roman* clearly responded to different sets of audience expectations in their formative period. Among these expectations were fairly distinct conventions of narrative content, which H. R. Jauss has catalogued in a now-classic essay on medieval genres.[2] It was this thematic component, however, that proved to be the most susceptible to variation in *chansons de geste* of the following centuries. Epics such as *Hervis de Mes* and *Huon de Bordeaux* challenge literary history's convenient binary oppositions between Carolingian and Celtic, heroic and courtly, collective and individual. When considered in the context of received narrative traditions, the choice of subject matter in *Hervis de Mes* reveals a good deal about the expressive possibilities of generic combination in the thirteenth century.

The individual components of the *tresse*, vestiges of the *Hervis* poets' thematic repertory, reveal a well-defined pattern that should come as no surprise to students of medieval narrative structure. Bipartition, that compositional staple of epic and romance storytellers alike, is a conspicuous feature of this text's generic make-up. Like many later *chansons de geste*, *Hervis de Mes* crowds the majority of its romance-oriented traits into one panel of a diptych. *Huon de Bordeaux*, *Floovant*, and *Aye d'Avignon*, for example, exploit epic

---

[2] Hans-Robert Jauss, *Toward an Aesthetic of Reception*, trans. Timothy Bahti, Theory and History of Literature 2 (Minneapolis: University of Minnesota Press, 1982) 85-86. The chapter on "Theory of Genres and Medieval Literature" first appeared in German in *Grundriss der Romanischen Literaturen des Mittelalters* 6 (Heidelberg: Carl Winter, 1972). The generic function that Jauss labels "unities of the represented" is grounded in oppositions formulated by Hegel, Frye, Todorov, Greimas, and Köhler.

schemata in the beginning as a framework for subsequent romance conflicts, characters, and decors.³ We shall see that the design of *Hervis de Mes* is just the reverse: although a degree of "mixing" is evident throughout the text, the hero's dubbing and concomitant acquisition of the duchy of Metz constitute a generic turning point, orienting the remaining half of the narrative in the direction of traditional epic matter.

Comparative studies of epic and romance generally divide narrative content into discrete categories, the number of which varies considerably from one analysis to another.⁴ Such an approach is also useful in the context of "bipartite" epics that exploit generic variation for poetic and didactic purposes. The following discussion will consider the five components most permeable to change in *Hervis de Mes* and other *chansons de geste* of the thirteenth century: a) matter; b) adventure vs. action; c) love and the woman's role; d) secondary characters; and e) the diegetic universe.

MATTER

Jehan Bodel's oft-quoted prologue to the *Chanson des Saisnes* demonstrates that in the thirteenth century, vernacular narratives could be differentiated on the basis of their matter and its supposed provenance. Bodel asserts that the *matière de France* is "voir chascun jour aparant," and his song reflects this preference.⁵ Indeed, the Old French epic usually derived from French historical events or personages, although poetic transposition often obscures the ves-

---

³ Rossi 205. On bipartition in *Aye d'Avignon*, see also Ellen Rose Woods, *Aye d'Avignon: A Study of Genre and Society* (Geneva: Droz, 1978).

⁴ In his article "Chanson de geste et roman courtois," Jauss considers a) the relationship between text and history; b) the role of the *merveilleux*; and c) the conception of the hero and his relationship to the action. The same author, in *Toward an Aesthetic of Reception*, provides an outline of four "modalities" or functions that epic, romance, and the novella fulfill in different ways. One of these functions, "Construction and Levels of Significance (Unities of the Represented)," offers the following categories: a) action; b) characters and social status; c) represented reality (83-87). William Calin, in his "Rapport introductif" to "Rapports entre chanson de geste et roman au XIIIe siècle," considers the following "content-oriented" categories: a) *la femme*; b) *le réel*; c) *le romanesque*. See *Essor et fortune de la chanson de geste dans l'Europe et l'Orient latin*, vol. 2 (Modena: Mucchi, 1984): 407-24. The typology that follows owes its orientation to all of the above analyses.

⁵ Jehan Bodel, *La Chanson des Saisnes*, ed. Annette Brasseur, 2 vols., Textes litteraires français (Geneva: Droz, 1989) v. 11.

tiges of annalistic fact. Scholars have succeeded in identifying the "kernel of truth" in most early epics, tracing the monumental battle of Roncevaux to a rather insignificant skirmish and the figure of Guillaume d'Orange to a number of real-life prototypes. The Loherain cycle, however, has proved more resistant to historical analysis. Ferdinand Lot was loathe to admit that he could find no solid historical foundation for the principal events and characters in *Garin le Loherain*; nevertheless, he did not eliminate the possibility that such a foundation existed: "Le fond historique, si tant est qu'il existe, n'est sans doute qu'une querelle locale entre personnages trop insignifiants pour que l'histoire nous ait conservé leurs noms."[6]

Lot did furnish possible antecedents for a number of minor characters in *Garin*, including Anseÿs of Cologne, who appears throughout the Loherain cycle.[7] Some thirty years later, Alexander Eckhardt suggested a link between the Hervis of *Garin le Loherain* and the historical figure Heriveus, bishop of Reims between 900 and 922: both Hervis and Heriveus defend Lorraine against Hungarian invasions, and both champion the cause of a King Charles against his barons.[8] Originally, then, the "matière de Lorraine" may have sprung from tenuous connections with history. The continuations, however, have never been the objects of serious historical conjecture: "il n'est point douteux qu'elles. . . ne constituent de simples fabrications."[9]

If *Hervis de Mes* has so often been designated as a "romance of adventure," it is partly because the early part of the text is not rooted in the traditional *matière de France* and has little in common even with the "matière de Lorraine." In fact, episodes such as the hero's profligacy, the heroine's abduction, and the sale of the embroidered cloth have been traced to Oriental folk motifs.[10] Certain-

---

[6] Ferdinand Lot, "L'élément historique de *Garin le Lorrain*," *Etudes d'histoire du moyen âge dédiées à Gabriel Monod* (Paris: Cerf, 1896) 220.

[7] Lot 217 and note 2 on the same page. It was Gaston Paris who first identified Anseÿs with Ansegisus, an ancestor of the Carolingians. See "La légende de Pépin le Bref," *Mélanges Julien Havet* (Paris: Leroux, 1895) 604-07.

[8] Alexander Eckhardt, "Franco-Hungarica," *Mélanges d'histoire littéraire générale et comparée offerts à Fernand Baldensperger* (Paris: Champion, 1930) I: 218-19.

[9] Lot 201. See also Maurice de Pange, in his introduction to Philippe de Vigneulles' prose translation, XII: ". . . la fantaisie y occupe une place qui le tient d'un bout à l'autre à l'écart du domaine de l'histoire."

[10] Leo Jordan, "Die Quelle des *Hervis von Metz*," *Archiv für das Studium der neueren Sprachen und Literaturen* 114 (1905): 432-40; Walther Benary, "*Hervis von Metz* und die Sage vom dankbaren Toten," *Zeitschrift für romanische Philologie* 37 (1913): 57-92 and 128-44; G. Huet, "Le retour merveilleux du mari," *Revue des traditions populaires* 32 (1917): 97-109 and 145-63.

ly, medieval romance did often glean its material from the foreign mythologies of the Celtic or Oriental world. Such *contes*, described by Bodel as "vain et plaisant," have nothing in common with French matter: "n'i a nul semblant" (vv. 8-9). Jehan Bodel's own topical choice was not based, however, upon historical fact, but rather the appropriateness of French matter to his intentions, which he describes as the expression of "chevalerie, amours, cembiaus." In the Middle Ages, veracity depended largely upon the poet's moral and intellectual decision to represent certain types of events and characters. The *roman*, too, laid claim to accuracy, but it was the text itself that created its own truth, a moral truth to be extracted from fictional events.[11] While the *chanson de geste* generally favored the immediacy of French historico-legendary matter, this choice was governed by the epic's primary social function, i.e. the commemoration and glorification of the community's past. In many epics of the thirteenth century, this function was fulfilled by means of an increasingly diverse matter.

Whether or not the Loherain heroes and their struggles have any basis in fact, medieval audiences did perceive them as historical and true. Evidence of this phenomenon comes primarily from the Lorraine region. In the fourteenth century, for example, the Duke of Lorraine designated the tenth of February as the date upon which the people of Nancy would celebrate the anniversary of Garin le Loherain's death.[12] In his *Chronique*, Philippe de Vigneulles insists on the historical truth even of *Hervis de Mes*, assuring his readers that the tombs of Hervis and Biatris might still be seen in the monastery of St. Arnoult.[13] These assertions of historical veracity, of course, are commonplaces of the medieval chronicler's prologue; nonetheless, Philippe's choice of subject matter is authenticated by his own self-proclaimed purpose:

> "Laquelle [euvre] je, Philippe de Vigneulle, le merchant et citains de Metz, ait deliberés, moyennant la grace de Dieu, que, a la louuange d'icelluy et a l'honneur de la noble cité et de tous les bons seigneurs et recteurs d'icelle, de ycy dire, traicter et raconter aulcune chose d'icelle dicte noble cité, tant de sa premiere

---

[11] See Douglas Kelly, "Topical Invention in Medieval French Literature," *Medieval Eloquence: Studies in the Theory and Practice of Medieval Rhetoric*, ed. James J. Murphy (Berkeley: University of California Press, 1978) 237-38.

[12] Gittleman 17.

[13] De Pange 2; Bruneau 3.

fondacions comme de ceulx qui depuis, longtemps apres, l'ont acreue, agmentee, regentee et habitee."

Despite its lack of factual foundation, *Hervis de Mes* was originally conceived and transmitted in this same commemorative spirit. Anchored to the rest of the cycle by genealogy and by relatively precise topographical indications, the early part of the text integrates new kinds of matter into the epic tradition of France and Lorraine.[14] The Tyrian slave-princess Biatris is linked both to the *chanson de toile* and Oriental folk tales by her name and her extraordinary skill in weaving. Philippe Walter perceives in her character the luminous figure of the *fée*, the mythical antecedent of the medieval romance heroine.[15] Yet Biatris is transported to Metz, and the jongleur declares her to be not only the mother of Garin le Loherain, but also the great-aunt of Charlemagne himself (vv. 616-24). By conjoining familiar proper names to the schemas of romanesque matter, *Hervis de Mes* combines the romance "truth" extracted from foreign folk tales with the epic "truth" consecrated by the community's past.

This process of integration is not without its textual traces. In order to authenticate his "sources," the poet makes use of traditional epic formulas, namely "ce dist la geste" (vv. 250, 1447, 2287, 2396, 5105) and "si con la chanson dist" (vv. 498, 2669). "Geste" in this context designates a vague written source, and is often invoked by epic poets to corroborate story events; the reference to a "chanson" fulfills a similar function, posing an oral source as the authority.[16] The actual existence of these sources has not been documented – and, curiously, all of these formulas appear in the first half of the story.

In most instances, the truth assertions accompany accounts of the Loherain heroes' births and/or anticipations of their future exploits in *Garin le Loherain* (vv. 250, 2287, 2396, 5105); these formu-

---

[14] On the precision and function of topography in *Hervis de Mes*, see Philippe Walter, "Géographie et géopolitique dans la légende d'*Hervis de Metz*," *Olifant* 13 (1988): 141-63. On *Garin le Loherain*, see Ruth Parmly, *The Geographical References in Garin le Loherain* (New York: Columbia University, 1935).

[15] Philippe Walter, "*Hervis de Metz*: le griffon et la 'fée'," *Vox romanica* 45 (1986): 157-67.

[16] "Geste" and "chanson" may even refer to the work itself. See Edmond Faral, ed. and trans., *La Conquête de Constantinople*, 2 vols., Classiques de l'histoire de France au Moyen Age 18 (Paris: Belles lettres, 1938) 9n.

las serve to link *Hervis de Mes* with the "matière de Lorraine." In addition, the phrases often function to corroborate a hyperbolic statement relating to the hero's exemplary good looks or to his horse's exceptional strength (vv. 2396, 2665, 5105). Finally, one instance of "ce dist la geste" authenticates the story of the three "demoisel de pris" who attempt to kidnap Biatris (v. 1447). Centuries later, Philippe de Vigneulles, too, found it necessary to prove one of the heroine's abductions to his readers. Although some people might find it difficult to believe, grants Philippe, such events were quite commonplace in the old days: ". . . ce n'estoit que chose toute commune pour celluy tampts de ainsy faire."[17]

The use of "authority" formulas in *Hervis de Mes* corresponds, then, to a well-known epic convention: the poet invokes a source whenever he needs to give credence to something that might seem exaggerated. Since these phrases are limited to the first half of the text, it is likely that the *Hervis* poets, like Philippe de Vigneulles, sensed the need to authenticate that portion of the story which had so little in common with the matter of the cycle. By inserting "documented" references to events from *Garin le Loherain* and invoking a source for the folkloric episodes of *Hervis*, the text guarantees the veracity of those episodes most lacking in historical or epico-legendary "truth."

The second half of the story, on the other hand, introduces a conflict that needs little justification, for it has its roots in Loherain legend. As soon as Hervis is dubbed, he enters into a war with Anseÿs de Cologne. The introduction of this quasi-historical figure serves to connect *Hervis de Mes* with the political conflicts of *Garin le Loherain*. In the latter work, Anseÿs temporarily assists Hervis in driving the Hungarian invaders from Lorraine, since Pépin le Bref has refused to aid his vassal. When Hervis is killed in battle, however, the King of Cologne immediately betrays him and seizes the duchy of Lorraine. Ferdinand Lot interprets this episode as an attempt at historical explanation: Anseÿs (derived from Ansegisus, an ancestor of the Carolingian kings) offers the *Garin* poet "un moyen commode de s'expliquer le fait que de son temps la Lorraine ne dépendait plus du roi de France."[18] The second part of *Hervis de Mes* provides a prehistory of this legendary conflict by presenting the antecedents of the characters' antagonistic relationship.

---

[17] De Pange 3.
[18] Lot 217.

Finally, although this portion of the poem contains no instances of the formulas "ce dist la geste" and "si con la chanson dist," the jongleur does present the fierce battle between Anseÿs and the Loherains as the immediate source of a primary epic song:

> Quant les II os s'ajoustent d'ambe part,
> Po en i ot qui as oelz ne plourast,
> Ne si hardi qui ne s'en esmaiast. [...]
> *Uns clers a dit que canchon en fera,*
> Et il ce fist, moult bien la devisa.
> Jamais jougleres millor ne cantera.
> (vv. 6631-33, 6637-39)

These lines recall the much-debated "Bertolais" passage in *Raoul de Cambrai*: "Bertolais dist que chançon en fera / Jamais jougleres tele ne chantera." [19] Similarly, in the *Chanson de Roland*, Roland and Turpin urge on their companions by citing the possibility that a "malvaise cançun" might otherwise be composed about them. [20] Traditionalists, of course, have cited such declarations as evidence that primary witnesses composed proto-epic songs to commemorate noteworthy events. Modern scholarship has not confirmed the literal veracity of such indications. Indeed, the passage in *Hervis de Mes* is particularly open to suspicion, since the battle in question is not corroborated by any historical document. It is more likely that the affirmation of an eye-witness account contributes here to a general aura of historical verisimilitude; the commemorative task of the (warrior?) cleric conforms to the conventionally "epic" subject of feudal warfare. Paradoxically, the second part of the text creates and validates the referent for "la geste" and "la chanson" cited in the earlier half of the narrative.

Although *Hervis de Mes* may well represent a pure fabrication, then, the text is presented as a prehistory of the mighty Loherain lineage. Rather than transgressing a generic code, the Hervis poet(s) merely responded to a change of expectations with regard to mate-

---

[19] *Raoul de Cambrai*, eds. Paul Meyer and Auguste Longnon, Société des anciens textes français 17 (Paris: Picard, 1882) vv. 2442-43. For a discussion of the "Bertolais" passage, see Pauline Matarasso, *Recherches historiques et littéraires sur Raoul de Cambrai* (Paris: Nizet, 1962) 20-21 and 81-90.

[20] *La Chanson de Roland*, ed. Gérard Moignet (Paris: Bordas, 1985) vv. 1014, 1466, 1517.

rial choices. Like other thirteenth-century epics, such as *Huon de Bordeaux* and *Aye d'Avignon*, *Hervis* temporarily broadens the epic framework to accommodate the aesthetic appeal of exotic romance matter. Where folklore elements outweigh allusions to historical or legendary events, frequent reference to "la geste" compensates for an actual lack of epic matter. The second part of the story recounts events that are no less "fictional" in the minds of modern readers, yet the war waged by Anseÿs of Cologne provides an epically verisimilar framework in which the narrative is able to generate its own source of truth.

NARRATIVE EVENTS

Early Old French epic and romance also differ in the events they choose to portray as well as the hero's relationship to those events. The *chansons de geste* of the eleventh and twelfth centuries typically evoke a collective action, subordinate to the interests of the community; the epic hero accomplishes a series of actions that transcend his own destiny. In the core text of the Loherain cycle, for example, the concerns of Garin and Bégon exemplify the interests of an entire lineal network. Moreover, the early epic hero's character generally does not evolve; although he actualizes his potential in the course of the story, his fixed identity permits him only to become "more like himself."[21] Finally, since the early *chanson de geste* is concerned with collective interest, the conflicts it portrays tend to be of a political and/or religious nature, usually deriving from an overall opposition between good and evil. "Good" is embodied in the hero's service to God, *seigneur*, and lineage. "Evil" appears in the form of heathen forces, the treachery of a trusted ally, the weakness of a sovereign, or the perfidiousness of an opposing clan.

Despite the presence of numerous "romance-like" episodes, the first part of *Hervis de Mes* is not entirely lacking in typical epic content. Traditional motifs are particularly evident in the very beginning of the story when Duke Pierre and the King of Spain each hold a *conseil* to discuss matters of state (vv. 44ff., 638ff.). Duke

---

[21] Eugene Vance, *Reading the Song of Roland* (Englewood Cliffs: Prentice-Hall, 1970) 11.

Pierre's financial dilemma recalls the opening conflict in the older *Garin le Loherain*, in which the impoverished Charles Martel must beg the wealthy clergy for assistance.[22] Similarly, in the twelfth-century *Charroi de Nîmes*, Guillaume demands a fief from King Louis, whom he has served loyally for many years. The hero's lack of revenue prevents him from exercising the noble function of largess, and thus strongly resembles Duke Pierre's plight:

CHARROI: 'Con longue atente a povre bacheler
Qui n'a que prendre ne autrui que doner!'[23]

HERVIS: 'Je suis si povres, sor sains le puis jurer,
N'ai que despendre, ne n'en ai que donner.'
(vv. 50-51)

The Spanish King's abrupt desire to marry is likewise typical of a (minor) epic conflict. In *Garin le Loherain*, it is Pépin who suddenly decides to take a wife, Blancheflor (vv. 6006-7); the lady has been and continues to be the object of a feudal dispute among Loherains, Bordelais, and Pépin.

Like typical epic *conseils*, those in the early portion of *Hervis de Mes* have repercussions for an entire community. Duke Pierre's plight affects the whole duchy of Lorraine and could mean the end of his lineage, for he can find no prince to marry his only child: "'Il n'en ait prince en la crestienté / Qui ost ma fille prendre ne espouser'" (vv. 58-59). The prospective marriage between Biatris and the Spanish King causes the latter to convert himself and all his barons to Christianity: "'Crerrai en diu le roy de maïsté / Et mon barnage estoverait lever'" (vv. 680-81).

Both of these *conseil* episodes, however, are followed by the departure of a character or characters whose absence ushers in modes of action that savor of twelfth- and thirteenth-century romance. After resolving his dilemma, Duke Pierre undertakes an expedition to the Holy Land. During his lengthy absence, the narrative turns to the indirect result of the earlier *conseil*, i.e. Hervis. In this portion

---

[22] *Garin le Loheren According to Manuscript A*, ed. Josephine Vallerie (Ann Arbor: Edwards Brothers, 1947) vv. 15-44. All subsequent quotations are drawn from this edition.

[23] Duncan McMillan, ed., *Le Charroi de Nîmes* (Paris: Klincksieck, 1972) vv. 81-82.

of the tale, the focus shifts from the community to an individual (though exemplary) protagonist whose "biography" recalls in some ways that of a romance hero. Many of the events, for example, do not result directly from the hero's actions or decisions, but rather *happen to* him. *Hervis de Mes* thus admits the adventure, which Jauss describes as "une constellation fortuite, bien qu'ayant une signification cachée, de plusieurs accidents que le chevalier isolé rencontre sur son chemin et que lui seul peut rencontrer."[24] In typically romanesque fashion, these adventures are organized in the form of a quest, during which the hero progressively proves his valor in the eyes of his peers and his lady.

Similarly, after the *conseil* in Spain and its immediate results, Biatris's parents set out on a long journey. Their departure for Hungary is followed by the abduction and sale of their daughter, which, as we have seen, recalls an Oriental narrative schema. The twelfth-century romance *Floire et Blancheflor* adapts a similar configuration to the story of two young lovers separated by the boy's father, who secretly kidnaps Blancheflor and sells her to Babylonian merchants.[25] In *Hervis de Mes*, the abduction serves rather to unite the hero and heroine and bring their love interest to the fore. Succeeding episodes depict the encounter of Hervis and Biatris, obstacles to their union, and the "happenings" or adventures that prove the hero worthy of his lady's love.

This portion of the narrative recalls the romances of Chrétien de Troyes in several respects. While traveling through a forest, Hervis must defend himself and his lady against the attack of three sinister would-be kidnappers; like Enide, Biatris warns her companion of the imminent danger and facilitates his victory.[26] Once the hero has secured his bride, he sets out in search of tournaments and other adventures, like the newly-married and restless Yvain. The temporal configuration of this development follows the pattern of adventure and transgression in Chrétien's *Chevalier au lion*. While Hervis's first adventure is recounted in much detail (vv. 2354-2777), others are merely summarized:

---

[24] Jauss, "Chanson" 72.
[25] Jean-Luc Leclanche, ed., *Le Conte de Floire et Blancheflour*, Classiques français du moyen âge 105 (Paris: Champion, 1980) vv. 415-44.
[26] Daniel Poirion notes the resemblance as well in Préface, *Hervis de Metz: Roman du moyen âge adapté par Philippe Walter* 8.

> Desor s'en va Hervis contreval le regnei.
> Querre tauble reonde sovent et ajouster,
> Maint cheval gaaigna, maint cheval a doné.
> (vv. 2778-80)

This particular segment evinces a great temporal disparity between *récit* and *histoire*, since a few short lines serve to recount the activities of nine months; a subsequent passage summarizes seven years of adventure (vv. 2866-69, 2872a-b). A similar time frame appears in the *Chevalier au lion*: the hero, lured away from his wife by the carefree Gauvain, spends over a year at tournaments that the narrator refrains from describing:

> Car as tornois s'an vont andui
> Par toz les leus, ou l'an tornoie.
> Et li anz passe tote voie...[27]

The nature of these adventures is irrelevant to the heroes' progress, for the real quest has not yet begun. What is important in this phase is the lapse of time (in *Yvain*) and the depletion of resources (in *Hervis*). Like Yvain, Hervis carries his taste for adventure too far, neglecting other essential duties. Hervis's duties, however, are familial and financial: the expenses of the tournaments and the hero's excessive largess reduce the entire family to dire straits, thereby moving Biatris to impose upon her husband a solitary quest to replenish the family resources. Like many Arthurian knights, Hervis accomplishes his quest by concealing his identity and by engaging in a final, decisive series of *épreuves*.

The quest sequence, which includes Hervis's first journey to Tyre and his encounter with the giant Hinbaut, is noteworthy for its mixture of romance and epic modes of the *merveilleux*. The embroidered cloth recalls the non-supernatural marvel of *lai* and romance, i.e. an extraordinary object that generates and emblematizes story action. When Hervis arrives in Tyre, he guards his secret treasure with such care that his host demands: "'Sont ce reliques que dedens aves mis?'" (v. 3297). The extraordinary value of the cloth is recognized by all who lay eyes on it: "Dix con l'esgardent li jone

---

[27] Chrétien de Troyes, *Yvain (Le Chevalier au lion)*, ed. T.B.W. Reid (Manchester: Manchester University Press, 1942) vv. 2670-72.

et li barbez!" (v. 3460); the members of Biatris's family swoon when they behold the object (vv. 3490-91, 3684-85, 3802). Remarkable events come to pass because of the cloth: Hervis becomes fabulously wealthy and the two Baudris recover their lost wealth. Finally, the embroidered portraits of Biatris and her family represent, in crystallized form, one of the principal narrative forces in the text, i.e. the disintegration and subsequent reunification of the Tyrian royal family. This amazing object, then, participates in a set of romance narrative conventions. Like the nightingale in *Laüstic*, it communicates a message and preserves the memory of a lost union; like the bird of Jean Renart's *L'Escoufle*, the *drap* serves as a narrative stimulus: without it, there would be no adventure.[28]

The subsequent confrontation between Hervis and Hinbaut, as we shall see in our study of secondary characters, also includes a romanesque *merveille*, for Hinbaut himself is a superhuman adversary in the manner of Celtic marvels. This segment further contains, however, a classic example of the epic *merveilleux chrétien*, wherein the intervention of divine Providence serves to confirm the exemplary strength and valor of the hero by portraying him as the champion of God's own cause.[29] Hervis benefits from such divine intervention in his struggle against the evil bandit:

> La fist miracles li roys de maïsté:
> Que li solaus qui luisait bel et cler,
> Adedevant de Hervi le membré,
> Par le miracle le roy de maïsté
> Est li seloil d'autre part trestournés.
>
> (vv. 4165-69)

The episode recalls a similar event in the *Chanson de Roland*, during which God assists Charlemagne by arresting the sun's "movement."[30] The Hervis of *Garin le Loherain* is also blessed by a sign from God: during a fierce battle against the pagan hordes, he miraculously procures a floating black cross and transports it to the "mostier Saint-Orsin" where it will inspire future warriors and pilgrims (vv. 531-51). Similarly, the Christian marvel in *Hervis de Mes*

---

[28] The narrator is explicit on this matter. See Jean Renart, *L'Escoufle*, ed. Franklin Sweetser, Textes littéraires français (Geneva: Droz, 1974) vv. 9086-91.

[29] Jauss, "Chanson de geste et roman courtois" 69.

[30] *Roland* vv. 2458-59.

reinforces the hero's roots in a religious and political cause that unites the community. As Hervis's romance quest draws to an end, then, his status approaches that of an epic hero: he becomes the protector of God's people and the earthly representative of divine will.

Upon the completion of the hero's quest, the story reintroduces Duke Pierre, who performs the rather belated dubbing rite for his grandson. Now, in both the epic and romance traditions, the *adoubement* generally precedes the period of exploits or adventures. Gérard Noiriel interprets the delay as a reflection of actual economic conditions, for by the thirteenth century, the ceremony had become much more costly.[31] Indeed, Hervis himself explains the postponement in these terms: " '. . . ce m'a fait povretés' " (v. 5268). However, one does not have to resort to external reality in order to justify the tardiness of this episode, for its place does have a distinct narrative function. The dubbing rites – and simultaneous acquisition of the duchy – culminate the series of adventures and thus the romanesque portion of Hervis's story. What follows, i.e. the war against Anseÿs of Cologne, may be characterized rather as conventional epic action. Duke Pierre's role in this transformation is noteworthy: as his departure ushered in a series of romance-oriented events, his return heralds the reappearance of the *geste*. This character acts then as a sort of generic catalyst, inducing modifications in the nature of story events by his very presence or absence in the narrative.

The "epic" character of the second half of *Hervis de Mes* is not conditioned only by the figures of Duke Pierre and King Anseÿs. The kinds of events portrayed and the hero's relation to those events change rather dramatically just after the dubbing ceremony. When Hervis goes to war with Anseÿs, he undertakes an action that affects not only his own destiny, but also that of the Brabant people. On the one hand, Hervis is offered the opportunity to distinguish himself and preserve his right to the duchy of Brabant. On the other, his presence in Brabant is considered "secours" by the Brabançons, who do not wish to pay homage to the King of Cologne. Now that Hervis has been dubbed, he becomes the champion of the community, guaranteeing the rights of his family and his vassals.

---

[31] Gérard Noiriel, "La Chevalerie dans la geste des Lorrains," *Annales de l'est* 28 (1976): 183.

Moreover, the war includes typical epic motifs, such as preparations for battle, general and single combat, and pillaging. The conflict centers on common epic themes that are particularly frequent in the *geste des Loherains*, namely problems of lineage and feudal rights.

The second conflict in Part Two, the dispute over Biatris, also transcends the realm of individual concerns. Whereas the earlier journey to Tyre represented a personal quest to reconcile noble pursuits with the preservation of family resources, the second journey creates an entirely different impression: ". . . le voyage final du héros. . . pour reprendre sa femme, enlevée par le père [*sic*] de celle-ci, a en partie le caractère d'une expédition militaire."[32] Indeed, Hervis is accompanied by an entire army of his countrymen, who consider the cause of their *seigneur* to be their own: "'Si requerrons *nos* anemis mortex!'" (v. 8361). Furthermore, when the King of Spain lays siege to the city of Metz, the defense of Biatris is linked to the survival of Metz itself. Hervis defines his duty only in terms of saving his city: "'Il me convient cest grant siege adosser / Pour a secourre ma mirable cité'" (vv. 10,260-61).

The second part of the story, then, introduces supra-personal conflicts that present Hervis as the champion of Brabant, Metz, and Lorraine against the unlawful invasions of German, Spanish, and Tyrian forces. The hero clearly completed any evolution of character in the earlier portion of the narrative. In Part Two, he is and remains the protector of the community; the conflict shifts to the *interpretation* of his status by his enemies. The Loherain interpretation prevails when Anseÿs, the Spaniards, and the Tyrians ultimately acknowledge Hervis's right to both his wife and his dominion.

LOVE AND THE WOMAN'S ROLE

Amorous relationships, conspicuous by their virtual absence in the Oxford *Roland* and *Gormont et Isembart*, do nonetheless have their place in many early epic narratives. The sentiment is often aroused in a feminine character by the beauty and prowess of the hero; if the lady must be won, it is only in the military sense. Most often, however, such events do not constitute the narrative core of

---

[32] Huet 161. Note, however, that Biatris is kidnapped by her brother, not her father.

the work; witness the *Prise d'Orange*, in which Guiborc is merely an additional prize in the conflict between Christians and Saracens, or *Garin le Loherain*, in which Blancheflor serves mainly as the focal point of a nascent feud. William Comfort describes the early epic hero's relationship to his lady by negating the terms of a typical romance conflict:

> He does not banish himself for her, he does not do penance for discourtesy to her, he does not fight in tournaments to win her favors, he does not undergo hardships upon land and sea to gain her love, he does not blindly follow his passions and marry her before the rites of the church have been fulfilled.[33]

Moreover, the woman's role may diminish once the couple is married: she then serves merely to produce offspring in order to continue the lineage, as in *Garin le Loherain*. Occasionally, however, as in *La Chanson de Guillaume*, the epic wife may take on leadership responsibilities in her husband's absence. Frappier considers Guillaume and Guibourc to be the epic couple *par excellence*: they are bound by reciprocal love as well as by an ideal of heroism and sacrifice.[34] Since the love relationship serves the epic community, the early *chanson de geste* is characterized almost exclusively by examples of conjugal or pre-conjugal love.

Conversely, both Arthurian and non-Arthurian romances of adventure frequently place the love relationship at the very center of the hero's quest. With the notable exception of Béroul's *Tristan*, most verse romances portray *fin'amors*, a love that is chosen rationally, based on the merits of the beloved; it is a sentiment that gives rise to much analysis and introspection.[35] Love awakens the hero to great aspirations and provides the motivation for his actions. Typically, the culmination of the quest coincides with physical or spiritual (re)union. Love relationships in medieval romance may be adulterous, as in the case of Lancelot and Guinevere; pre-conjugal, as in *L'Escoufle*; or conjugal, as in *Erec et Enide*. However, even when the romance couple is married, their *fin'amors* does not typically produce offspring.

---

[33] William Comfort, "The Essential Difference between a *chanson de geste* and a *roman d'aventure*," PMLA 19 (1904): 71.

[34] Jean Frappier, *Les Chansons de geste du cycle de Guillaume d'Orange*, I:9.

[35] Jean Frappier, "Structure et sens du *Tristan*: version commune, version courtoise," *Cahiers de civilisation médiévale* 5 (1963): 265.

The importance of love in the romance of adventure tends, of course, to enhance the role of women in this genre.[36] In many Arthurian tales, it is she who inspires the quest for self, since the ideal knight cannot be whole without balancing the exigencies of his lady and those of his knightly vocation. In the non-Arthurian *L'Escoufle*, the woman exhibits great initiative in the search for her lost lover, settling in his native land and earning her own living to continue her own quest.

One particular feminine function appears in romance of all kinds, in both the twelfth and thirteenth centuries: the woman is noted for her capacity to make and perceive images. That is, the romance woman is conventionally endowed with *engin*, the ability to imagine ruses and strategies to be carried out by the hero. Thus, while the heroines of both early epic and romance may assist their lovers in times of need, the frequency and context of this assistance distinguishes the two genres in the early texts: the epic wife occasionally contributes to the military exploits of her husband, while the romance woman often serves as an inspiration and source of imagination for her lover's or her own personal quest.

The evolution of the *Hervis* legend provides ample proof of generic "confluence" in the *chansons de geste* of the thirteenth century.[37] Hervis's betrothal and marriage are first recounted in *Garin le Loherain*, but with the characteristic terseness of twelfth-century epic aesthetics. In this text, the hero takes advantage of a brief period of relative peace to request that the Abbot of Gorze find him a bride. The appeal is brief and functional: " 'Querez moi fame, mes cors mestier en a' " (v. 768). When the accomodating abbot asks if Hervis might offer any suggestions, the hero obliges:

> 'Droit a Couloigne i pucelle a;
> De haute jent et grant parenté a.
> C'est Aheliz; el mont plus belle n'a;
> Suer est Gaudin qui tante honor fait m'a.
> Tel chevalier en cest siecle n'en a.'
> (vv. 772-6)

---

[36] For an overall view of women in medieval texts, see Joan M. Ferrante, *Woman as Image in Medieval Literature* (New York: Columbia University Press, 1975).

[37] The term is used by Donald Maddox in "Les figures romanesques du discours épique et la confluence générique," *Essor et fortune de la chanson de geste dans l'Europe et l'Orient latin*, vol. 2: 517-22.

The maiden is brought directly to Metz, where the wedding festivities take place; the poet accords the event one line (v. 784). A final glimpse of the relationship between Hervis and Aelis is furnished by an account of the children born to the couple (vv. 786-819). In *Garin le Loherain*, the role of Aelis is thus strictly limited to her ability to produce offspring for the great Loherain lineage.

The later *Hervis* poet changes more than just the name of the hero's wife. *Hervis de Mes* recounts in detail the "courtship" and marriage of Hervis and Biatris. Furthermore, Biatris herself assumes a much greater role in the narrative. Philippe Ménard estimates that three quarters of the text is devoted to this character, although this includes conflicts in which she plays a passive role. Moreover, Philippe de Vigneulles refers to the text in his early sixteenth-century journal as "le livre de la belle Biautris."[38] *Hervis de Mes* represents, then, a significant departure from the earlier epic portrayal of love and womanhood.

We have seen that choice of matter and modes of action divide the generic structure of *Hervis de Mes* into two fairly distinct parts. The role of love, however, does not offer such a clear dichotomy, for this factor is granted a privileged position in the narrative as a whole. Nevertheless, the function of Biatris in the couple does undergo a transformation once she has been successfully integrated into the Metz community: these changes complement and support the shift to conventional epic modes of action.

The text has frequently been cited for the "romanesque" and even fairy-tale character of the love between Hervis and the Princess of Tyre.[39] Hervis is first struck by the exquisite beauty of Biatris, who, incidentally, is initially mistaken for a "fée" by her abductors (v. 924). The maiden's loveliness casts Hervis into that state of awed stupor so characteristic of courtly lovers: "Quant il coisi la bele o le cler vis / De sa biauté par fut toz *esbahis*" (vv. 1252-53). The hero does not remain long in this tongue-tied state, however, for he is just as concerned with the maiden's background and virtue as he is with her beauty. When Biatris refuses to divulge her full identity, Hervis contents himself with the assurance that she is a vir-

---

[38] See "'Berte" 119-20.
[39] See, for example, Alfred Adler, "*Hervis de Mes* and the Matrilineal Nobility of Champagne," *Romanic Review* 37 (1946): 156; and Micheline de Combarieu du Grès, *L'idéal humain et l'expérience morale chez les héros des chansons de geste des origines à 1250* (Aix-en-Provence: Université de Provence, 1979) 375.

gin. Although he has already decided to purchase her, he does give Biatris a choice in the matter:

> 'Quant pucelle estes, ici con m'avés dit,
> Vous plairoit il – gardés n'i ait menti! –
> Que vous accate et d'argent et d'or fin?'
>   (vv. 1346-48)

He later asks if she wishes to marry him (vv. 2190-92), and gives her the opportunity to choose the marriage all over again after she has been kidnapped by her family and returned to Tyre (vv. 7980-82). Finally, Hervis further proves himself worthy of his lady's love by vowing to preserve her virginity until they are married (vv. 1355-57). Despite his purchaser's claim on the maiden, he keeps his word and endures eight months of abstinence before the wedding takes place (v. 2176).[40]

Biatris, for her part, is too overwhelmed by her abduction to respond immediately to her suitor's outpouring of affection. Nonetheless, she soon comes to love Hervis for both his *biauté* and his *bonté*; like Hervis, she chooses her lover on the basis of physical and moral attributes:

> 'Et s'il est biax, encore a plus bonté.
> [...]
> [A Lagny] m'accata Hervis li bacelers
> Quinze mil mars que d'argent que d'or cler.
> Mais ainc ne volt gesir a mon costé,
> Ma douce meire, ne mon cors avillé
> Tant qu'il m'ot a moullier espouzé.'
>   (vv. 7690, 7697-7700)[41]

In addition, Hervis's status as heir to the duchy of Lorraine impresses her deeply (vv. 1355-63).

Thus, the love between Biatris and Hervis is one that is chosen rationally, according to the merits of each partner. This bond does display, however, a curious admixture of amorous and commercial ties. Biatris is consistently portrayed as both an object of desire and an object of trade, first by her abductors and then by Hervis. The

---

[40] In the other manuscripts, Hervis must wait only one month.
[41] The line "Ma douce meire..." is added by ms. E.

latter frequently justifies his union with Biatris on the basis of his transaction with the ten kidnappers: "'Car ele est miene, car je l'ai accaté'" (v. 1581; cf. vv. 1654-56, 8835-37). Such assertions are typically followed, however, by the expression of more tender sentiments appropriate to the conjugal mode of *fin' amors*:

> 'Vous estes miene *en vendre* et en doner,
> Vos cors est miens, quant je l'ai *accaté*.
> Si m'aiut dix, vous estes mes *cateus*,
> U que je voise, avoec moi en venrés.
> Se je jeüne, avoec moi junerés
> Et mal et bien avoec moi prenderés.
> (vv. 1654-59)

By introducing bourgeois values of exchange into the *service d'amors*, the text appears to subvert the lofty ideals of courtly love. In a recent study of the *Chevalier au lion*, however, Eugene Vance unveils the "mercantilist" underpinnings of Chrétien's courtly discourse.[42] Analyzing the "ideologies of change and exchange" in the Yvain-Laudine-Lunette relationship, Vance sees in the fiction of courtly desire a "metaphorization ... of a burgeoning new commercial economy."[43] Whereas the interference of courtly and merchant codes operates on a metaphorical level in the romance of the twelfth-century Champenois, *Hervis de Mes* realizes the latent potential of this "economy of love." We shall see later that this coupling of love and commerce is an integral part of the text's didactic strategies; for now, let us simply note its ties with the discourse of earlier romance.

Unlike Chrétien's intrusive narrator, the narrator-jongleur of *Hervis de Mes* does not intervene to philosophize about the vicissitudes of love, nor does he generally penetrate the thoughts and feelings of the two characters. Nonetheless, the text does contain indices of love's effects, particularly on the hero. He repeatedly risks his life for Biatris, he willingly submits to the ostracism of his community in order to marry her, and he obediently undertakes a quest at her command. These demonstrations of love are less surprising

---

[42] Eugene Vance, "Chrétien's *Yvain* and the Ideologies of Change and Exchange" in *Mervelous Signals: Poetics and Sign Theory in the Middle Ages* (Lincoln and London: University of Nebraska Press, 1986) 111-151.

[43] Vance, *Mervelous* 122.

in the earlier portion of the story, for they are consistent with romance-oriented modes of action. Even in the second part, however, Hervis continues to display the symptoms of an enamored romance hero. During a fierce battle in Brabant, for example, Duke Pierre has only to utter the name of Biatris to stimulate his grandson's prowess:

> 'Biax tresdouz niés, en cest estor mortel
> De Biatris, por deu de maïsté,
> Sovigne toi, qui tant ait biauté.'
> Hervis l'antant, le boinc branc aceré,
> At mis ou fuere, s'ait I espie couré,
> Les rens trespasse par vive poësté.
> (vv. 6734-38)[44]

Micheline de Combarieu du Grès cites this passage as an extremely rare phenomenon in the *chanson de geste*.[45] Generally, the epic hero succeeds on the strength of duty and force alone; it is the knight of courtly romance who is spurred to victory by love and thoughts of his lady. Once again, Chrétien's romances offer a chivalric model for Hervis's comportment: in the *Charrete*, it is only when Lancelot's attention is drawn to Guinevere that he gains the necessary strength and boldness to defeat Meleagant: "et force et hardemanz li croist / qu'Amors li fet molt grant aïe."[46] Indeed, Hervis takes this form of inspiration one step further during his battle against the emissaries of the Spanish King, when, at his wife's request, he pauses in mid-combat to kiss her (vv. 8534-44). Finally, when Hervis is separated from Biatris, he pines away like an exemplary courtly lover. As the squire Thieri informs Biatris:

> 'Puis icele heure que il oït parler
> Que vos cors fut et raviz et amblez,
> Ainz puis ne po dormir ne repozer,

---

[44] The line "Ait mis ou fuere..." is added by ms. E.
[45] Combarieu du Grès, *L'idéal* 375.
[46] Chrétien de Troyes, *Le Chevalier de la Charrete*, ed. Mario Roques, CFMA 86 (Paris: Champion, 1981) vv. 3720-21. It is true that the Queen's presence initially diverts Lancelot's attention from battle, causing him to lose ground temporarily. When he is reminded of his duty, however, Love begins to help rather than hinder his efforts.

> Riens ne li plaist quanqu'il puet esgarder,
> Cans de pucelle ne deduis de jongler.'
> (vv. 7989-92)[47]

Throughout the narrative, then, the hero's well-being and prowess are inextricably linked to his love for Biatris. In this respect, Hervis could hardly be further removed from the hero of the Oxford *Roland*, whose attention never strays from thoughts of his conquests, lineage, and *seigneur*. At the same time, the lack of analysis and introspection reduces the model of courtly love to a set of outward representations; allusions to familiar poetic patterns of love behavior are merely symptomatic. For all its innovative coupling of epic heroism and courtly love, *Hervis de Mes* may be said to represent only a partial synthesis of the two ideals. The text incorporates a limited number of signifiers, such as psychosomatic ailments and love-induced prowess, whose signified, *fin'amors*, can be grasped only in relation to its fuller representation in romance texts. Intertextual echos cannot take the place of a romance narrator's *glose* or a character's inner monologues. *Hervis* thus provides a veneer of the courtly love tradition without truly assimilating it into its narrative structure.

Although the love relationship itself does not alter perceptibly in the course of the story, the role of Biatris does undergo substantial changes after her husband is dubbed and named Duke of Lorraine. In Part One, as we have seen, she briefly assumes the "guardian angel" function granted to Chrétien's Enide. Unlike Erec, however, Hervis accepts his lady's advice somewhat graciously and thanks her for saving his life: "'Li vos consaus m'ont de la mort tensé'" (v. 1667). As Daniel Poirion has noted, Biatris corresponds even more closely to the "femmes avisées des romans d'aventure" such as Aelis in Jean Renart's *L'Escoufle*.[48] Like Aelis, Biatris is remarkably shrewd and resourceful, concocting ruses to put gold in her family's treasury. Although she fulfills this function briefly in Part Two, when she arranges for Hervis to steal the dowry that was intended for the Spanish King, the most developed representation of her *engin* occurs in the first part of the story during the episode of the embroidered cloth. It is Biatris's capacity to produce images

---

[47] The line "Que vos cors fut..." is added by ms. E.
[48] Poirion, Préface 8.

that links her so closely with the female protagonists of romance. Like Solomon's wife in the *Queste del saint Graal*, Biatris responds to a dilemma posed by her husband and produces the necessary forms to solve the problem:[49]

> 'Mais se j'avoie I seul drap de samin
> Et fil de soie et fil d'or autressi
> Sus qai ouvrasse le drap seignori,
> Tex IIII formes i voudroie establir.'
> (vv. 2926-29)

Unlike Solomon's wife, Biatris is fully aware of both the meaning and destination of her forms. In this respect, her function resembles that of Marie de Champagne in Chrétien's prologue to the *Charrete*: Biatris provides *matiere* and *san*, while Hervis carries out the scheme with his own *painne*.[50]

The thirteenth-century version of Hervis's wife represents, then, a positive and courtly example of female *engin*, a complementary force that supplements her lover's temporary deficiencies. When Hervis accomplishes his quest with her guidance, he integrates her forms and her shrewd commands with his own action: Biatris constitutes a principle of unity, a guide to the realization of the hero's potential ... perhaps the hero's other self.[51] In this sense, the text may not truly be considered the *livre de la belle Biautris*, for although the heroine plays a vital role in the story's development, her actions in Part One contribute essentially to the growth, education and prosperity of Hervis.

Once Biatris becomes duchess of Lorraine, however, her function acquires a more socio-political bent. Her status increases with regard to the other characters, for it has been discovered that she is the daughter of a king. It is, therefore, Biatris who will confer a superior strain of nobility upon Garin and Bégon, just as Aelis endowed her son Hervis with matrilineal nobility.[52] This emphasis on lineage tends to alter the representation of Biatris in Part Two; slipping out of the romance model, she takes on the traditional trap-

---

[49] *La Queste del saint Graal*, ed. Albert Pauphilet, CFMA 33 (Paris: Champion, 1978) 221-23.
[50] *Charrete* vv. 26-29.
[51] cf. Ferrante 2-3 and 73.
[52] Adler, "*Hervis de Mes*" 159.

pings of the epic wife and mother of heroes. While her function as child-bearer was mentioned in Part One with the birth of each child, the events of Part Two magnify the maternal element. When Biatris is kidnapped by her brother Floire, she is concerned primarily about her children: "Dix con regrete Garinet le membré / Et Begonnet, sa fillete autretel!" (vv. 7357-58, cf. v. 7685). During the siege of Metz, which adumbrates the future exploits of Garin and Bégon, Biatris appears as a sollicitous mother figure: like Guibourc in the *Chanson de Guillaume*, she tries in vain to persuade the *pueri senes* that they are not yet old enough for battle.[53]

Biatris also acquires in Part Two the duties of a duchess. In the absence of Hervis, she assumes responsibility for decisions concerning war and the governing of Metz. The people of the city report the siege directly to her:

> 'Puis icele ore que damedix fu nés
> Voir de la virge qui porta damedé
> Ains plus grans [os] ne fu mais esgardés,
> Qu'il a, ducoise, devant Mes *vo cité*.'
> (vv. 9820-23)

When the bourgeois begin hoarding food and wine, the "gent menue" appeal first to Biatris (vv. 10,374-75). As the narrative progresses, then, the role of the heroine shifts perceptibly: guardian angel to the enamored and immature Hervis in Part One, she becomes in Part Two the protectress of future heroes and of the community they will serve.

In essence, the "slippage" in Biatris's generic character parallels that of her husband. Just as the hero's personal quest gives way to more global exploits in the name of Lorraine, the object of his affections acquires the status of prize in an epic conflict.[54] In Part One, obstacles to the couple's union are construed as barriers to Hervis's personal happiness; in Part Two, the possession of Biatris becomes a question of legal rights and finally of brute force. Inspiration of a *quest* in her husband's "developmental" stages, Biatris ultimately becomes the object of a *conquest*: "'Chi vient Hervis vos fix li dus membrés / Biatrix ait sa femme *conquesté*'" (vv. 9005-06).

---

[53] *La Chanson de Guillaume*, ed. Duncan McMillan SATF 87 (Paris: Picard, 1949-50) vv. 1526-32.

[54] cf. Woods, *Aye d'Avignon* 46.

As the arena of conflict expands to include matters of diplomacy and succession, the union fulfills an increasingly suprapersonal function. Now the primary and auxiliary guarantors of society, Hervis and Biatris come to form an epic couple, linked, like Guillaume and Guibourc, by common ideals of lineage, justice, and heroism.

SECONDARY CHARACTERS

1. *Entourage*

The distinctions between secondary characters in early epic and romance derive largely from their diverging modes of conflict. In the *chanson de geste*, owing to the predominance of lineal and military concerns, the protagonist is typically surrounded by other warriors of his homeland or his lineage. He is frequently associated with a close friend or brother who serves as his *alter ego*: Roland and Olivier are, of course, the best-known examples of this phenomenon. Similar relationships appear in the Loherain cycle, notably the complementary Garin and Bégon, whose combined virtues constitute a model of chivalric perfection.[55]

Although the hero is closely associated with his family, the epic often portrays conflictual family relationships, particularly between father and son. Between maternal uncle and nephew, however, there generally exists a sympathetic bond; celebrated examples include Charlemagne and Roland as well as Guillaume and Vivien. These kinship patterns have been characterized as a sentimental survival of early Germanic matriarchal traditions.[56] Regardless of their origins, such patterns clearly fulfill an essential function in the Old French epic: they furnish a recognizable narrative substructure capable of generating and defining relationships between male characters.

The "Enfances Hervis" portion of *Hervis de Mes* offers a remarkable instance of the matriarchal kinship patterns present in

---

[55] See Gittleman 31.
[56] W.O. Farnsworth, *Uncle and Nephew in the Old French Chansons de Geste* (New York: Columbia University Press, 1913) 239. See also Claude Lévi-Strauss, *Anthropologie structurale* (Paris: Pion, 1958) I: 55.

early Old French epic. The relationship between Hervis and Thieri is extremely antagonistic: when the young man fails to do his father's business at the fair in Provins, Thieri strikes him so violently that the boy's face is covered with blood (vv. 520-23). Reconciliation is effected only through the intervention of Aelis, who threatens to ban Thieri from her bed if he does not make amends (vv. 551-58). Later, when Hervis has been exiled for his second offense, Aelis assures her husband that if her son dies in exile, Thieri will have to answer to her powerful kinsmen:

> 'Par diu, prevos, s'il est a mort livrés,
> La mort l'enfant te ferai demander
> A com de Bar qu'est de mon parenté
> Et a duc Sance de Monrial le ber,
> A mon lignage et mon fier parenté.'
> (vv. 1936-40)

The hero's encounters with his three paternal uncles mirror his quarrels with Thieri. Conversely, he establishes strong ties with his maternal relatives, particularly the count of Bar whom he assists in the Senlis tournament. Family associations, then, situate even the early portion of *Hervis de Mes* within an epic tradition that poses the mother's male relations as the son's natural protectors and allies.

At the same time, these conventional rifts and affiliations take on a new function in their romanesque context and even contribute to its creation. The negative relationship between father and son does not result in territorial disputes or blood feuds, but rather generates the son's quest for adventures and Round Tables. A very similar pattern appears in the twelfth-century Arthurian *Romance of Fergus*: the young hero, son of a *vilain* and a noblewoman, disagrees bitterly with his father about his future as a knight. As in Hervis's case, the noble mother intervenes, citing the aristocratic and chivalric heritage of the boy; he is finally allowed to join Arthur's entourage and ultimately to set out in search of adventure.[57] By sublimating adolescent rebellion into knightly *épreuve*, both Fergus and Hervis ultimately surmount the formidable obstacle posed by an unworthy paternal figure.

---

[57] Guillaume le Clerc, *The Romance of Fergus*, ed. Wilson Frescoln (Philadelphia: William H. Allen, 1983) vv. 461-517.

Even the positive relationship between Hervis and his maternal relatives does not conform to epic models in the early episodes of *Hervis de Mes*. At first, the bonds of kinship are not portrayed on a true battleground, but rather on the lists of the Senlis tournament. Moreover, the relatives are unaware of the young man's true identity, since Hervis prefers (like many romance heroes) to remain anonymous during his early exploits. The blood ties that later unite the lineage in territorial conflict are thus in a latent stage during the first part of the text. The Count of Bar's cause serves here as a means to a romanesque end, namely Hervis's desire to "cevaucier et errer" (v. 2320).

Indeed, the "adventure" portion of *Hervis de Mes* portrays the hero's entourage (or lack thereof) predominantly in terms of romanesque patterns. Hervis's adventures are often solitary: he sets out for the fairs at Provins and Lagny with his paternal uncles, but abandons them each time on arrival. He is attended by the young squire Gerart at the tournament in Senlis, but he participates alone. Moreover, he is unaccompanied on his mission to the city of Tyre. While he engages twenty *valets* to help defend his treasure on the return trip, his encounter with Hinbaut is an individual effort: "'Jou voel mon cors vers le sien esprover'" (v. 4047). Like many an Arthurian knight, Hervis engages in a self-defining quest that temporarily separates him from his family and his peers.

In Part Two, however, members of Hervis's lineage assume a greater role, and the hero associates himself to a much greater degree with these other warriors. First of all, his most important maternal relative, Duke Pierre, accompanies him to Brabant and assists him in their mutual struggle. Pierre does not, of course, represent the sort of companion that Roland found in Olivier; Hervis makes it clear that young blood is supplanting the old guard, particularly on the battlefield: "'Nous jovenchel si legier baceler / Souffrir devommes les vens et les orés'" (vv. 6256-57). In addition, however, the other relatives and allies of Aelis reappear as soon as Hervis returns from the Tyre adventure, at which time the Count of Bar and Sanson de Monroial both participate in their young cousin's dubbing ceremony. These maternal relatives will continue to serve as military allies for the remainder of the text. Along with the Counts of Aspremont and Montbeliart, they command battalions in Brabant; they gather a special defense unit to protect Hervis against the treacherous ambush of King Oudart's

Scottish army; and later, they volunteer to assist Hervis in recovering his wife: "'Nos parens es et nos carnex amis / Ne te faurrons tresc'a membres tolir'" (vv. 7542-43).

The second half of the narrative thus portrays the constituents of the hero's entourage as faithful members of a kinship group. Like the companions of Roland and Guillaume, they display great prowess in their own right, distinguishing themselves in combat. In addition, however, they function as a backdrop for the superior valor and strength of the epic hero. As the narrator announces, Hervis will eventually surpass his entire lineage: "Puis fu il d'armes si vassaus esprovés / Qu'il sormonta trestout son parenté" (vv. 5106-7).

2. *Adversaries*

In the Old French epic, adversaries most often appear in the form of the hated Saracen, a title that encompasses heathens from all lands. Pagans occasionally resemble the Christian knights in strength, valor and social organization; their only deficiency is devotion to Mohammed: "Fust chrestïens, asez oüst barnet."[58] However, epic texts stress most often the otherness of the heathen enemy by associating Saracens with exotic names, far-away lands and a strange appearance: representative figures include the evil Chernubles de Munigre in the *Chanson de Roland* and Corsolt in the *Couronnement de Louis*. Other enemies include members of an opposing lineage: in *Garin le Loherain*, Fromont de Lens exemplifies the malevolence of a treacherous line of Bordelais. On occasion, internecine warfare poses a former ally as an enemy, as in *Raoul de Cambrai*.

Romance displays a somewhat more colorful array of adversaries, partly because it exploits the resources of the Celtic *merveilleux*. The romance hero defends the defenseless against dragons, trolls, giants, and a variety of other fabulous creatures. In addition, humanly evil knights serve to test the protagonist's valor: particularly in the non-Arthurian romance of adventure, opponents may appear in the form of human obstacles to the happiness of two lovers. In tournaments, finally, competitors may be the hero's associates (often in disguise) as well as kings and barons from far-away lands.

---

[58] *La Chanson de Roland*, ed. Moignet, v. 899.

The adversaries encountered by Hervis contribute to the generic division we have already observed. The "adventure" segment features typical romance adversaries: three wicked young men who attempt to appropriate the heroine, an unsympathetic parent who poses obstacles to young love, the Count of Flanders and his knights, who compete with Hervis and the Count of Bar for the prize in a tournament, and the giant bandit Hinbaut.

This last opponent is perhaps the most illuminating, particularly since he represents a rare instance of the supernatural *merveilleux* in *Hervis de Mes*:

> XI piés ot li glous en son ester,
> La char ot noire com armens destemprés
> Et les iex rouges con carbons embrasés.
> (vv. 3999-4001)

That Hinbaut is a giant does not situate him exclusively within the romance tradition. In the *Chanson de Roland*, for example, Baligant's allies include "des jaianz de Malprose" (v. 3253). Hinbaut has even more affinities with the giant Corsolt faced by Guillaume in the *Couronnement de Louis*: "Lez et anches, hideus comme aversier / Les eulz ot roges com charbon en braisier."[59] What distinguishes Hinbaut from these epic giants is not supernatural size and hideousness but rather social orientation and context. Corsolt is a pagan king who resides in a fortress; he therefore represents a threat to Christianity and a territory to be conquered for France. Hinbaut, on the other hand, is a *larron* whose function corresponds to that of the bandits in *Fergus* (vv. 628-712, 3091-3406). Like these bandits, and indeed like many a romance adversary, Hinbaut resides in the forest, guarding a bridge which travellers cannot cross without being robbed. This enemy therefore represents a threat to individual adventurers, an obstacle to be overcome in the course of a quest, and a means of proving the hero's valor.

In the second part of the story, changing modes of conflict condition the appearance of opponents more appropriate to the epic ethos. Anseÿs of Cologne, related by marriage to Duke Pierre, constitutes an intra-familial enemy in a territorial dispute. Uistasse,

---

[59] Yvan G. Lepage, ed., *Les Rédactions en vers du Couronnement de Louis* (Paris: Droz, 1978), Rédaction AB, vv. 508-9. All further references to the *Couronnement de Louis* will be drawn from this edition.

Floire, and the Kings of Portugal, Navarre, and Aragon also embody feudal and lineal concerns: bound by their contractual and vassalic obligations to the King of Spain, they must join forces to assert his claim on the fair Biatris.

Significantly, Hervis encounters a second giant during the latter portion of the tale: this adversary, King Oudart of Scotland, offers a striking contrast to his romanesque counterpart in the Hinbaut episode. It is true that Oudart and Hinbaut are of precisely the same height; a messenger describes the former as follows: "·XI· piés a li rois en son ester / Gaians ressamble, tant est grans et formés" (vv. 9150-51). Nonetheless, two significant contextual markers distinguish Oudart: first, like the epic giant Corsolt, he is an enemy king; second, he is the son of Anseÿs' sister. The sympathetic relationship between Oudart and his maternal uncle corresponds to similar configurations in the Loherain camp, where Hervis is supported by his maternal cousins and grandfather. Like the pagan kings in the *Chanson de Roland*, then, Oudart and Anseÿs resemble their righteous enemies in social organization. If only they weren't "traïtor mortel" (v. 9484), they might be fit companions for the Loherain heroes.

THE DIEGETIC WORLD

Hans-Robert Jauss characterizes the fictional universe of the early *chanson de geste* as symbolic: "Only a few symbols for the outer world (*pin*, *olivier*) frame the portrayal of heroic acts."[60] Among these objects are the hero's sword and horse, each of which generally has a name and is closely associated with the exploits of its possessor; less differentiated are the various pieces of armor evoked by the jongleur before and during battle. Descriptions of landscape often direct the reader/listener's attention to the imminent danger or profound significance of ensuing action, as in the celebrated lines "Halt sunt li pui e li val tenebrus / Les roches bises, les destreiz merveillus" (*Roland*, vv. 814-15). Stephen G. Nichols has eloquently demonstrated the function of place and relic in accounts of the Roncevaux disaster: by systematically conjoining topographical configuration and sacred symbolism, the Oxford *Roland* "displaced

---

[60] Jauss, *Toward* 86.

the meaning and the function of the site from military denotation to religious connotation."[61] Topography may also contribute to plausibility and to the affective link between text and receiver: in the *geste des Loherains*, the relatively precise and accurate geographical indications serve largely to establish a bond of familiarity with the audience.[62] All in all, however, descriptions of the heroes' surroundings are rather sparse in the early *chanson de geste*.

When considered in its entirety, *Hervis de Mes* corresponds to the French epic tradition in its evocation of the diegetic universe. References to the characters' surroundings are rather sparse, and the high frequency of verbal locutions attests to the overwhelming supremacy of action in the text. The fictional world is present only in nominal glimpses, including animals, armor, booty, and a few articles of clothing. Like the other songs of the Loherain cycle, *Hervis* amplifies the role of geographical detail: Philippe Walter has demonstrated the significance of Metz as the locus of a "geopolitical" mythmaking process:

> ... on peut lire à travers la légende d'*Hervis* les affinités profondes de la monarchie française et de la terre lorraine. On peut y percevoir également le singulier destin stratégique qui attend cette ville-symbole, berceau des Carolingiens et terre d'enjeu entre le monde roman et le monde germanique.[63]

By means of symbolic redirection, then, a real site translates the historical and political forces at work in thirteenth-century Lorraine. Whereas "Roncevaux" directs our attention upward, "Metz" evokes a horizontal axis linking the present with a mythical pre-Carolingian past. This metaphorical transformation of real topography, a constant feature of Old French epic, operates throughout the *Hervis* narrative.

The first half of the text, however, displays on occasion a predilection for the milieux and descriptions associated with romance. The first and most notable instance occurs in the prelude to Biatris's first abduction. Left to her own devices while her guardian attends mass, the maiden enters a "vergier," the *locus amoenus* of

---

[61] Stephen G. Nichols, *Romanesque Signs: Early Medieval Narrative and Iconography* (New Haven and London: Yale University Press, 1983) 159.
[62] See Ruth Parmly, *The Geographical References*.
[63] Walter, "Géographie" 162.

amorous adventure in both courtly love lyric and romance; the site is intertextually appropriate, as she has just asserted her desire for a "legier baceler" (v. 867). Accompanying indications conform to the traditional disposition of the *locus amoenus*:

> Ce fu en may que on dist en esté
> Biaus est li tens et verdissent li prez,
> Chil oisel cantent doucement et souef
> (vv. 856, 856a, 857)

In addition, the text provides us with rare details concerning the heroine's attire:

> Une cemise blance con flors de pré
> Ont lors vestue Bïatris au vis cler,
> Puis li vestirent I bliaut d'or ouvré
> Et une gipe de gris sans arrester.
> Et puis li ont I mantel afublé
> D'un chier dïaspre, moult par fut bien foré,
> A bendes d'or estoit molt bien ovré.
> A II filz d'or ont ces crins galonez,
> Que plus resplandent que orfrois esmerés.
> (vv. 880-89)[64]

Such descriptions are common in romance and, according to Paul Zumthor, serve to fix a certain tonality: a stylized evocation of magnificent clothing conforms to the general aura of beauty and elegance appropriate to the amorous context.[65] Of course, at this stage, the heroine's desire is temporarily transferred to the beholders of the scene, namely the ten wicked squires who become enamored of the "'fee en cel vergier ramé'" (v. 924).

We have already alluded to other objects and milieux that recall those of courtly romance. The *drap* serves as an example of the *merveilleux* by virtue of its splendor and its effects on narrative development. A dangerous forest sets the scene for the hero's various *épreuves*: the bridge guarded by the giant Hinbaut, for example, recalls the menacing Other World of Arthurian tales, a fictive space in which the forces of chivalry confront antagonistic values. Erich

---

[64] Ms. E omits line 888 of Stengel's edition: "Et pardeseure erent sorargenté."
[65] Zumthor, *Essai* 354.

Köhler interprets this fabulous and demonic *Autre monde* as the fictional projection of real social antagonism: only the elected hero is able to dominate these forces and effect a return to stability.[66] Here, the generous Hervis confronts the avarice that has long haunted the forest:

> Dedens le bos u suelent converser
> En une creute qu'iere d'antiquité,
> Ilueques estoient li ceval establé,
> Et tant d'avoir i avoit amassé
> Dont il avoient marcheans desrobés,
> Maint pelerin, [maint] evesque et abbé.
> (vv. 4112-17)

The moral dangers of pure gain are thus projected onto the obscure, wooded decor that so often frames the chivalric adventures of romance.

At the same time, the Hinbaut episode once again represents a transition between epic and romance narrative content. Just as the giant himself incorporates components from both traditions, the arena of conflict displays a certain generic mixture. Just before Hervis reaches Hinbaut's lair, imminent danger is evoked in a vertically-oriented landscape reminiscent of Roncevaux: "Haut sont li tertre, moult font a redouter" (v. 3990). The typological potential of this epic motif is immediately diminished, however, by the appearance of a typically Arthurian locus:

> Parmi I val le convint trespasser,
> De V journees environ de tous les
> N'i puet nus hom par le païs passer
> Fors par I pont, dont parfont sont li gué,
> XXX larron qui font a redouter ...
> (vv. 3992-96).

The hero's final adventure, then, places him at the crossroads of epic and romance.

Unlike *Huon de Bordeaux* and other "hybrid" epics of the thirteenth century, however, *Hervis de Mes* does not accord a signif-

---

[66] Erich Köhler, *L'Aventure chevaleresque: Idéal et réalité dans le roman courtois*, trans. Eliane Kaufholz (Paris: Gallimard, 1970) 38.

icant role to the Celtic marvel. Rather, the text is perhaps best known for its depiction of daily life in thirteenth-century Lorraine, particularly in the fair episodes.[67] For this reason, *Hervis* has been compared to the non-Arthurian adventure romances of Gautier d'Arras and Jean Renart, both of whom seem to have reacted against the *merveilleux* by augmenting the function of everyday details and decors.[68] Indeed, the mundane, practical considerations that receive so much attention in *L'Escoufle* do occupy a rather remarkable place in the first half of *Hervis de Mes*. A preoccupation with basic human needs is striking: the procurement of ordinary bread, for example, is a repeated theme. Biatris grows hungry in the forest and obliges Hervis to seek bread from a herdsman; the clerics held captive by Hinbaut are dying of hunger and beg for a bit of bread; Hervis's children go hungry because of their father's extravagant spending, and Biatris laments the lack of bread; the reformed bandit Thieri takes pity on the children and provides Biatris with the wherewithal to purchase bread.

Frequent and precise notations of money are also striking in this portion of the story. We are told exactly how much gold Hervis spends at the fairs: one thousand marks on entertainment, three thousand marks for his steed and hunting animals (minus ten pounds sterling left over for the return voyage), and sixteen thousand marks for Biatris (minus twenty pounds sterling for the return voyage). The sums are often weighed: "Trestot l'avoir fait a balance peser" (v. 1451). The frequency and preciseness of these indications distinguish *Hervis de Mes* from earlier *chansons de geste*, in which one rarely encounters "la monnaie sonnante et trébuchante."[69]

Nonetheless, claims to "realism" – for both *Hervis* and the romances to which it has been compared – have been somewhat exaggerated: descriptions still remain highly stylized and correspond to a limited number of typical configurations. The fair episodes in *Hervis de Mes* are not, in fact, a document of medieval economic life; like the decors of romance, they serve a didactic purpose, thereby contributing to the "sen" of the text. The narrator-jongleur generally sets forth only those details which contribute to the elab-

---

[67] Edmund Stengel speaks of the "wertwollen Angaben über das mittelalterliche Marktwesen und Marktleben, welche unser Dichter mit behaglicher Ausfuhrlichkeit zu wiederholten Malen schildert ...," *Vorwort* V.

[68] Poirion, "Préface" 7-8.

[69] Combarieu du Grès, *L'idéal* 25.

oration of the exemplum: the enumeration of foods and gifts lavished upon Hervis's guests, as well as the precise sums spent at the fairs, function principally to illustrate the young hero's excessive spending habits.

Only a few vestiges of romanesque decors and objects remain in the second part of Hervis's story. The rescue of Biatris, for example, is effected with the help of a ring that assures the heroine of Hervis's identity; such tokens frequently facilitate encounters between the lovers of romance.[70] The rescue also takes place in a setting that briefly recalls the earlier Hinbaut episode: the Loherain contingent must negotiate "I· iaue. . . Moult perillouze" by means of a bridge whose passage will ensure their safety (vv. 8594-98). Finally, one episode evokes the practical details of the previous fair episodes: Floire's expedition to Metz occasions brief references to meals and money, since he duplicates Hervis's earlier ruse by disguising himself as a Norman merchant. Significantly, all of these instances involve abbreviated reflections of events occurring in the first portion of the narrative. As we have seen, the second abduction/rescue of Biatris as well as the second disguised-merchant ruse are played out in a predominantly epic context; the diminished role of romance motifs is underscored by the recurrence of similar events.

Indeed, the second half of the text strongly favors settings and objects gleaned from the epic tradition. Between battles, the knights retire to their "trefs" and "encubes"; battles themselves take place "pres du castel," and the surroundings are often evoked with reference to pillage and destruction: "Copent ces vingnes, s'ont les leuz desartez" (v. 9815); "Que bués que vakes que moutons autretel" (v. 6208). Hervis is no longer associated with sums of money, but with his mighty horse, Rufin and especially with his sword, Florence:

> Lonc est l'espee et moult ot de biaté,
> N'avoit millor en la crestïenté
> Que chevaliers peüst adonc porter;
> Durandars a point d'or noielé
> N'estoit forgie ne Cortains autretels.
> (vv. 5562-66)

---

[70] The later manuscripts N and T amplify this episode by adding a second ring with magical powers. See *Anlage VI* in Stengel's edition (pp. 439-40).

The allusion to other legendary swords situates Florence in the tradition of symbolic objects associated with great epic heroes.

* * *

The first half of *Hervis de Mes*, then, selects a significant portion of its content from the romance tradition, while the second half departs less frequently from the parameters of earlier *chansons de geste*. All five categories examined above are clearly interdependent: certain modes of conflict lend themselves to certain types of matter, characters, and decor. Within the binary structure of the work, transitional episodes effect a relatively smooth passage from "romance" to "epic" content: the presence or absence of Duke Pierre seems to favor generic transformations, and the pivotal Hinbaut episode represents a curious mixture of epic and romance traits.

This narrative flexibility suggests that the generic distinctions perceived by modern scholars are valid only if considered as broad tendencies, susceptible to variation very early in the history of vernacular French literature. The combinatory patterns in *Hervis de Mes* represent a relatively early stage in the development of recorded *chansons de geste*; its processes of variation and expansion mediate the transition between the Oxford *Roland*, *Garin le Loherain*, and the epic poems of the fourteenth and fifteenth centuries.

CHAPTER TWO

NARRATIVE STRUCTURE AND THE
POETICS OF LINEAGE

Like many *chansons de geste* of the second generation, *Hervis de Mes* has been criticized for a lack of narrative organization: Paulin Paris, for instance, deemed the story a disjointed amalgamation of episodes "sans ordre, sans motifs, et sans résultats."[1] Such judgments, of course, are based mainly on modern novelistic expectations of textual coherence that were not shared by medieval readers or listeners. Upon close examination, the text reveals a carefully constructed pattern designed to pose and solve a fundamental social problem: the hero's mixed lineage generates a confrontation between aristocratic and bourgeois value systems, and it is this confrontation that informs the work's narrative organization.

Paulin Paris was, however, justified in citing a certain lack of structural unity in *Hervis*, for the bipartition we have observed in the nature of discrete story elements is also manifest on the level of narrative composition. Indeed, the locus of generic division corresponds to a distinct transformation in the overall organization of story events: while the first part is primarily constructed as a consecutive sequence, the hero's dubbing ceremony is followed by the systematic weaving of two related plots. Although the two parts share a common hero and a common theme, the text does display a certain measure of compositional disjunction.

Morever, each part is structured around a different solution to the problem of the hero's mixed lineage. This discrepancy is largely responsible for diverging critical interpretations of the work: the first half of the story tends to justify the "bourgeois hero" thesis, while the second half asserts the purity of the hero's nobility. A clos-

---

[1] Paulin Paris, "Trouvères, chansons de geste," *Histoire littéraire de la France* 22 (Paris: Didot, 1852) 602.

er look at the two diverging modes of composition and conflict resolution will reveal the didactic possibilities inherent in this bipartite organization.

MODES AND PRINCIPLES OF COMPOSITION

The *chanson de geste* does not always lend itself to a smooth division into parts, particularly since formal divisions (such as laisse boundaries) do not correspond systematically to changes in episode. In order to facilitate the analysis of narrative composition, however, we have outlined the major narrative articulations of *Hervis de Mes* according to the following criteria: First of all, the limits of an "episode" may be determined by significant spatial or temporal displacement; therefore, the hero's journeys to the fairs are distinct from their preparation in Metz. Secondly, conventional epic themes and motifs (in the Rychnerian sense) as well as typical romance schemas mark the boundaries of many episodes; thus, the *conseil* and the *tournoi* represent obvious divisions. Secondary motifs, such as the dispatch and arrival of messengers, are generally subsumed under larger categories; although such events are discrete units of the epic tradition, their impact on the story is predicated upon the larger episodes to which they belong.

While separate episodes tend to occupy at least fifty lines of the poem, certain events, regardless of the paucity of textual space devoted to them, affect the course of the narrative in a significant way and thus constitute distinct units. The marriage of Aelis and Thieri, which occupies a mere eight lines in the text, is representative of this category.

Larger divisions or "sections" may be dictated by obvious turning points in the narrative. These junctures are generally marked by major spatial or temporal shifts as well as momentous advances in the development of the plot. The hero's expedition to Tyre, for example, transports him to the Orient and redirects the fortune of his family; this sequence thus constitutes a separate series of adventures. Finally, as we have seen, the text displays a large-scale division into two roughly equal "parts" that favor diverging thematic and compositional devices. Appendix A provides a detailed outline of narrative articulations in *Hervis de Mes*.

* * *

Structuralist narrative theory continues to offer a useful point of departure for the analysis of principles governing the composition of stories. According to Tzvetan Todorov, represented events may be organized according to three fundamental modes: *enchaînement*, a relationship of consequence and/or consecution; *enchâssement*, the embedding of one narrative within another; and *alternance*, the alternation of two or more plot lines.[2] Since embedding does not play a significant role in *Hervis de Mes*, this analysis will focus on the two remaining processes.[3]

Although no medieval genre is associated exclusively with any particular compositional mode, consecution characterizes the overall temporal structure of most early *chansons de geste* and verse romances.[4] Certain epics, such as the *Couronnement de Louis*, contain a consecutive series of episodes without causal connection, linked primarily by the presence of the same hero; others, such as the *Chanson de Roland*, are said to exhibit a "dramatic" structure with a central conflict, preparation, and dénouement.[5] Verse romances generally contain a series of episodes that constitute a particular hero's quest; this quest is often marked by a gradation of adventures.

When scholars consider alternation in medieval texts, they most often use the term "interlace" (*entrelacement*).[6] This label, however, is not universally employed to designate the same procedure. Ferdinand Lot's canonical definition of interlace was conceived in the context of the thirteenth-century prose *Lancelot*:

---

[2] Tzvetan Todorov, *Littérature et signification*, Langue et langage (Paris: Larousse, 1967) 72.

[3] Embedding is used only occasionally and on a very small scale, e.g. when messengers relate their messages and when characters give brief accounts of past events. See, for example, vv. 2485-2507, where Hervis's host relates events from Thieri's past.

[4] Despite this tendency toward consecutive ordering, early medieval narratives do tend to de-emphasize sequential relations in favor of analogical, "spatial" form. See Norris J. Lacy, "Spatial Form in Medieval Romance," *Yale French Studies* 51 (1974): 160-69 and "Spatial Form in the *Mort Artu*," *Symposium* 31 (1977): 337-45. This technique is discussed below with regard to symmetrical sequences in *Hervis de Mes*.

[5] Jean Rychner, *La Chanson de geste: Essai sur l'art épique des jongleurs*, Société de publications romanes et françaises 53 (Geneva: Droz, 1955) 39, 44-45. The "structure" of the Oxford *Roland* is, of course, subject to a wide variety of critical interpretations.

[6] Portions of this discussion appear in "*La Tresse*: Interlace in the *chanson de geste*," to be published in *French Forum* 15.3 (1990): 261-75.

> Aucune aventure ne forme un tout se suffisant à lui-même. D'une part des épisodes antérieurs, laissés provisoirement de côté, y prolongent des ramifications, d'autre part des épisodes subséquents, proches ou lointains, y sont amorcés.[7]

According to Lot, interlaced texts such as the *Queste del saint Graal* are characterized by a systematic imbrication of adventures, none of which could be eliminated from the whole. Some scholars consider Lot's model to be the only pure manifestation of interlace, thereby excluding many texts from the structural category.[8]

While this definition is still useful for the study of the *Lancelot-Graal*, it does not account for the looser form of "weaving" found in many romances and *chansons de geste*. Other studies have attempted to broaden the category, occasionally to the extent that "interlace" has lost its specificity: scholars have associated the device even with twelfth-century epics such as the *Couronnement de Louis*.[9] In a recent article on the *Enfances Renier*, María L. D. Fernández offers the most cogent analysis to date. She isolates three narrative conditions essential to the use of interlace in any text, i.e. multiple characters, temporal imbrication, and spatial displacement; nonetheless, she does not venture to generalize about the relationship between the different narrative strands.[10] In fact, no single construct takes into consideration all of the factors shared by the group of texts that scholars have traditionally described as "interlaced."[11]

---

[7] Ferdinand Lot, *Etude sur le Lancelot en prose* (Paris: Champion, 1918) 17.

[8] See, for example, François Suard, *Guillaume d'Orange: Etude du roman en prose*, Bibliothèque du XVe siècle 44 (Paris: Champion, 1979) 181.

[9] Charles Altman, "Medieval Narrative vs. Modern Assumptions: Revising Inadequate Typology," *Diacritics* 4 (1974): 14.

[10] María Luisa Donaire Fernández, "*Enfances Renier*: l'entrelacement: une technique du roman, *Essor et fortune de la chanson de geste dans l'Europe et l'Orient latin*, Actes du IXe congrès de la Société Rencesvals, vol. 2 (Modena: Mucchi, 1984) 490-93. The article also considers the linguistic dimension of interlace, comparing epic and romance transition formulas.

[11] William Ryding, in his *Structure in Medieval Narrative* (The Hague and Paris: Mouton, 1971), applies Lot's definition to a group of medieval narratives from Chrétien's *Perceval* to the works of Ariosto. Charles Altman, in his critique of Ryding, calls for a more precise definition of interlace. He distinguishes two types: "alternation between two interdependent plot lines, and more or less random combination of less closely related sequences" (14). His distinctions, however, are based solely on considerations of spatial displacement, change of characters, and "narrative interest." These broad parameters account for his curious comparison between *Aucassin et Nicolette* and the *Couronnement de Louis*, whose narrative structures are actually quite different.

In fact, many non-consecutive medieval texts are situated on a continuum whose extremes are represented by the *Couronnement de Louis* and the *Queste del saint Graal*. At one end of the spectrum we find a certain number of works characterized by simple alternation. The *Couronnement de Louis*, for example, does present an occasional shift of focus; however, each instance occurs within a single episode (frequently a battle), and the shift occupies only part of a laisse for a maximum of 35 lines. Both spatial displacement and temporal imbrication are minor: our attention shifts only to the other side of the battlefield, and events overlap by an hour or less. This text cannot, therefore, be said to display systematic interlace: rather, a temporary oscillation functions to present two opposing views of the same episode. While the alternation device is rather frequent in epics of the twelfth century, no early *chanson de geste* employs inter-episodic weaving as a major structural technique.[12]

By contrast, the *Queste del saint Graal* represents an intricate, systematic form of alternation. This romance alternates the adventures of many different characters for the greater part of the story. We follow individual knights for sequences of episodes that occupy long passages in the *récit*. The characters are separated by space, and their adventures overlap by long periods of time in the *histoire*. As for the relationship between narrative strands, Lot has demonstrated the extent to which the various quests are thematically and structurally interdependent.[13]

A large group of narratives, both epic and romance, fall somewhere in between the categories of simple alternation and large-scale interlace of inextricably linked events. These intermediate works employ inter-episodic alternation over a significant portion of the narrative; their characters are dispersed to remote geographical locations, or to locations perceived as remote by the characters; events that overlap by long periods of time in the story are recounted successively; and the alternating events are linked, if not inextri-

---

[12] According to Fernández, ". . . l'entrelacement n'est pas utilisé par l'épopée médiévale française avant la fin du XIIe siècle" (507). In a recent study of *Garin le Loherain*, Jean-Pierre Martin explores a transitional device, i.e. "plurilinear narration." *Garin* contains no true flashbacks, and the time schema is often quite vague; but the poet does occasionally recount roughly simultaneous maneuvers of the same principal action, notably the first phase of the Loherain-Bordelais feud. See Jean-Pierre Martin, "Sur le jeu des motifs dans *Garin le Loheren*: une narration plurilinéaire," *Revue des langues romanes* 91 (1987) 81-90.

[13] Lot, *Etude* 27.

cably bound, by conflict, character or theme. Texts composed under these conditions display a definite weaving pattern, and therefore must be included in the structural category of "interlace."

These interlaced narratives may be further divided into two subtypes. In some texts, alternating strands could theoretically exist as independent units; nonetheless, their combination is not random, for they are joined by structural links such as principal character or thematic considerations.[14] Chrétien's *Perceval* and a number of later epics share this classification. While the dual or multiple plots do not always form an entirely dependent chain, they do exhibit what might be called "associative interlace": narrative strands are held together by mutual association with the protagonist and/or recurring themes. Another form of the technique (less frequent in epic than in romance) involves the alternation of *complementary* and interdependent threads, as in *Ami et Amile* or *Aucassin et Nicolette*. In such texts, alternation generally arises from the separation of protagonists involved in a mutual search for the lost other(s), and thus the whole is contingent upon each narrative thread. It must be noted that these compositional strategies are not mutually exclusive; the later *chanson de geste* often exploited both subtypes within the same story.

COMBINATORY STRATEGIES IN *HERVIS DE MES*

The composite design of *Hervis de Mes* demonstrates that thirteenth-century epic poets were experimenting with different forms of narrative organization within the same textual unit.

The first two sections of Part One, which prepare the eventual meeting of Hervis and Biatris, clearly display a very similar pattern. Hervis and Biatris are each victims of a council that proposes marriage as a solution to a lord's dilemma; in both cases, the solution serves to create further conflict: The "mixed marriage" of Thieri and Aelis produces a son who struggles with his heritage, and the marriage proposed by the elderly Spanish King is distasteful to the young Biatris. Moreover, the latter conflicts both generate a rebellion against paternal authority. After the departure of Duke Pierre,

---

[14] It should be recalled that Altman described this sort of combination as "more or less random" (14).

Thieri asserts the dominance of merchant values and attempts to instill these values in his son; Hervis, however, actively resists his father's will, deliberately disobeying Thieri's wishes: "'J'accaterai mon bon et mon devis'" (v. 608). Biatris, for her part, plays a more passive role: she silently opposes her father's nuptial agreement with the King of Spain, not daring to voice her objections: "N'osa la belle son panser descovrir" (v. 813). After her parents' departure, she indicates her preference for a "legier baceler" (v. 867); this desire is fulfilled (somewhat obliquely) by her subsequent abduction, which ultimately unites her with the "baceler" Hervis.

The parallel structure of sections A and B may be schematized as follows:

> exposition → *conseil* → wedding (plans) → departure of (grand) parents → conflict with father → removal to Lagny

Such patterns of symmetrical development are typical of the "spatial form" of composition described by Norris J. Lacy.[15] The Oxford *Roland*, for example, opens with two parallel sections that take place in the opposing camps of Marsilie and Charlemagne; each section depicts a *conseil* followed by the dispatch of an ambassador. Like the *Roland*, *Hervis de Mes* evinces here a deliberate symmetry, designed to reveal similarities and contrasts between characters and eventually to bring the latter into some kind of confrontation. In *Hervis*, the two sequences function to move the hero and heroine along parallel trajectories and ultimately to effect their "chance" encounter.

The parallel opening sections of *Hervis de Mes* do differ from those of the *Roland* in one important respect, namely the ordering of events on the levels of story time (*temps de l'histoire*) and narrated time (*temps du récit*). In the *Roland*, the symmetrical sequences represent consecutive time periods on both levels; in *Hervis*, however, there is a marked disparity between *histoire* and *récit*. While the text does not always furnish precise or consistent temporal indications, it is clear that Section B opens with events that occurred well before the last episode of Section A: the *récit* provides background information on both Hervis and Biatris before uniting them

---

[15] See Note 4.

in the same time frame. The opening sections of the story thus contain the rudiments of complementary interlace, i.e. two lengthy, interdependent sequences of events, separated by space, and displaying a measure of temporal overlap.

The text immediately abandons this form of composition, however, as soon as the hero and heroine are joined in Lagny. Thus, the two plot lines are not truly permitted to alternate; rather, they fuse, for the remainder of Part One, into a unified, consecutive narrative thread constituted by Hervis's early adventures.

It is true that a certain degree of temporal and spatial alternation may be observed within episodes: as in the *Couronnement de Louis* and *Garin le Loherain*, the story occasionally shifts focus to the actions of related characters. In the episode of the failed kidnapping, for example, the narrator relates first of all Hervis's purchase of Biatris, then the simultaneous machinations of the wicked young men overhearing the transaction. After the hero's confrontation with the would-be kidnappers, the scene shifts temporarily to Lagny, whose provost has lost a son in the skirmish. The different articulations are punctuated by the typical transition formulas "Or vous devons conter" and "vos vorromes parler."

Intra-episodic alternation, then, permits the narrator to recount different aspects of the same event. On a large scale, however, the episodes in sections C through F display a linear progression that spans nearly four thousand lines (in the *récit*) and approximately eight years (in the *histoire*). It is consecution, therefore, that characterizes Part One as a whole: the initial presentation of separate plot lines fuses into a unified, consecutive chain of events relating to the hero's quest to overcome his mixed heritage. As noted in the preceding chapter, these adventures are gradated to provide the hero with increasingly challenging adversaries: first, the three wicked young men (Section C-3), then the Count of Flanders and his allies (D-1), and finally the giant Hinbaut with his group of bandits (E-8). The passage of time reflects the gradual development of a rather brash youth into the mature Duke of Lorraine. The composition of the first half of the narrative, then, corresponds generically to the nature of its discrete story components: romance features are organized in typical romance fashion.

Hervis's ascension to the rank of *chevalier* and duke is followed by a rupture in the consecutive mode of composition. The more conventionally "epic" material in Part Two is organized by a technique widely used in thirteenth-century prose romance, namely the systematic interlacing of related plots. The device permits the fragmented narration of simultaneous story events occurring in different arenas: while Hervis faces Anseÿs of Cologne in a feudal conflict over Brabant, the King of Spain struggles to gain possession of Biatris. The jongleur punctuates the narrative by ten plot junctures, shifting back and forth between the two trajectories and continually deferring resolution. Conventional transition formulas recall the metaphor of the narrative "trace" or trail found in the prologue: the jongleur frequently interrupts his tale in the midst of one character's voyage to follow the travels of another:

> Or vous *lairons* chi des essauz aler,
> Et de Hervi le gentil baceler,
> A poc de terme i vorrai *retorner*,
> Il *cevauchoit* avoec lui son barné,
> Des II paumiers vos vorrommes parler,
> Qui tant avoient *cevauchiet* et erret.
> (vv. 5881-86)

By means of strategic departures and returns, the narrator weaves the itineraries of separate characters into a textual whole – "*tote* la tresse."

At first, this pattern is characterized by the alternation of large narrative blocks. Section A, which depicts the beginning of the war in Brabant, treats this subject almost exclusively for 1310 lines, with only a brief interlude to prepare the abduction of Biatris. Similarly, Section B devotes its 2156 lines to the kidnapping and rescue of the heroine; the scene shifts to Brabant only to depict the hero's discovery of his wife's disappearance and Anseÿs's plans to exploit Hervis's absence.

Section C, however, inaugurates a more rapid form of alternation, as the narrative oscillates back and forth between the two plots every few hundred lines. Dramatic tension builds as the jongleur interrupts his account of the siege of Louvain in order to relate the siege of Metz; battle in Louvain gives way to battle in Metz. Finally, the two plots are resolved – successively in the *récit*, simultaneously in the *histoire*.

It is clear that the war in Brabant and the dispute over Biatris could theoretically exist as separate entities; indeed, the poet(s) may well have culled them from different sources. Far from constituting a disjointed amalgamation, however, the narrative is designed in a symmetrical pattern that poses Hervis as a structural link between alternating sequences.

First of all, both disputes arise from a challenge to the hero's rights and possessions. The war in Brabant questions his right to inherit that duchy; the dispute over Biatris sets the marital and property rights of Hervis against a formal agreement concluded by the King of Spain. In each case, the hero must take defensive action:

(of Brabant): 'Mienne est la terre, li dons m'en est donnés.
Non ai Hervis, ensi sui apellés,
Je te chalons la terre et le regné.'
(vv. 6099-6101)

(of Biatris): 'Rois de Navare, cel ceval me tornez,
Je vous caloing Biatrix au vis cler.'
(vv. 8498-99)

Hervis's enemies each have dual motives for challenging his claims: Anseÿs maintains that Brabant belongs to him through his wife, niece of the deceased duke of Brabant (vv. 6370-74), and Biatris's family cites an obligation to the King of Spain (vv. 5936-40, 8817-49). Both, however, consider Hervis inadequate for another significant reason, namely his lineage:

ANSEŸS: '*Fix de vilain* certes ne doit tenir
Tel ducee; car n'afiert pas a lui.'
(vv. 6376-77)

KING OF TYRE: 'Ce fut damages, grans duels et grans vité,
Fix de vilain jeut onques a son costé.'
(vv. 8821-22)

Hervis and his advocates consistently respond to this charge by citing his matrilineal nobility:[16]

---

[16] See Alfred Adler, "*Hervis de Mes* and the Matrilineal Nobility of Champagne," *Romanic Review* 37 (1946): 150-61.

78 THE NOBLE MERCHANT

> HERVIS: 'Se vilains a le mien cors engenré,
> Sire, *ma mere* Aeliz a vis cler
> *Fille est de duc* et *de grant parenté.*'
> (vv. 8824-26)

> THIERI: 'Hervis mes sires qui tant fait a loer,
> *Filz est par deu la ducesse* au vis cler.
> *La fille au duc* de Mes la fort cité.'
> (vv. 6382-84)

> QUEEN OF 'Si m'aït dix, quique l'ait engenré,
> COLOGNE: *Depar sa mere* est *de grant parenté.*'
> (vv. 6919-20)

Hence the alternating plots present similar conflicts motivated by related concerns. Hero, narrator, and reader/listener must divide their attentions between Germans and Tyrians/Spaniards as the Loherains and their allies struggle to defend Hervis's fief, wife, and lineage.

As both conflicts arose from similar issues, both are resolved in similar fashion. While military strength contributes to the conclusion of the two wars, it is the appeal to common *lineage* that brings peace to Brabant and Metz. Hervis's grandfather begs Anseÿs to consider their family ties:

> 'Roys Anseÿs,' dist il, 'or m'entendés!
> Tu as ma niece a moullier esposé.
> Pour coi me voels ensi deshyreter?'
> (vv. 9302-04)

Ultimately, Anseÿs of Cologne gives in to this repeated plea:

> 'Li vostre fil qui moult ont de biauté,
> Rois orguillous, sont mi ami carnel.'
> Dist li rois: 'Sire, vous dites verité.'
> (vv. 10,332-34)

Back in Metz, the King of Tyre succumbs to a similar argument from his grandson Bégon:

> 'Hé rois de Tir, u estes vous alés?
> Fix sui vo fille Biatrix au vis cler,
> Ne me devés faillir per loiauté.'
>
> (vv. 10,441-43)

In the end, all recognize the validity of matrilineal nobility, doubly secured for the future heroes Garin and Bégon by both their mother and grandmothers.

The narrative threads in Part Two are thus joined by analogous motives, developments, and conclusions, producing an associative signifying network. Far from being a disjointed amalgamation, textual composition reveals the form of a *tresse*:

> Le texte, pendant qu'il se fait, est semblable à une dentelle de Valenciennes qui naîtrait devant nous sous les doigts de la dentellière: chaque séquence engagée pend comme le fuseau provisoirement inactif qui attend pendant que son voisin travaille ... L'ensemble ... constitue une tresse (*texte, tissu*, et *tresse*, c'est la même chose)....[17]

The process is not unlike Biatris's fabrication of the embroidered cloth, that marketable family souvenir fabricated with "fil de soie et fil d'or autressi" (v. 2927). Weaving disparate strands into a coherent whole, *Hervis de Mes* traces a narrative trajectory designed to validate the Loherain heroes' noble ancestry.

This *tresse* – as narrative path, genealogical continuation, and braid – marks an important juncture in the development of Old French epic storytelling.[18] In the early *chanson de geste*, as Howard Bloch has demonstrated, there exists a close relationship between genealogy and linear narrative: "... the epic stands both as the poetic transposition of a straight line and the literary equivalent of lineage."[19] Although cyclical production did allow the genre to maintain a linear superstructure throughout its history, *Hervis de Mes* and many other succeeding epics trace (internally) a sinuous narra-

---

[17] Roland Barthes, *S/Z* (Paris: Seuil, 1970) 165-66.

[18] While the word *tresse* does not appear unambiguously as "braid" in *Hervis de Mes*, tonic blocked /E/ is stable: see *destrece*, v. 541. This suggests that the words for "braid" and "trace" were homophonic.

[19] R. Howard Bloch, *Etymologies and Genealogies: A Literary Anthropology of the French Middle Ages* (Chicago and London: University of Chicago Press, 1983) 98.

tive path. The *tresse* maintains the epic equivalence of text and genealogy, prolongs the epic search for origin and continuation. At the same time, by fragmenting and deferring the narrative trajectory, the interlaced epic problematizes the notion of lineage. What Bloch has said of later medieval romance thus applies equally to this text and to many a late *chanson de geste*: such works are characterized by "a constant tension between the possibility of a certain filial and narrative continuity as against its interruption."[20]

The transition to traditional epic content, then, does not entail a shift to traditional epic composition; both parts of the text demonstrate the structural convergence of epic and romance in the thirteenth century. However, compositional bipartition does underscore the generic transformations exhibited on the "represented" level. This fusion of two rather distinct textual systems is by no means a rare phenomenon in thirteenth-century literature; one need only recall the structural duality of the *Roman de la Rose*. When coupled with a dual ideological framework, such shifts in narrative repertory and technique allow for reinterpretation and correction within the confines of a single work.

PATTERNS OF CONFLICT

The Old French epic is often conceived as a battle between two diametrically opposed socio-political groups or world views. In this context, most scholars consider the didactic function of *Hervis de Mes* as a struggle between merchant and noble values.[21] The importance of this theme in twelfth- and thirteenth-century literature is linked to the economic and social revolution of the epoch. With the rise of cities and the increasing role of the marketplace, the merchant's function – which had traditionally been defined in terms of avarice – came to be gradually rehabilitated. While the feudal lords regarded the merchant's power and values as an economic and cultural menace, Danielle Buschinger has demonstrated that some poetic texts of the period betray a new social conscience according to

---

[20] Bloch 212.
[21] See, for example, *Hervis de Metz: Roman du moyen âge adapté par Philippe Walter*, preface by Daniel Poirion: 5-9, afterword by Philippe Walter: 197-202.

which the merchant is partially accepted and integrated into society.[22] Such is the case in Part One of *Hervis de Mes.*

The noble/merchant dichotomy informs the text from the outset. Immediately following the jongleur's prologue, a double exposition presents the two opposing influences that will determine the hero's heredity:

(of Pierre):
Avoit ·I· duc *qui moult fist a loër.* . .
Li dus fu larges et *courtois* pour donner,
Per Loherainne fait les tornois crïer,
Lai ou les seit per estrainge regney,
Li dus porte armes et il et ces barnez.
Tant despendi li frans dus naturez,
Qu'il endeta si fort la ducee.
(vv. 9, 16, 16 a-c, 17-18)[23]

(of Thieri):
·I· prevost ot *qui moult fist a loër.* . .
Sage et *courtois* pour bon conseil donner. . .
Si grant tresor, seignor, ait *assamblei,*
Que il n'en seit plus le conte nombrer.
(vv. 22, 24, 36-37)

The elements of this opposition merit a brief formal analysis. It is noteworthy that an identical formula, "qui moult fist a loër," is associated with both characters. This serves, however, only to highlight the numerous distinctions between Duke Pierre and the bourgeois Thieri. First of all, the gap in social status is reflected in the choice of "li dus" and "li prevos" rather than the use of proper names. Secondly, both men are described as "courtois," but each context assigns a different connotation to the word. In the case of Duke Pierre, "courtois" is connected with the exclusively noble quality of largess ("pour donner"), and thus participates in the system of characteristics associated with the ideal nobleman. Duke Pierre is "courtois," then, in the sense that he is generous, as befitting a man of his rank. Thieri, on the other hand, is "courtois" in a manner consistent with his own social status: his function is to give advice to the duke ("pour bon conseil donner") concerning the

---

[22] Danielle Buschinger, "L'Image du marchand dans les romans de Tristan en France et en Allemagne," *Tristania* 10 (1984-85): 43-51.

[23] The lines "Per Loherainne. . . ces barnez" are added by E.

government of Metz. "Courtois," in Thieri's case, evokes therefore a certain graciousness in the fulfillment of his duties. Thirdly, the parallel constructions "Tant ... que" and "Si. . . que" reflect a significant disparity between the two characters' past actions. The verbs in the principal clauses are at opposite poles ("despendi" / "ait assamblei"). Similarly, the result clauses indicate inverse movements, i.e. incurring debts (Pierre) and being unable to count all of one's assets (Thieri).

Thus, the poet represents the noble and the merchant in traditional fashion, opposing aristocratic *distribution* and bourgeois *accumulation*. The antithesis receives its coherence from a cultural and poetic model immediately recognizable to a medieval audience. Traditionally, this opposition clearly favors noble distribution and condemns any form of gain for its own sake. For the nobleman, "la recherche des biens est légitime parce qu'elle s'ordonne non pas à l'intérêt propre de son possesseur ou à son simple plaisir, encore plus vain, d'entasser, mais à celui des autres."[24] Moreover, the advice given to nobles by bourgeois characters in early medieval narrative is generally portrayed as an evil influence. The term *vilain*, which may designate a non-noble in general or a peasant in particular, is often used in a pejorative sense for bourgeois characters who have attempted to penetrate the aristocratic world. In the *Couronnement de Louis*, for example, Charlemagne admonishes the young emperor:

> 'Que de vilain ne faces conseillier,
> Fill a prevost ne de filx a voier:
> Il boisereient a petit por loier.'
>
> (vv. 207-9)

Similarly, in the romance *L'Escoufle*, the Holy Roman Emperor loses his authority because he has favored *vilains* at the expense of his own courtiers. Richard of Normandy rescues the emperor and cautions him:

> 'Car haus hom est honis et vix
> Qui de soi fait nul vilain mestre.

---

[24] See Micheline de Combarieu du Grés, *L'idéal humain et l'expérience morale chez les héros des chansons de geste des origines à 1250*, Etudes littéraires 3, Thesis Aix-en-Provence (Aix: Publications de l'Université de Provence; Diffusion Paris: Champion, 1979), I: 27.

>   Vilain! et comment porroit estre
>   Que vilains fust gentix ne frans?'
>   (vv. 1628-31)[25]

Hervis de Mes, however, initially represents the bourgeois/noble opposition in a very different light. Duke Pierre's largess has been so extreme that he is in danger of losing his lands; moreover, he cannot hope to marry his daughter Aelis to a prominent noble because of his great debts (vv. 49-60). The duke actually values his prevost Thieri for the latter's counsel, his loyalty, and even his capacity for accumulation: "'Et gaaignié et le sien amassé / Et j'ai le mien folement aloué'" (vv. 85-86). In fact, neither value system is presented here as an exclusively positive or negative model.

The opposition merchant/noble is temporarily neutralized by the marriage of Aelis and Thieri, which benefits both classes: the duke is able to maintain his position with the help of bourgeois funds, and the merchant is able to approach the boundaries of the noble world. Although Duke Pierre views the union as a necessary evil, the marriage is generally portrayed as a favorable solution. The true conflict between bourgeois and aristocratic values emerges after the birth of Hervis, for the combined heritage of Thieri and Aelis juxtaposes the elements of the opposition within a single individual. It is noteworthy that other epics of the period portray similar struggles between bourgeois fathers and their half-noble sons; if mixed marriage is a necessary evil, mixed heritage fosters bitter strife.[26]

Because Hervis has inherited his maternal grandfather's noble instinct for distribution, the opposition *despendre / gaaignier* now generates quarrels between the young hero and his father and pa-

---

[25] See also the *Roman d'Alexandre*, ed. E.C. Armstrong, D.L. Buffum, Bateman Edwards, L.F.H. Lowe, Elliott Monographs 37 (Princeton: Princeton University Press; Paris: PUF, 1949) Br. IV, vv. 1652-68.

[26] In *Aiol*, for example, Antiaume is the son of a usurer and a poor noblewoman. His father, Hunbaus, is unable to divert the boy from noble pursuits such as chess, hunting, and the *adoubement* ceremony. As in *Hervis*, family conflicts arise, and the noblewoman desperately regrets the mixed marriage arranged by her father. See *Aiol*, ed. Jacques Normand and Gaston Raynaud, SATF 7 (Paris: Didot, 1877) vv. 7062-74, 7105-26, 7265-68.

In the *Enfances Vivien*, a similar conflict arises between Vivien and his adopted merchant father. Like Hervis, he squanders the merchant's money at the fair. Like Aelis, the stepmother intervenes on behalf of the boy. See *Les Enfances Vivien*, ed. Alfred Nordfelt (Upsala: Librairie de l'Université; Paris: Librairie Emile Bouillon, 1895) Ms. B, vv. 828-1319.

ternal uncles. Despite his father's warning, "'Qui ne *gaaigne*, tost seroit espovris'" (v. 294), Hervis follows his grandfather's example: "Tant *despendi* li damoisiaus gentis" (v. 360). Indeed, most of Part One functions to oppose these two socio-economic behavior patterns and offer the hero a choice between them:

> Entre une noblesse qui ne sait que distribuer l'argent qu'elle ne produit pas et une bourgeoisie qui produit la richesse sans la distribuer, un fossé semble se creuser et deux conceptions de l'existence s'affronter.[27]

Hervis obviously favors the aristocratic half of his heritage: like Duke Pierre, he is unmatched in his largess, and his extravagance leads to financial ruin. His merchant ancestry, however, is not entirely suppressed in Part One. In fact, narrative development indicates that the hero manages to achieve a synthesis of the two social roles he has inherited. Textual manifestations of this synthesis include the pattern of the three fair episodes: Provins, Lagny, and Tyre.

The episodes in question join diverse motifs from folklore and courtly romance to the problematics of social differentiation. Portions of these episodes recall popular legend, particularly that of the Grateful Dead, variations of which were circulating throughout Europe in the thirteenth century. The fair episodes correspond roughly to the common framework uniting the legend's numerous variants: 1) A young man is sent by his merchant father (uncle) on a commercial voyage; instead of making the required purchases, he spends all his money elsewhere. (In the Grateful Dead legend proper, he uses this money to pay the debts of a dead man who has not yet received proper burial; the hero's generosity provides for this interment, and, in a future time of need, the corpse comes to the hero's rescue.) 2) The merchant father (uncle) is angry with the hero, and sends him on a second commercial voyage. This time the hero purchases a beautiful slave woman who has been kidnapped from her Oriental homeland; she was betrothed before her abduction. 3) The father exiles his son and the beloved slave. 4) Since the couple now has no resources, the woman embroiders a cloth that

---

[27] Walter 199.

will be recognized by her family, and sends the hero on yet another commercial voyage.[28]

Hervis de Mes transforms the Grateful Dead story by clothing it in an ideological conflict between father and son; instead of aiding a corpse, the hero reveals a noble instinct for hunting, fine horses, and women of high birth.[29] Furthermore, the role of the kidnapped slave takes on an added dimension in the *Hervis* story: Biatris, as we have seen, is portrayed as the courtly woman who guides the hero to a full realization of his potential. The curious blend of love and commerce that characterizes their relationship stems from the integration of popular legend, courtly traditions, and an ideological matrix, i.e. the confrontation of bourgeois and noble values.

This fusion of diverse matter and contemporary social propaganda is largely accomplished by the use of parallel configurations. The Provins and Lagny episodes constitute symmetrical sequences with identical stages of development.[30] On both occasions, the hero deliberately disobeys his father's wishes, rejects the advice of his paternal uncles, spends lavish sums on entertainment, makes an extravagant purchase, and is ultimately upbraided by his father. The repetition suggests that Hervis is trapped by his mixed heritage into a mechanical iteration of the same behavior patterns. As Alfred Adler puts it, "The nobleman in Hervis absurdly handicaps the businessman, and vice versa; this at a time and in a locality where noblemen and businessmen needed as well as hampered each other."[31]

It is undeniable that the values of the nobleman receive a distinctly more favorable portrayal than those of the merchant. Hervis's noble instincts guide him to buy animals that ultimately prove to be worth their weight in gold. The same instincts govern his purchase of Biatris: although he does not know empirically that she is a princess, Hervis declares her to be a "proude femme" (v. 1802). Similarly, the noble Aelis is immediately drawn to the Tyrian

---

[28] Walther Benary, "*Hervis von Metz* und die Sage vom dankbaren Toten," *Zeitschrift für romanische Philologie* 37 (1913): 57-92 and 128-44; Gédéon Huet, "Le retour merveilleux du mari," *Revue des traditions populaires* 32 (1917): 97-109 and 145-63.

[29] Traces of the generosity motif may also be seen at the beginning of the Tyre episode, when Hervis gives his last *denier* to two grateful lepers at the city gate (vv. 3180-90). See Benary 88-89.

[30] A formal analysis of this sequence will be presented in Chapter Three.

[31] Adler, "*Hervis de Mes*" 155.

slave for her striking beauty (" 'Il n'a plus bele en LX citez,'" v. 1927) and her apparent noble birth ("'Qu'elle pert bien que soit de parenté,'" v. 2127). This innate sense of true worth thus contrasts sharply with the petty values of Thieri and his brothers, who interpret the hero's purchases in an entirely different light. The merchants insist that the commodities were overpriced, disdaining the expensive animals ("Tout ne vaut mie XX livres d'estrelins," v. 476) and misconstruing Biatris's status altogether:

> 'T'as acheté une putain miautrix
> Que comunal estoit ele a Ligni,
> Nus n'en voloit avoir le sien plaisir,
> Pour II deniers n'en eüst a devis.'
> (vv. 1788-91)

Given the audience's greater knowledge (and superior judgment), the latter "miscalculation" is particularly damning.

Nevertheless, the hero's predilection for extravagant spending does precipitate the financial ruin of his family; his predicament thereby resembles the initial problem of Duke Pierre. This time, it is Biatris who provides a solution to the nobleman's dilemma. When Hervis follows her instructions at the fair in Tyre, disguising himself as a merchant from Normandy, he is able to satisfy both his desire to spend and his need to acquire. As in the previous fair episodes, he entertains the local merchants, multiplying the number of guests each day (v. 3339-54). When the time comes for him to sell the embroidered cloth, however, he displays a remarkable talent for bargaining, continually doubling the price until he sells the cloth for 32,000 marks.

Leo Jordan has criticized this bargaining session on the grounds that the repeated price increments are unmotivated. Comparing the *Hervis* episode with a similar episode from *Nûr al dîn*, a variation on the Grateful Dead legend, Jordan maintains that the *Hervis* poet simply misunderstood his source. In *Nûr al dîn*, the hero is obliged to raise his prices repeatedly in order to prevent a certain one-eyed hunchback from purchasing the heroine's embroidery. Since *Hervis de Mes* includes no such reason for the price increase, Jordan dismisses it as a "seltsame Art zu handeln."[32]

---

[32] Jordan 437.

In fact, this motif is essential to the structure of the Tyre episode, for it demonstrates that Hervis has now mastered both distribution *and* accumulation. His pattern of spending (for all three fairs) was characterized by systematic augmentation; the bargaining session in Tyre reveals the same pattern, but this time the flow of gold is diverted into the hero's pocket. His acquisition will permit him to restore the fortunes of both Baudri of Tyre and Baudri of Metz (vv. 3786-87, 4845-47), resume the noble function of largess (vv. 4580-84, 4619-20) and finance the war in Brabant (vv. 5794-5808). And while the first two fairs terminated in a family quarrel, the fair in Tyre leads to a reconciliation between Hervis and Thieri.

Thus, the opposition *despendre / gaaignier*, which generated most of the conflict in Part One, is transcended at the midpoint of the story. With the guidance of Biatris, Hervis is able to integrate the functions of merchant and noble within himself: he has proved himself both in the marketplace (in Tyre) and on the battlefield (against the three would-be kidnappers, the count of Flanders, and Hinbaut). Once he reaches this synthesis, both paternal and maternal relatives join in the dubbing ceremony: the merchant Thieri provides the feast, and the noble Duke Pierre performs the rite. At this juncture in the narrative, then, the great ancestor of the Loherain lineage seems to have adapted some of his father's practical, merchant values to noble pursuits and ideals.

This hypothesis is further corroborated by the motif of *resemblance*, which appears in seven different episodes. The problem of the hero's identity is translated into a series of comparisons whose progression reinforces the merchant-noble opposition and final synthesis:

Early in the tale, one of the hero's adversaries affirms that Hervis resembles a Lombard (v. 1567). This comparison is ostensibly motivated by the hero's size ("'tant est grant et formez,'" v. 1567); however, Lombards were also known in the thirteenth century for their activities at the fairs, particularly at the fair in Lagny, where they engaged in usury. On another occasion (vv. 2520-21) the people of Senlis perceive the same resemblance. In both cases, the comparison Hervis-Lombard dwells on the merchant half of his heritage. Similarly, Baudri of Metz notes the extraordinary physical resemblance between Hervis and Thieri (vv. 2103-04). This comparison is reiterated by the host in Senlis (vv. 2505-06) and the Count of Montbeliart (vv. 2810-12). Despite his noble pretentions,

Hervis is consistently associated with the bourgeoisie during his early adventures.

Once he has succeeded in freeing the clerics from the clutches of the giant Hinbaut, however, Hervis is seen to resemble his grandfather, the Duke of Metz (vv. 4424-26). This comparison, strategically placed at the end of the hero's quest, corrects the previous "merchant" references by highlighting his aristocratic heritage.

Finally, during the celebration preceding the hero's dubbing, the Count of Bar and Duke Sanson insist that Hervis resembles the anonymous hero of the Senlis tournament: (vv. 5184-5209); at this time, Hervis is finally obliged to reveal his identity. Transcending the dual image of his merchant and noble relatives, Hervis ultimately comes to resemble himself:

> 'Voir vous dirai, ja n'en iert trestourné. [...]
> Au tournoi ving entesé l' grant pel,
> *Je fiz* le conte a ceval remonter.
> Tant li aidai en bone loiauté
> Qu'il ot secours et son rice barné.
>
> (vv. 5237, 5241-44)

With his emphatic "*je fiz*," Hervis appropriates his own heroic actions, and ceases to be identified by his family resemblances. The quest for an integrated social identity is seemingly resolved, allowing the hero to project his own image onto the community.

In Part One, then, the hero grapples with two value systems, neither of which is represented according to a clear-cut *parti pris*. The monologism of the early Old French epic, manifest in a strongly polarized conflictual structure (Christian/Pagan, Hero/Traitor), is for the moment conspicuously absent.[33] Like Guillaume in the

---

[33] On this "deep structure" in the *chanson de geste*, see P. Van Nuffel, "Problèmes de sémiotique interprétative: l'épopée," *Lettres romanes* 27 (1973): 150-62. Van Nuffel's adaptation of Greimas's semiotic square also incorporates the theories of Julia Kristeva, *Le Texte du roman* (La Haye: Mouton, 1970). Critical responses to Van Nuffel appear in the following articles: Larry S. Crist, "Deep Structures in the *chansons de geste*: Hypothesis for a Taxonomy," *Olifant* 3 (1975): 3-35; Minnette Grunmann-Gaudet, "From Epic to Romance: The Paralysis of the Hero in the *Prise d'Orange*," *Olifant* 7 (1979): 22-30; and John W. MacInnes, "Gloriette: The Function of the Tower and the Name in the *Prise d'Orange*," *Olifant* 10 (1982-83): 24-40. The latter studies demonstrate the movement away from monologism in the epics of the late twelfth and early thirteenth centuries.

Prise d'Orange and many heroes of courtly romance, Hervis succeeds in reconciling the oppositions within himself. This portion of *Hervis de Mes* exhibits an underlying structure of "non-disjunction," allowing opposing world views to reach at least a temporary synthesis.

It soon becomes apparent, however, that the hero's dubbing marks only a provisional solution to the problem of his mixed lineage. In Part Two, the unresolved conflict of the Spanish King and the new conflict in Brabant reopen the question of the hero's social role.

Part Two continues to adapt elements of the Grateful Dead legend to the contemporary social problem of mixed lineage. *Hervis de Mes* shares with this tale two remaining points: 1) The embroidered cloth allows the heroine's family to follow her traces and recapture her; 2) the hero travels to the Orient to recapture the heroine, establishing contact by means of a token. By adducing the problem of mixed lineage to these elements, and weaving them with the parallel epic conflict in Brabant, the second part of the text dissolves the neat synthesis proposed earlier. Such dissolution is suggested by the continued use of symmetrical motifs that recall earlier narrative patterns only to modify their function and signification. This time, however, the intratextual repetition pairs episodes from the text's two structurally distinct parts.

Floire's voyage to Metz, for example, displays remarkable parallels with Hervis's earlier trip to the fair in Tyre. Like Hervis, Floire disguises himself as a merchant from Normandy (vv. 6989-92); he entertains the local merchants (vv. 7095-7116); and he accomplishes his mission by means of a ruse:

> 'Se par engien ne le puis conquester
> Ne la porai per deu de maïsté
> Ne la porai a nul jor conquester.'
> (vv. 5943-44, 5944a)[34]

Like Hervis and Biatris in Part One, he regrets the use of deception, but considers it vital to maintaining his primary obligations:

---

[34] Ms. E adds the third line.

BIATRIS: 'Sovent estuet maint preudome mentir
Por covenense en autre liu tenir.'
(vv. 3022-23)

FLOIRE: 'Ja sui jou rois, doi couronne porter,
Je ne devroie mentir si m'aït dex,
Pour nul avoir c'on me seüst donner;
Mais pour ma suer Bïatrix a vis cler,
M'estuet mentir, vrais dix, outre mon gré.
Hé rois d'Apaigne, qui tant fais a doter!'
(vv. 7024-29)

Finally, as Hervis depended on Baudri of Tyre's need for a paying guest, Floire relies on the greed of a host to accomplish his mission. Thieri, who has repented of his earlier misdeeds, nevertheless retains his love of gain and thus welcomes the stranger with open arms: "Li prevos a lor avoir goulouzé" (v. 6996).

Hervis's parallel scheme in Part One ended in a triumphant alliance between merchant and noble behavior patterns. Despite the similarities between the schemes of Hervis and Floire, however, the latter's actions are condoned by neither jongleur nor characters. When Floire arrives in Metz, we are told that he greets Thieri "de fantil cuer" (v. 7037). Moreover, the young Garin senses the evil intentions of the disguised Floire. Upon seeing the stranger in church, Garin assumes the traditional role of *puer senex*, and suddenly strikes Floire with such force that the latter is stunned into awed admiration: "'Hé enfanchons, se tu vis par aé / Con tu avras et prouece et bonté!" (vv. 7162-63). Of course, the unsympathetic portrayal of Floire is necessary to the favorable representation of the love between Hervis and Biatris; Floire presents an obstacle to this ideal conjugal relationship. Nevertheless, the implicit condemnation of this character has more deep-seated causes: unlike Hervis, King Floire lowers himself to the merchant level in assuming the merchant's disguise. Like Thieri, who earlier misinterpreted the status of Biatris, Floire fails to discern true nobility: he sees in Hervis only a "fix de vilain," refusing to recognize the worthy ancestry of the Dukes of Lorraine. Thus, the ruse of the merchant's disguise, which previously facilitated a merchant-noble synthesis, now comes to represent an ignoble descent to the flawed perceptions and values of the bourgeoisie.

The rejection of the synthesis is also suggested by the pattern of Biatris's second abduction, which presents many parallels with the abduction episode in Part One. First of all, both episodes include a premonitory dream: the first constitutes a *somnium alienum*, a dream foretelling the fate of another.³⁵ Before learning that her daughter has been kidnapped by ten squires, the Queen of Tyre dreams that Biatris is swept away from a *verger* by ten griffons (vv. 1015-31). Similarly, before she is abducted by her brother Floire, Biatris recounts a *somnium proprium*, a dream foretelling her own fate: she has dreamed of being kidnapped from a *verger* by an eagle and rescued by a griffon (vv. 7257-69). The *somnium* motif therefore links two episodes which are separated by six thousand lines in the text.

Biatris is rescued on both occasions by the actions of Hervis. It is here, however, that the two episodes offer radically different outcomes. In Part One, Hervis rescued Biatris from the ten evil squires by means of a commercial transaction; his bourgeois blood accounted for his presence in the marketplace, while his noble blood allowed him both to sense the true worth of Biatris and disregard the sum of money she cost him. In Part Two, he sheds his merchant role altogether and appropriates Biatris in a manner befitting the Duke of Lorraine, a mighty warrior who wages battle on those who do not accept his status:

> Fiers fut li caples et ruiste la mellee
> Et la bataille cremue et redoutee.
> Es vous Hervi el poing destre l'espee!
> Cui il consut moult a courte duree.
>
> (vv. 8435-37)

It is also significant that Hervis acquires a large treasure as a result of this rescue mission, namely the dowry that was intended for the King of Spain (vv. 8568-90). This occurrence recalls the earlier Tyre episode, in which the hero succeeds in acquiring 32,000 marks from his wife's family. On both occasions, it is Biatris who suggests the object and means of acquisition. Yet whereas Hervis *bargained*

---

³⁵ For an in-depth analysis of epic *songes*, see Herman Braet, *Le songe dans la chanson de geste au XIIe siècle*, Romania Gandensia 15 (Ghent: University of Ghent, 1975).

for the Tyrian treasure acquired in Part One, he *conquers* a treasure in Part Two. As the Spanish King's ambassadors explain (rather sheepishly) to their lord:

> Li rois de Tir s'est vers vous acquités;
> Il nous carga Bïatrix au vis cler
> Et tel present qui moult fist a loër:
> Tresc'ai L· sommiers trestous toursés
> D'or et d'argent et de paille roei,
> Ours et lions, viautres encäynés
> Que vous volait li bons rois presenter.
> Nos encontrames, biax sire, I· baceler,
> Non a Hervi, voir si est de Mes nez,
> C'est uns des miudres de la crestïenté.
> V· mille estoient acompliz et passez,
> Et nous estiemes X· mille ferarmé,
> Nos ne poïmes encontre iaus contrester.
>
> (vv. 8909-21)

This means of accumulation is more in keeping with the nobleman's traditional role; Hervis no longer acquires his wealth in the marketplace, but appropriates it – against formidable odds – on the battlefield.

Finally, although Hervis is no longer said to *resemble* other characters in Part Two, his identity is systematically represented in terms of filial ties. We have observed that Hervis's enemies consistently refer to him as a "fix de vilain" throughout this half of the text. Hervis and his allies, however, employ such expressions as "'Neiz. . . [au] duc de Mes'" (v. 6095), "'Nevout a duc qui tant fait a loër'" (v. 6349), and "'Filz. . . la ducesse'" (v. 6383). Once he has conquered his enemies, the appellation "fix de vilain" is obliterated from his identity, leaving only the noble extraction of the Duke of Lorraine ("'Nobiles dus,'" v. 10,325). The bourgeois paternal heritage essentially disappears from consideration at the story's conclusion.

It seems, therefore, that whereas Part One allowed the hero to combine the best of merchant and noble characteristics, Part Two strives to eliminate the first element of the opposition. Indeed, the conflict has shifted from the ideological struggle beteween merchant and noble to an internal conflict among members of the noble class. Like *Garin le Loherain* and succeeding branches of the *geste des Loherains*, Part Two opposes the feudal rights of rival houses. Good and Evil are represented respectively by the claims of Lorraine (based on the matrilineal nobility of the hero), and the claims of Tyre/Cologne (based on the rejection of matrilineal nobility). These opposing claims are characterized by exclusive disjunction and can therefore be schematized according to P. Van Nuffel's Greimasian model of the *chanson de geste*:

```
defend Loherain claims ---------- defend Tyre/Cologne claims
                          \    /
                           \  /
                            \/
                            /\
                           /  \
                          /    \
reject Tyre/Cologne claims ---- reject Loherain claims
```

Unlike epics which portray internal treason, *Hervis* does not generate narrative development by movement along the diagonal axis of contradiction. (However, like Bramimonde in the Oxford *Roland*, the female members of the Tyre and Cologne groups do ally themselves along the vertical axis of implication: both Biatris and the Queen of Cologne reject the claims of their homeland and accept the matrilineal nobility of the hero.) As in most early *chansons de geste*, resolution is achieved only by the victory of one term of the opposition: the Tyre and Cologne parties reverse their allegiance as do the converts in religious epic.

Surface manifestations of didacticism operate therefore in a similar fashion throughout *Hervis de Mes*. The systematic return of similar narrative patterns – both within and between the two parts – generates conclusions about the lesson to be drawn from the *tresse*. Nonetheless, the two distinct textual units represent radically different conceptions of ideological problem-solving on the level of deep structure. Part One opposes two social value systems only to bring them into harmony; although the bourgeoisie definitely suffers in the balance, the merchant's tools are recognized as an auxiliary means to the noble ends of largess and military strength. Part Two, on the other hand, no longer acknowledges the resourcefulness or even the necessity of the merchant; only the noble warrior can succeed in this battle of feudal rights, and conflict may be resolved only through the defeat of the opposition. Rather than reflecting social reality, i.e. the rise of the merchant class, this part of the text attempts to suppress it.[36]

---

[36] Lévi-Strauss describes a similar process in the elaboration of myths. See *Anthropologie structurale* (Paris: Plon, 1958 & 1973) I: 241-42.

It is therefore not surprising that *Hervis de Mes* has given rise to conflicting modern interpretations: ambivalence is inherent in its bipartite structure. This ambivalence may well have served a pragmatic function in the thirteenth-century reception of the text. As audiences became more heterogeneous, particularly in Eastern France, such a narrative may have elicited different responses:

> . . . qu'un pauvre bachelier parte à l'aventure et découvre une lointaine princesse, belle et riche, voilà de quoi satisfaire les désirs de tous les cadets de famille frustrés dans leurs ambitions. Qu'un chevalier, d'origine vilaine par son père, triomphe de plusieurs rois en se conduisant plus noblement qu'eux, voilà de quoi satisfaire les riches bourgeois récemment parvenus à la noblesse et désireux d'intégrer les valeurs chevaleresques.[17]

Furthermore, these ruptures in composition and conception raise questions about the origins of *Hervis de Mes*. It is indeed possible that one or more redactors assembled different legends of the first Loherain hero into a single text. Diverging modes of composition and conflict may well indicate the presence of disparate origins; structural links, such as symmetrical patterns and the central problem of lineage, suggest a redactor's efforts at unification. These questions will be considered in more detail in Part Two of the present study, which examines the formal level of the text.

---

[17] Gérard Noiriel, "La Chevalerie dans la geste des Lorrains," *Annales de l'Est* 28 (1976): 195.

PART TWO

"LA CHANSON"

> Bone canchon plast vos a *escouter?*
> Des Loherens vos voromes *chanter.*
> (*Hervis de Mes,* vv. 2-3)

The prologue of *Hervis de Mes* carries an additional promise that reflects the work's formal dimension: the poet-jongleur offers to deliver the *tresse* in the form of a *chanson* designed to please a listening audience. Indeed, the greater part of the text is composed of assonanced decasyllabic lines marked by a 4/6 caesura and grouped in laisses of varying length. This formal mode aligns *Hervis* to a certain degree with conventions of the early *chansons de geste*, conventions that derived from the exigencies and aesthetics of a well-established oral tradition.[1]

Nevertheless, *Hervis de Mes* does represent a distinct departure from earlier epic technique. Substantial modifications in laisse structure and formulaic style, particularly in the more "romanesque" half of the text, suggest that the notion of *chanson* must be reevaluated in the context of thirteenth-century epic production. Moreover, by generating and reinforcing other types of bipartition, poetic form serves the particular signifying mechanisms of this binary epic. The modulations of strophe, meter, stereotyped expression and narrative discourse contain vestiges of the text's performative dimension as both "song" and message.

---

[1] See Jean Rychner, *La Chanson de geste: Essai sur l'art épique des jongleurs,* Société de publications romanes et françaises 53 (Geneva: Droz, 1955); Martin de Riquer, "Epopée jongleresque à écouter et épopée romanesque à lire," *La Technique littéraire des chansons de geste,* Actes du Colloque de Liège, 1957 (Paris: Belles Lettres, 1959) 75-84; Joseph Duggan, "Die zwei 'Epochen' der Chansons de geste," *Epochenschwellen und Epochenstrukturen im Diskurs der Literatur- und Sprachhistorie,* Hans Ulrich Gumbrecht et al., eds. (Frankfurt: Suhrkamp, 1985) 389-408; and Paul Zumthor, *La Lettre et la voix: De la 'littérature' médiévale* (Paris: Seuil, 1987).

CHAPTER ONE

LAISSE STRUCTURE AND FORMULAIC STYLE

Any study of formal composition in the Old French epic must take into account the indispensable research of Jean Rychner.[2] His penetrating essay on the relationship between poetic form and conditions of production and dissemination laid the foundation for many fruitful analyses of epic technique.[3] The works studied by Rychner, however, represent a relatively early stage of the *chanson de geste* tradition; moreover, his principal frame of reference is the Oxford *Roland*, which he considers to be the model of epic perfection.[4] This standard, shared by many modern scholars, has hampered the appreciation of later epic technique. Works that do not conform to the strophic structure of the *Chanson de Roland* are considered as mutant forms, which could just as easily be composed in another generic mode:

> Peut-on d'ailleurs parler encore de structure strophique, lorsque certaines laisses atteignent presque deux cents vers? Autant vaudrait composer en couplets d'octosyllabes![5]

The fact that such works were *not* composed in romance form, however, indicates that epic versification and composition still re-

---

[2] Rychner 68-158.
[3] See, for example, the collection of papers in *La Technique littéraire des chansons de geste*, Actes du Colloque de Liège 1957 (Paris: Belles lettres, 1959); Anne Iker Gittleman, *Le Style épique dans Garin le Loherain*, Publications romanes et françaises 94 (Geneva: Droz, 1967); and Marguerite Rossi, *Huon de Bordeaux et l'évolution du genre épique au XIIIe siècle*, Nouvelle Bibliothèque du Moyen Age 2 (Paris: Champion, 1975) 121-204.
[4] Rychner 124-25, 150-51.
[5] Rychner 110. The author refers here to the *Moniage Guillaume*, a twelfth-century epic whose *laisse* structure anticipates thirteenth-century forms. *Garin le Loherain* also falls into this category.

tained a distinct poetic function in the thirteenth century. While it is probable that many later *chansons de geste* were not composed orally, recent studies provide convincing evidence that these texts were performed – read aloud or even sung to an audience.[6] The survival of the assonanced laisse and traditional formulas thus provides a formal link between texts such as *Hervis* and the already familiar conventions of epic poetics. This link is inherent in both the production and reception processes: by proclaiming *Hervis* a "chanson" and maintaining the contours of the *chanson de geste*, the poet/performer consciously situates his work in a specific tradition; the audience, perceiving the structural and rhythmic echoes of a familiar form, automatically relates the text to this known tradition. In its treatment of strophic technique and formulaic composition, *Hervis de Mes* furnishes abundant evidence of both stability and change in this "horizon of expectations."[7]

* * *

THE LAISSE

The study of the laisse is closely tied to the relationship between narrative and lyric functions in the *chanson de geste*. The narrative component of an epic text may be defined as the progressive unfolding of a story; this progression involves the accretion of details that serve to advance the fictional chronology or to expand our knowledge of circumstances and related events. The lyric dimension, on the other hand, concerns the epic's status as song; the refrains, repetitions, and parallels which link consecutive laisses tend

---

[6] Duggan, "Epochen"; Zumthor, "Voix"; see also Robert Francis Cook, "Unity and Esthetics of the Late Chansons de geste," *Olifant* 11 (1986) 111; Nico van den Boogaard, "Le caractère oral de la chanson de geste tardive," *Langue et littérature françaises du Moyen Age: Etudes réunies par R.E.V. Stuip* (Assen: Van Gorcum, 1978) 25-38.

[7] The term is essential to the critical vocabulary of Hans Robert Jauss, who counsels the literary critic to examine individual texts "within the objectifiable system of expectations that arises for each work in the historical moment of its appearance, from a pre-understanding of the genre [and] from the form and themes of already familiar works." *Toward an Aesthetic of Reception*, trans. Timothy Bahti, Theory and History of Literature 2 (Minneapolis: University of Minnesota Press 1982) 22.

to decelerate narrative progress or even to obscure the sequence of events.

For Rychner, the model laisse is one which balances narrative progression and incantation: he praises the short strophe, framed by a "timbre d'intonation" and a "timbre de conclusion," which describes one unified action such as a single combat or a discourse. (These narrative units are much smaller than the "episodes" defined in the previous chapter.) Composite laisses, which contain more than one incident, are met with disapproval.[8]

Furthermore, he favors *chansons* characterized by the predominance of lyric halts. These effects are produced by the use of strophic devices that Rychner terms *enchaînement* (the narration of the same action at the end of one laisse and the beginning of the following laisse); *laisses parallèles* (a series of two or more laisses which present analogous actions in a similar form); *laisses bifurquées* (two or more laisses beginning with the same action, but offering two different conclusions of this action); and *laisses similaires* (two or more laisses which present the same action in a slightly different perspective, with little or no narrative progress). According to Rychner, all of the above criteria are necessary to the achievement of "la vraie hauteur épique":

> En somme, conserver à la laisse son caractère de *strophe*, c'est vraiment composer une *chanson*; offusquer ses contours, ne respecter ni le découpage naturel qu'elle devrait imposer à la narration, ni l'ordre qu'elle devrait apporter à la disposition des reprises, l'allonger démesurément, c'est altérer le caractère premier du chant.[9]

In fact, more recent studies have shown that the great majority of extant *chansons de geste* do not conform to the norms established by Rychner; only the Oxford *Roland* comes close to fulfilling these modern expectations.[10] Moreover, it was not mere poetic artifice

---

[8] Rychner 69-74, 107-125.

[9] Rychner 125.

[10] For a reevaluation of Rychner's assumptions and typology, see Dominique Boutet, *Jehan de Lanson: Technique et esthétique de la chanson de geste au XIIIe siècle* (Paris: PENS, 1988); Edward A. Heinemann, "'Composite Laisse' and Echo as Organizing Principles: The Case of Laisse 1 of the *Charroi de Nîmes*," Romance Philology 37 (1983): 127-38; and Barbara Schurfranz, "Strophic Structure versus Alternative Divisions in the *Prise d'Orange*," Romance Philology 33 (1979): 247-64.

that led medieval poets to present as "chansons" works containing very long laisses and a distinct emphasis on narrative progression. For poets and audiences of the Middle Ages, these factors obviously did not significantly alter the epic's function as song. Indeed, the lyric dimension is far from negligible in works such as *Hervis*; rather, the poets have adapted the compositional techniques of earlier epics to longer, more complex narratives.

In the following pages, we shall observe the mechanics of this adaptation in the two parts of *Hervis de Mes*. It is not surprising that the bipartition we have discerned on the level of the *tresse* is also evident on the level of song: the first half of the text represents a greater departure from early epic form, while the second half exhibits a marked return to convention. However, the formal divisions of the text do not correspond precisely to the divisions of the narrative; although the locus of generic disjunction may be situated after the dubbing rites on the levels of theme and narrative construction, this event occurs in the midst of the longest laisse in the text. Laisse structure dictates a binary division approximately four hundred lines after the dubbing, at the beginning of the war in Brabant (v. 6016, L. 44). We shall see that this point marks a distinct transformation in the composition of individual laisses and in the links between them.

A detailed chart of Laisse Statistics is provided in Appendix B.[11]

Part One

Daniel Poirion has noted the relative absence of epic "incantation" in the first part of *Hervis*; he attributes the lack of lyricism to the didactic nature of this segment, i.e. the logical demonstration of opposing value systems. Traditional epic style, according to Poirion, does not really surface until Hervis goes to war in Brabant.[12]

The validity of this judgment is undeniable, for Part One is characterized by the predominance of straightforward narration

---

[11] Since the forthcoming edition of Ms. **E** is not yet available, I have based my statistics on Stengel's composite edition. This edition does, however, retain the essential structure of Ms. **E**; the additions of **N** and **T** are relegated to the Appendices.

[12] Daniel Poirion, Préface, *Hervis de Metz: Roman du moyen âge adapté par Philippe Walter*, Editions Serpenoise (Nancy: Presses Universitaires de Nancy, 1984) 6-7.

over lyric pause. The very length of the laisse precludes the strophic play characteristic of works such as the Oxford *Roland*, for assonances rarely change and the laisse does not usually function as a discrete narrative unit; the majority of strophes are "composite" in Rychner's sense.[13] This portion of the text shows an average of 140 lines per laisse (compared to 14 for the *Roland*, 43 for the *Couronnement de Louis*, and 100 for *Garin le Loherain*[14]), which certainly diminishes its capacity for lyric effects. In this very general sense, then, the formal texture of the first part displays a tendency toward the composition of verse romance. The narrative unfolds within the constraints of a certain horizontal framework – meter and assonance – but vertical progression is relatively uninhibited by strophic division.

Nevertheless, narrative progression is occasionally interrupted and transcended by complementary surges of lyricism. These lyric effects fall into two distinct categories: the occasional deployment of traditional strophic techniques, and the more frequent adaptation of conventional lyric devices to the longer laisse. Let us consider first of all the remnants of earlier compositional features.

First of all, many laisses begin with a marked "timbre d'intonation," a line which signals a new strophe in one of various ways: 1) by naming a character or intoning the epithet used to designate him/her; 2) by employing epic inversion of subject and verb; 3) by entreating the audience to listen.[15] Witness these examples from Part One:

> Liés fu Thieris li prevos naturés (v. 181)
> Li damoisiaux qui tant fist a loër (v. 258)
> Tresor cevauce li damoisiaus Hervis (v. 1774)
> Or escoutés dou bon prevost gentil! (v. 584)

Less frequent but still noteworthy is the "timbre de conclusion," a line which closes the strophe with a commentary or the conclusion of an action:[16]

---

[13] Rychner 107-110.
[14] Rychner 68 and Rossi.
[15] The first two instances are taken from Rychner 71-72. For a different typology of intonation verse, see Boutet 22.
[16] Rychner 72-73. See also Boutet, who nuances four different types of conclusion: 31.

'Et j'en ferai dou tot a vo devis.' (v. 109a)[17]
'Par diu, mi frere, je cuit bien dit avés.' (v. 583)
'Ci a bataille et grans estours esté.' (v. 4559)

Secondly, there are several instances of linking or *enchaînement* in this first half. The reprise is occasionally specific, i.e. formally similar and limited to one line:

. . .
Passent les terres, s'unt lo val avalé,
Tant cevaucha Hervis li bacelers.

Tresor cevauce li damoisiaus Hervis.
Ses oncle ataint qui en vont le cemin.
. . .

(vv. 1772-75)[18]

Most often, however, the repetition is more general and spans two or more lines. At the end of Laisse 4, for example, the provost Thieri falls at Duke Pierre's feet in gratitude, for the latter has just offered his daughter in marriage; this action is repeated at the beginning of Laisse 5:

. . .
'Par saint Esteve ou Jesus est servis,
Quant jugié l'ont mi home et mi ami,
Autre que vous, frans prevos seignoris,
N'avra ma fille qui tant a cler le vis.'
Li prevos l'ot, au piés li va caïr.

Liés fu Thieris li prevos naturés,
Quant oit le duc son sairement jurer
Que il aurait Ayelis a vis cler.
Au piés len chiet par grant humilité.
. . .

(vv. 176-84)[19]

---

[17] Ms. **E** adds a line before the conclusion.
[18] The later manuscripts **N** and **T** add a line at the end of the first laisse quoted here. This addition, "Qu'il voit ses oncles a I val avaler," lengthens the repetition to a two-line reprise.
[19] Ms. **E** adds the line "Quant jugié ont . . .".

This conventional form of epic repetition tends to obscure modern notions of narrative frequency. In Genette's terms, it is not clear whether this is a *récit répétitif* (one action told n times) or a *récit singulatif* (n actions told n times).[20] Indeed, the question is unimportant, for the function of this device lies rather on the level of song. Like many lyric reprises, this repetition serves to signal an important event, namely the properly humble attitude of Thieri before his marriage (as opposed to his subsequent presumptuousness).[21] Moreover, it is widely believed that the device of *enchaînement* originally served two pragmatic functions: on the level of production, it facilitated oral improvisation; on the level of reception, it attracted the attention of a boisterous, ambulatory audience. The latter function clearly remained even in the later written epic, for oral performance continued to require frequent repetitive signals.

It is tempting to link the strategy of *enchaînement* in *Hervis de Mes* to the text's typically epic motifs, for many instances are to be found in *conseils* and battles. However, the device also occurs in the more "romanesque" episodes, such as the purchase of Biatris: the final portion of Laisse 17 relates Hervis's offer to the ten squires, which is repeated in the beginning of Laisse 18:

>...
>'Seignour,' dist il, 'vers moi en entendés!
>De ceste dame qu'avés chi amené
>Pour son cors vendre a ceste feste anvel
>XVI·M mars que d'argent que d'or cler,
>C'on me carga dedens Mes la cité
>A ceste foire pour des dras accater
>Et vair et gris et fres hermines clers.'
>
>'Franc escuier,' ce dit l'enfes Hervis,
>'De ceste dame c'ait a non Beatrix,
>Qu'amenez si por vendre a Ligni,
>Je l'accatrai volentiers non envis;
>...
>
>(vv. 1371-81)

---

[20] Gérard Genette, *Figures III*, Collection Poétique (Paris: Seuil, 1972) 146. Genette does distinguish between the *récit singulatif* proper (one action told once) and its variant (n actions told n times).

[21] Duggan maintains that the sort of repetition present in *laisses similaires* and *enchaînements* constitutes a hypotactic movement at the narrative level which compensates for parataxis on the syntactic level. See *The Song of Roland: Formulaic Style and Poetic Craft* (Berkeley: University of California Press, 1973) 105-106.

Once again, the repetition blurs modern conceptions of narrative "logic" and serves to highlight a dramatic moment in the story.

Curiously, the later manuscripts **N** and **T** tend to increase the number of *enchaînements*. This may be indicative of the sort of voluntary archaism characteristic of many later redactions; composers and revisers often sought to retrieve the style of the early *chansons de geste* by multiplying lyric repetition.[22]

Only one tenuous example of *laisses parallèles* may be found in *Hervis de Mes*, and this instance does not involve entire laisses; rather, parts of two strophes exhibit a parallel development:

> ...
> Hervis le fiert de si grant poësté,
> Que nulz haubers ne le puet contrester,
> Parmi le cors li fist l'espiel passer,
> Tant con tint l'anste, l'abat mort enversé.
> L'ame s'en part, or l'emporte malfez.
> 'Outre traïtres,' dist Hervis li gentiz
> ...
>
>
> ...
> Grant cop li done sor le hiame flori,
> Que flors et pierres contreval abbati,
> L'elme et la coife li a parmi parti,
> Treque en dens le fendi et parti,
> Mort le trebuce dou bon cheval sovin.
> A vois escrie li damoisiax Hervis:
> 'Seignor gloton et fel et de put lin,
> Mar me gaitastes pour mon avoir tolir.'
> ...
>
> (vv. 4176-83; 4194-4201)

Significantly, this doubling of the single combat pattern in two succeeding laisses occurs at the boundary of thematic division, i.e. during the Hinbaut episode. As Hervis makes the transition from adventure to epic exploit, the text's formal pattern adumbrates the techniques to be used in the later part of the poem.

Despite the presence of opening and concluding timbres, numerous *enchaînements*, and two roughly parallel laisses, the con-

---

[22] See Rossi, *Huon* 159 and 609.

tours of each individual strophe do not receive the same prominence in the first part of *Hervis* as they do in such works as the Oxford *Roland*: the length of the laisse in *Hervis* greatly decreases the frequency of traditional framing and bridging devices. In fact, the majority of lyric effects in Part One are achieved by the transformation of certain early epic techniques. These transformations are characterized by two opposing tendencies, which may be termed *compression* and *dispersion*.

i) *Compression*

Compression is the presence within one strophe of lyric devices which framed or linked separate, consecutive strophes in the earlier *chansons de geste*; in the later works, that is, the interstrophic often becomes intrastrophic. Rychner notes the presence of one of these devices even in a twelfth-century epic with relatively long strophes, the *Couronnement de Louis*: laisses 33 and 42 of this work each present intrastrophic parallel developments. However, Rychner attributes the technique to poor composition: ". . . il reste étonnant que, d'une partie à l'autre, il n'y ait pas changement d'assonance, que l'on n'ait pas profité de cette reprise pour un découpage en laisses parallèles."[23]

It should be emphasized that my definition of later techniques with respect to typically earlier practices does not reflect this same critical bias: rather, it indicates a historical development. The compression of multiple timbres, bifurcation, and parallelism into single strophes increased with the passage of time and the progressive lengthening of the laisse.

Part One of *Hervis de Mes* presents many significant instances of compression. Very long laisses, such as the 1443-line laisse 43, are subdivided by internal intonations and conclusions, as the following examples demonstrate:

Internal Timbres of Intonation

Atant vient Hervis an son ostel (v. 4609)
L'anfes Hervis au coraige anduré (v. 4959)
Or escoutez dou boin prevost loé. (v. 5037)

---

[23] Rychner 113-14; quote 114.

Internal Timbres of Conclusion

Dïent li prince: 'Si con vos comandez.' (v. 5149)
'Sire,' font il, 'vous dites verité.' (v. 5706)

Such internal framing devices often serve to punctuate the multiple episodes and sub-episodes that comprise composite laisses of this sort.[24] Thus, certain types of phrases that fulfilled both narrative and lyric functions in the early *chanson de geste* come to serve a primarily narrative purpose in this later epic.

Other forms of "compression," however, retain their fundamental lyric effects. Notable in this respect are two examples of internal bifurcation, which adapt principles of traditional, consecutive *laisses bifurquées* to the long strophe. The first instance appears only in manuscripts **N** and **T**. They present, in laisse 5, two different conclusions of the same action, "Va s'ent li dus": in the first, Duke Pierre's departure is marked by a mass and a discussion between Pierre and Aelis; the second evocation of his leave-taking is characterized rather by a discussion between Pierre and Thieri (vv. 209-35). Although it is reasonable to assume that the two actions are consecutive, poetic form obscures narrative chronology. The repetition of "Va s'ent li dus" at the beginning of both segments de-emphasizes the importance of chronology and places the two actions on the same plane. This internal branching produces the same effects as the *laisses bifurquées*: ". . . cette forme. . . fait découler deux futurs du même présent."[25]

The second example of this phenomenon occurs on the level of narration. In Laisse 31, all three manuscripts open with the transition "Or vous lairons de Bïatris ester" (v. 3148). Since Hervis has just left for Tyre, we expect an account of his voyage and arrival. The *jongleur* does not, however, keep his promise, for the next thirteen lines present a scene between the forlorn Biatris and her hungry children. Line 3162 repeats the transition "Or vous lairons ci de la dame ester" (v. 3162), and this time the narrative does shift to the hero's voyage to Tyre (vv. 3163 ff.). Although this instance of bifurcation might seem a mere blunder, its presence in all three versions suggests that it was considered a necessary component of the text.

---

[24] For an analysis of framing devices in the *Prise d'Orange*, see Schurfranz 250-53.

[25] Rychner 81.

Indeed, it serves an essential narrative purpose: by affirming that the story is about to move on, the *jongleur* suggests that the following "afterthought" concerning Biatris occurred simultaneously with Hervis's voyage. The coincident events of the hero's departure and the heroine's lament underscore the pathos of the family's situation. At the same time, the repetition of "Or vous lairons de Biatris (la dame) ester" constitutes a lyric halt, an emphasis on the function of the *jongleur*: two separate accounts emanate from the same transitional chant, which takes on the value of an intonation timbre.

The third and final category of "compressed" lyric devices concerns parallel composition. Part One of *Hervis de Mes* contains several instances of intrastrophic symmetrical developments. Indeed, in the first half of the poem, this technique has largely replaced the *laisses parallèles* of earlier epic. The following two examples will illustrate the nature and function of the device.

In the midst of the lengthy laisse 8, Hervis has the opportunity to test his new hunting animals. The *épreuves* of the dog and the falcon follow the same narrative pattern and are described by many identical or similar hemistichs:

> a) Aprés son oncle en acuet son cemin.
> N'ot pas esré II liues et demi,
> Quand saut uns lievres fors del bruellet folli.
> Hervis le voit, li damoisiaus gentis,
> [...]
> Boins fu li chiens, tost ot le livrier [pris],
> [...]
> 'Levrier,' dist il, 'Ci ait m'ame merchi,
> Ne te donroie pour XM mars d'or fin.'
> (vv. 427-30, 433, 438-39)
>
> b) Isnelement accoilli son cemin.
> Les I estan uns mallars li sali,
> Prent son faucon li damoisiaus gentis,
> Apres le gete li damoisiaus gentis.
> Boins fu l'oisiax, n'ait pas del tot falli.
> [...]
> 'Si m'aït dix, oisiax,' ce dist Hervis,
> Ne te donroie qui me donroit Senlis.'
> (vv. 441-45, 452-53)

Rather than creating a bridge between strophes, then, compressed parallelism connects two incidents that occupy the same laisse. The functions of the technique are similar to those of *laisses parallèles*. First of all, the jongleur relates separate events in terms of their common denominators in order to signal certain important aspects. In this case, the essential characteristics of both events are the merits of the animals and the hero's recognition of their superior value; these factors will have contrastive value in the subsequent episode, when the *vilain* Thieri scoffs at his son's purchase. Secondly, the return to similar events and expressions tends to decelerate narrative progress by evoking echoes of a previous event: the story moves ahead, but emphasis is placed on lyric reverberation. Finally, the repetitions no doubt served a pragmatic purpose, facilitating oral performance and emphasizing important narrative developments for the audience.

Our second example multiplies the number of intrastrophic parallels, compressing seven symmetrical passages into one long laisse. In laisse 30, Bïatris conceives and elaborates the ruse of the embroidered cloth. Her instructions to Hervis are punctuated by the regular return of two initial elements, i.e. a frantic question raised by Hervis, followed by his wife's soothing response:

a) Hervis l'entent, pleure des iex del vis,
   Il en apelle sa femme Bïatris.
   'Que ferons nous, dame, pour diu merci?
   Ou merrons nous nos enfanchons petis?'
   [...]
   Bïatris l'ot, s'en a jeté I ris,
   [...]
   'Sire,' dist ele, 'ne vous esmaiés si!'

   (vv. 2904-7; 2910; 2913)

b) 'Que dites vos, dame?' ce dist Hervis.
   'Je n'ai ceval, palefroi ne ronci,'
   [...]
   'Sire,' dist ele, 'ne vous esmaiés si!'

   (vv. 2967-68; 2971)

c) 'Ma douce dame,' ce li a dit Hervis,
   De son drapel que vous avés chi mis
   [...]
   Qu'en ferai jou, douce suer Bïatris?'
   'Sire,' dist ele, 'j'ai le vos arai dit.'

   (vv. 2991-92; 2995-96)

d) Hervis l'entent, a po n'enrage vis:
   'Que dites vous, douce suer Bïatris?
   [...]
   Or voi je bien que tu me vués honnir.'
   'Non fas voir, biaus sire,' ce li a dit Bïatris.
             (vv. 3005-6; 3011-12)

e) Hervis l'entent, a souspirer en prist,
   Lors en apele sa femme Bïatris:
   'Dame,' dist il, 'quant je venrai a Tir,
   Que dirai jou a sou prince Baudri,
   Comment porrai son ostel retenir?'
   'Je vous dirai, sire,' ce dist Bïatris.
             (vv. 3016-21)

f) Hervis l'entent, a po n'enrage vis,
   [...]
   'Fole,' dist il, 'qu'est ce que avez dit?'
   [...]
   Bïatrix l'ot, s'en ait jeté un ris,
   Puis li respont doucement non envis,
   'Biax tresdous frere, et cor t'en va a Tir!'
             (vv. 3070, 3073, 3080-82)

g) 'Ma douce suer,' ce li a dit Hervis,
   De cest drapel que m'avés cargié ci,
   Qu'en ferai jou, quant je venrai a Tir?'
   'Sire,' dist ele, 'a l'estal sera mis.'
             (vv. 3088-91)

Once again, the effects of compressed parallelism are similar to those of *laisses parallèles*. The recurring schema serves in this instance to highlight the contrasting roles of the hero and heroine: multiple reprises confirm that it is Bïatris who advises and guides the helpless Hervis. The rhythmic return to the same patterns also articulates the narrative into seven distinct phases, which are rendered in the form of a question-and-answer refrain.

Compressed bifurcation and parallelism thus retain a measure of the lyric-narrative balance characteristic of their interstrophic counterparts. One notable transformation in the later technique is, of course, continuity of assonance. *Laisses parallèles* have always been admired for their virtuosity, since the poet must express similar themes or actions using a variety of assonances. By compressing parallel structures into one long strophe, the *Hervis* poet is able to repeat identical first *and* second hemistichs. Edmund Stengel considers this lack of assonantal variety a major compositional flaw.[26]

It is true that *Hervis de Mes* as a whole does offer a paucity of assonantal change. More than 83 % of the poem carries the assonance [e]; lines in [i] number 15 %, and none of the remaining assonances ([e]fem., [a], [ie], [a]fem., [u]fem., and [u]) occupies more than two laisses or twenty-one lines. Thus, versification as a whole exhibits a large-scale uniformity. The phenomenon is even more evident in the first half of the text, which incorporates only [e] and [i], the former occupying the great majority of lines.

This variation on epic form ought not, however, be attributed *ipso facto* to unskilled composition. The predominance of one assonance is in fact characteristic of the *geste* as a whole, although it is present to a lesser degree in the earlier works: the assonance [i] occupies 70 % of *Garin le Loherain* and 25 % of *Gerbert de Mez*.[27] Thus, the single-assonance mode appears to have had some aesthetic value for the composers and audiences of this cycle. Indeed, the frequent repetition of hemistichs and entire lines, considered monotonous by many modern readers, actually contributes to incantatory expression.[28] We shall see that the dominant assonance also plays a role in the second category of compositional transformation.

ii) *Dispersion*[29]

Whereas compressed parallelism densifies the structure of the laisse, the mechanism of dispersion diffuses the components of par-

---

[26] "Diese Künstelei hat bei ihm die schlimme Folge gehabt, dass bestimmte Versanfänge fortwährend wiederkehren ... ja dass ganze Verszeilen sich wörtlich genau oder mit nur ganz geringen Modifikationen Dutzende von Malen wiederholen." Stengel, Introduction, *Hervis de Mes*, V.

[27] Pauline Taylor, Introduction, *Gerbert de Mez: Chanson de geste du XIIe siècle*, Bibliothèque de la Faculté de Philosophie et de Lettres de Namur 11 (Namur, Lille, Louvain: Nauwelaerts, 1952) XLIV.

[28] See Gittleman, 84-87 and 99-100.

[29] This study of dispersion originally appeared in Catherine M. Jones, "Dispersed Parallelism in *Hervis de Mes*," *Olifant* 13 (1988): 29-40.

allel scenes over a span of several strophes and hundreds of lines. The repeated elements are thus separated by intervals of varying length. Part One of *Hervis de Mes* offers two notable examples of dispersion, both of which occur in the celebrated fair scenes.

In the previous chapter, we considered the symmetrical pattern of the Provins and Lagny episodes, which are characterized by nearly-identical stages and similar formulaic expression.[30] These parallel developments, however, do not appear consecutively; the stages of the fair in Lagny are fragmented and separated by intervals of one to three strophes and several hundred lines. The mechanics of this dispersion become evident when one examines the distribution of the motifs that comprise each fair episode:

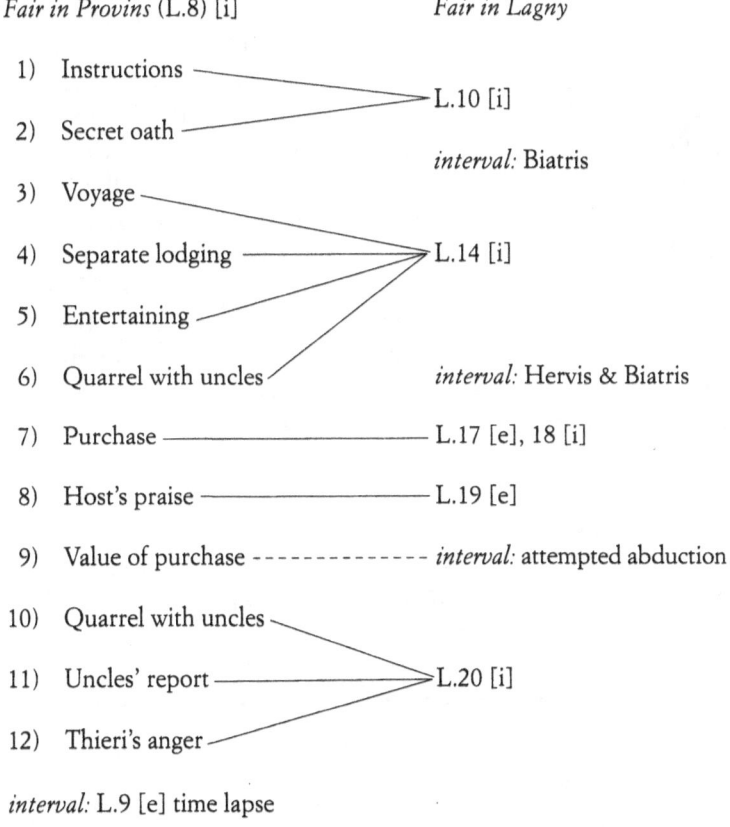

---

[30] The similarity of expression is somewhat variable; some parallel stages present identical hemistichs, while others offer more variety. On the whole, however,

The lengthy laisse 8 successively relates all twelve of the incidents connected with the fair in Provins, from Thieri's instructions to his angry reaction upon Hervis's return (vv. 298-565). The following short strophe indicates the passage of time between the fairs in Provins and Lagny (vv. 566-83).

Laisse 10 resumes the same assonance as laisse 8 [i], and begins a symmetrical account of the fair in Lagny; this strophe, however, relates only the first two stages (vv. 584-608). The remaining parallel components are delayed by a shift to the story of Biatris and the Spanish King. This interval occupies over three laisses and 589 lines, and contains the betrothal of Biatris as well as her abduction (vv. 609-1197). Laisse 14 resumes the account of the hero's adventures in Lagny, and echoes stages 3, 4, 5, and 6 of the Provins episode (1198-1234); this laisse again employs the assonance [i]. Another interruption follows: the end of Laisse 14, Laisses 15, 16, and the beginning of Laisse 17 portray the meeting of Biatris and Hervis and the latter's decision to purchase the lady (vv. 1235-1378). Laisses 17 and 18 contain parallel stage 7 (vv. 1379-94). Laisse 19 recounts at length a final narrative interval, the attempted abduction of Biatris by three wicked young men (vv. 1395-1724); parallel stage 8 is embedded in this segment (vv. 1521-24, 1539-43).[31] Finally, in Laisse 20, parallel stages 10, 11, and 12 conclude the episode of the fair in Lagny.

The function of dispersed parallelism is revealed by the diverging roles of intervals and repeated sequences in the Lagny episode. The *intervals* as a group serve a primarily narrative function: the story of the Spanish King furnishes a related plot sequence that will become important in subsequent episodes; the encounter between Hervis and Biatris initiates a union that generates future conflicts within *Hervis de Mes*, and also produces offspring whose exploits furnish the subject matter of subsequent epics in the cycle; finally, the attempted kidnapping of Biatris provides the hero with the first of many opportunities to distinguish himself in battle. The interludes thus expand the narrative to include simultaneous or subse-

---

each of these stages may be said to constitute a "fabricated motif," i.e. a repeated compositional unit that combines traditional formulas with a new context. See Rossi, *Huon* 172.

[31] Stage 9 of the Provins episode, the *épreuve* of the hero's hunting animals, presents general thematic parallels with this segment. Biatris warns Hervis of approaching danger and thus proves to be a "valuable" purchase in the hero's eyes.

quent conflicts; they serve to advance and amplify narrative movement in the text.

The parallels and repetitions, on the other hand, fulfill quite different functions which, like compressed parallel structures, correspond in many ways to the technique of *laisses parallèles*. We noted in the previous chapter that the symmetrical episodes fulfill a didactic function by encouraging reciprocal interpretation: both fair scenes contrast the petty values of the bourgeoisie with the nobleman's sense of true worth.

Secondly, the regular return of identical units of content and formal expression confers a lyric dimension upon the account of the fairs. These repetitions do not, however, produce the same effects of pathos evoked by parallel structures in such epics as the Oxford *Roland*. Rather, the litany of commercial transgressions and reprimands provides the fair episodes with a certain comic value by emphasizing the mechanical nature of the hero's actions and his father's reactions. Rupert Pickens has analyzed the potential for comedy inherent in early epic parallelism, demonstrating that certain characters in the *Couronnement de Louis* become "trapped in the automatism of the ... jongleur's parallel structuring."[32]

It is noteworthy that dispersed lyricism, like compressed lyricism, permits the consistent return to the same assonance. Intervals provide variety, while repeated elements often share identical opening and closing hemistichs. This consistency suggests that the composer(s) of *Hervis* generally associated parallel structuring with a dominant assonance.

Finally, the parallelism of the two fair episodes creates a bridge that ultimately acts to decelerate and even obscure narrative progress. Although the time lapse between the fairs is very clearly indicated in Laisse 9, the events in Provins and Lagny tend to blend into each other with the multiplication of parallels. While the two episodes never merge completely, the manuscripts eventually begin to confuse them, attributing the purchase of Biatris to the fair in Provins or the purchase of the horse to the fair in Lagny (Ms. E, v. 863; Ms. v, folio 12a). The separate fairs seem almost to fuse into a single episode with two different conclusions, much like bifurcated

---

[32] Rupert T. Pickens, "Comedy, History and Jongleur Art in the *Couronnement de Louis*", *Olifant* 11 (1986): 214.

structures. This sort of narrative confusion between parallelism and bifurcation has also been observed in earlier epics."

Thus dispersed parallelism retains some of the techniques and effects of consecutive parallelism, but adapts them to the exigencies of story-telling. While intervals permit the expansion and progression of the narrative, repeated elements open the text to its lyric dimension.

This mechanism of dispersion is most conspicuous in the episodes of Provins and Lagny. Nevertheless, it does appear in a less-developed form in a later episode, namely the bargaining sessions at the fair in Tyre. However, the insertion of a narrative interval is present only in the later manuscripts **N** and **T**. The following diagram illustrates the structure of dispersed parallelism in the bargaining sessions between Hervis and Floire and between Hervis and Uistasse:

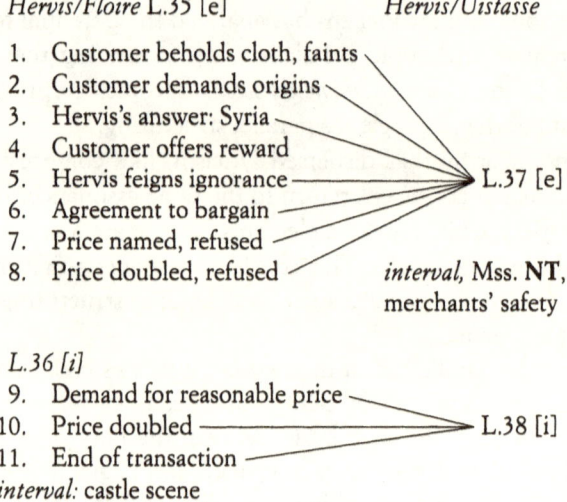

The hero's first customer is Floire, King of Hungary and brother of Biatris. The encounter between Hervis and Floire, which is characterized by eleven distinct stages, is recounted at the end of Laisse 35 and the beginning of Laisse 36 (vv. 3477-3575). A parallel bargaining session involving Hervis and Uistasse begins in the middle of the following laisse (vv. 3670-3765). The two sessions are sep-

---

" Pickens 212-16.

arated by an interval of nearly one hundred lines, and the last three parallel components are separated from the others (in Mss. **NT**) by an interval of two laisses for a total of sixty lines (L. 38a and 38b).[34]

Once again, the intervals contribute to narrative progression and motivation. Between bargaining sessions, the scene shifts from the fair to the castle, where the Queen offers her entire treasure to procure her daughter's embroidery. It is the Queen's initiative that will permit the purchase of the embroidered cloth. Furthermore, this scene prepares a later episode in which she insists that Hervis must know the whereabouts of her daughter; her demands lead to the eventual recapture of Biatris in the second half of the story (vv. 3887-3938).

The interval *between* parallel components plays a similar role. This sixty-line interlude involves a discussion between Hervis and the King of Tyre about the safety of merchants and their wares. When the King suggests that it is in his power to appropriate the silk cloth, Hervis insists that Tyre is known for the King's goodwill toward merchants. This conversation prepares a later episode, in which the King (influenced by the Queen) attempts to capture Hervis and force him to reveal information about Biatris; it is the merchants of Tyre who come to the hero's rescue by citing the standards of justice that have always prevailed in that city (vv. 3837-70). Both intervals, therefore, lay a narrative foundation for future events by increasing the number of logical indicators that link different events in the story.

The dispersed *refrains* of the bargaining process, on the other hand, transform this commercial transaction into an amusing and instructive chant. We have seen that the hero's repeated price increases reverse his previous behavior patterns and signal a unique mastery of commercial practices. Moreover, it is now the hero's adversaries who become the victims of the jongleur's automatism; thanks to the instructions of Biatris, Hervis assumes control over the mechanical stages of bargaining. Finally, it must be noted that the parallel structures once again share identical assonances, permitting the occasional repetition of hemistichs and entire lines.

---

[34] Appendix to Stengel's edition, pp. 430-32. Mss. **NT** present a variation of L. 38 in the edition, followed by an additional strophe which Stengel numbers 38a. These two manuscripts then return to the assonance and common material of L.38. Since the **NT** version actually adds two strophes, I have chosen to number them 38a and 38b.

Thus, dispersed parallelism once again tempers narrative progression with lyric effects. The intervals between parallel scenes and their components look forward to later events, while the repetitions recall and echo previous occurrences. This second example of dispersion is significant in that the narrative interpolations are present only in the later manuscripts; the intervals represent later additions to an originally consecutive chain. The interruption of parallel laisses reflects a general tendency on the part of Mss. **NT** to furnish additional motivation, thereby attenuating the occasionally paratactic narrative movement of the earlier manuscripts.

The mechanism of dispersion constitutes a definite departure from traditional epic modes of parallel composition. The scenes we have examined are composed with little regard for consecution or strophic boundaries; intervening laisses permit a consistent return to the same assonance; and narrative intervals delay the lyric effects of repetition. Moreover, whereas *laisses parallèles* are almost certainly linked to the exigencies of oral improvisation, our second example of dispersion indicates that this later technique may stem from the revisions of later redactors.

Nevertheless, even this altered form of parallelism links the episodes in question with compositional strategies of the epic tradition. The regular return of identical units of content in similar formulaic configurations brings epic tonality even to the affairs of the marketplace. By interspersing narrative advances and fragmented refrains, these passages create a new kind of balance between the dimensions of story and song.

One final aspect of composition in Part One remains to be examined here. The rather lengthy episode of the tournament in Senlis constitutes a formal rupture in all three principal manuscripts: although assonance is maintained, **E**, **N**, and **T** shift temporarily to twelve-syllable lines. This change in versification occupies 571 lines in **E** (vv. 2333-2895), 579 lines in **T** (vv. 2349-2908), and 573 lines in **N** (vv. 2351-2910).[35]

Heinrich Hub suggests that this episode is most likely the work of a later redactor, since both subject matter and versification re-

---

[35] The discrepancy in figures is due to my use of the verse numbers in Stengel's edition. The actual number of twelve-syllable lines in each manuscript may be found in Heinrich Hub, *La Chanson de Hervis de Mes: Inhaltsgabe und Classification der Handschriften*, Diss. (Marburg: Heilbronn, 1879) 37.

flect the transformations of later epic poetry.[36] Indeed, these narrative and formal indices attest to the presence of a separate origin for the Senlis episode, which may well have occupied only a few lines in the original version. Nevertheless, it is significant that all three manuscripts attempt to weave the segment into the narrative fabric of the text, so that the change in verse-length might be the sole indicator of disunity. The following passages indicate that the three versions accomplish this transfer with varying degrees of subtlety; junctures in each manuscript are marked by the symbol >:

> **E:** Hervis en vint arriere en son ostel,
> Voit son serourge, sel prent a apeller:
> 'Biax tresdous freres, vers moy en entendés!
> Forment m'ennuie dedens ceste cité.
> > Et tot pour le prevost c'ai fait le ban crïer,
> Que compaignie nule ne jone ne barbé
> Ne li osoient faire ne si ami charné.
> Or me convient cerorge deporter
> Aler en un tornoi an France le regné.'
> (vv. 2329-37)

The transition in this manuscript thus occurs in the midst of a laisse, indeed, in the midst of an utterance. However, the juncture is manifest not only in the change to twelve-syllable lines, but also in the failure to maintain consistent first-person discourse (v. 2335).

In the following excerpt from manuscript **T**, Hervis has just asked Baudri of Metz to look after Biatris and Garin during his absence:

> **T:** Et dist Baudris, 'que c'est que dit avés?'
> > Certes ne lor faurroie dusqu'a membres coper.
> Mais menés ent Gerart mon neveu l'alozé!'
> (vv. 2348-50)

Once again, the shift occurs within a discourse; this time, however, the transition does not exhibit any morphological discrepancies and thus effects a smoother shift to twelve-syllable lines.

Ms. **N** also offers a smooth transition, which appears two lines after that of Ms. **T**:

---

[36] Hub 37.

> N: 'Mais menés ent Gerardin l'alozé!
> \>   Fix est de ma seror, si le doi moult amer.
>   Frere, de bien servir e[s]t bien endoctrinés.'
>
>   (vv. 2350-51)

The Senlis episode provides two important pieces of information. First of all, it furnishes irrefutable evidence that even Ms. E of *Hervis de Mes* represents an amalgamation of at least two different traditions. Secondly, the mode of incorporation indicates that the redactors of *Hervis* attempted to efface the junctures to a certain extent: although they did not convert the twelve-syllable lines to decasyllables, they compensated for the formal rupture by maintaining the same strophic and (to varying degrees) the same discursive framework.

This procedure leads us therefore to speculate on the compositional process of the text as a whole. We have already observed significant narrative and structural differences between Parts One and Two of *Hervis*; this suggests the possibility that different legends or *chansons* were combined to form the text as we know it in Mss. E, N, and T. It seems quite likely that if such a combination occurred, the process was similar to the insertion of the Senlis episode: the poets or redactors attempted to efface certain junctures, weaving the disparate parts into a unified narrative fabric. Nonetheless, as we shall see in the following section, the formal rupture between Parts One and Two is still evident in the structure and function of the laisse.

                       * * *

The second part of *Hervis de Mes* continues to display many characteristics of late epic form. It contains a number of very long strophes, and the average number of lines per laisse (117) is still relatively high. Although dispersion is absent from this part of the text, the longer strophes exhibit techniques of compression similar to those we noted in Part One: internal timbres and intrastrophic parallelism continue to play a significant role in the structure of the laisse.

Nevertheless, Part Two marks a definite change in formal composition. First of all, the average number of lines per laisse (117) is significantly lower than that of the first half. While the strophic dimensions of Part Two are certainly much greater than those of the Oxford *Roland*, they are not very far removed from those of *Garin le Loherain*.[37] Moreover, the second part of *Hervis* includes a greater percentage of short laisses and much more assonantal variation. Although the alternation [e] / [i] remains dominant, six other assonances appear, all in short strophes of fourteen lines or less (L. 46, 47, 55, 58, 59, 60, 68, 69, 75). These strophes, and indeed short strophes in general, tend to be used in traditionally epic narrative segments, particularly in battle scenes.

Part Two also includes a greater number of conventional intonation and conclusion timbres. Epic inversion is more common as an intonation, especially in short laisses describing battle:

> Grans fu la noize et li estours mortex (v. 6640)
> Fiers fu li caples et li estours badiz (v. 6674)

This type of laisse also tends to use a vehement concluding timbre:

> Et dist Hervis: 'M'espee avés sentue.' (v. 6141)
> 'Mar le pensastes, se diu plaist et je vif.' (v. 9501)

The diverging tendencies of Parts One and Two are perhaps most apparent on the level of traditional interstrophic lyricism. The second part contains more instances of *enchaînement*, particularly of the following type:

> Li cevaus chiet, Hervis dessant el pré,
> Traite a l'espee au poing d'or ameré,
> . . .
>
> Or fu Hervis a pié el pre flouri.
> . . .
> (vv. 9518-19, 9523)

The two laisses both indicate that Hervis is on the ground, but they evoke two different aspects of the action: the process of being "unhorsed" and the resulting predicament of the hero. This technique is quite typical of the early *chanson de geste* characterized by dis-

---

[37] It is worth recalling that Part One of *Hervis* averages 140 lines per laisse, the Oxford *Roland* 14, and *Garin le Loherain* 100.

tinct strophic boundaries. Rychner describes a similar passage in the Oxford *Roland*:

> ... la pâmoison de Roland, envisagée d'abord sous l'aspect de son déroulement, l'est ensuite sous celui de son achèvement ... les deux aspects, le premier penché sur le futur, le second retourné sur le passé, soulignent très exactement la ligne de démarcation qui sépare les laisses.[38]

Part Two also exhibits many more examples of conventional parallelism. Laisses 68, 69, and 70, for example, display similar openings and developments: each strophe begins by evoking the general battle, and then portrays an individual knight in combat:

> 68: Fiers fu li caples et li estours mortez.
> Atant es vous Sance de Monroial,
> En sa compaigne maint nobile vassal...
> (vv. 8428-30)

> 69: Fiers fut li caples et ruiste la mellee
> Et la bataille cremue et redoutee.
> Es vous Hervi el poing destre l'espee!
> Cui il consut moult a courte duree.
> (vv. 8435-38)

> 70: Fier fu li caples et li estours mortels.
> Es vous Hervi, el poing le branc letré!
> Si con il va parmi l'estour mortel,
> Cui il consuit tout a son tans uzé.
> (vv. 8442-45)

Laisse 70 continues with a different sphere of action, thereby precluding perfect strophic symmetry. Nevertheless, the similar opening inversions and parallel developments accentuate strophic boundaries, thereby recalling and recreating the incantatory movement of the early *chansons de geste*.

Thus the technique of the laisse corroborates the bipartition we have discovered on other textual levels. Although the formal innovations of Part One cannot properly be termed "romanesque," they do diminish the role of the strophe in poetic composition. Part Two

---

[38] Rychner 78.

reflects rather a generic conservatism, a return to conventional molding of strophic contours and interrelationships. This tension between innovation and convention parallels the narrative and ideological framework of the text; modifications in subject matter and form appear to exercise reciprocal influence. A similar phenomenon will be observed in the following examination of formulaic style.

FORMULAIC STYLE

At the micro-compositional level, the *chanson de geste* is characterized by a highly stereotypical disposition of narrative elements and the phrases used to represent them. Jean Rychner has convincingly demonstrated the connection between this style of composition and the epic's original conditions of production and dissemination.[39] The jongleur, who improvised or memorized texts containing thousands of lines, composed his *chanson* by exploiting a common stock of narrative-linguistic systems that Rychner and his followers have described at various levels of detail.

The most global of these compositional units, called "themes", are roughly equivalent to the narrative divisions we have defined as "episodes"; common examples include the council and the battle. On a more detailed level than themes or episodes is the repertory of what Rychner terms "motifs."[40] Heinemann refers to these motifs as "networks of narrative details," usually occupying ten to twenty lines, which occur in a more or less fixed order and use similar forms of expression.[41]

The motifs catalogued by Rychner and other scholars are not all stereotyped to the same extent. The *repas* and the *voyage*, for example, display a good deal of variation on both the synchronic and diachronic axes. The "combat singulier à la lance" and the *planctus*, on the other hand, are clearly defined narrative units that vary little

---

[39] Rychner 126-128.
[40] Rychner 126-41.
[41] Edward A. Heinemann, "Network of Narrative Details: The Motif of the Journey in the *Chanson de geste*," *The Epic in Medieval Society*, ed. Harald Scholler (Tubingen: Max Niemeyer, 1977) 178-80. Marguerite Rossi uses the term "séquences narratives stéréotypées" to describe the epic repertory. See her article entitled "Les séquences narratives stéréotypées" in *Mélanges de langue et de littérature françaises offerts à Pierre Jonin* (Paris: Champion, 1979): 593-607.

from one epic to another.[42] The latter motifs are characterized by stable series of narrative details, which are represented by metrical-semantic-syntactic units known as "formulas."

The definition of an epic "formula" has been a subject of controversy for over half a century. Milman Parry, who pioneered studies in oral-formulaic style, defined the formula broadly as "a group of words which is regularly employed under the same metrical conditions to express a given essential idea."[43] Since Parry's definition, scholars have alternately expanded and limited the scope of what constitutes a formula. Some definitions rely heavily on semantic properties, while others consider the formula to be a primarily syntactic unit.[44] Joseph Duggan, in his computer-generated formula analyses, limits the concept to repeated word groups within the same poem.[45]

The elaboration of a satisfactory definition of the epic formula is well beyond the scope of the present study, which seeks principally to examine the phrases comprising specific motifs in *Hervis de Mes*. To this end, we have adopted a modified synthesis of the above formulations. A "formula" will here designate any hemistich or line that is employed at least twice within the poem to express a given narrative detail; phrases exhibiting only minor syntactic or lexical deviations will be deemed members of the same formula system.[46] For example, the following lines belong to the same stage of the "armement" motif, i.e. the suspension of the knights' shields:

> A lor cols pendent les fors escus bendés (v. 8371)
> Au col li pendent I fort escu doré (v. 9453)

---

[42] See Rychner 130 & 139. For a detailed study of the *planctus*, see Paul Zumthor, "Les *planctus* épiques," *Romania* 84 (1963): 61-69; and Joseph Duggan, *The Song of Roland* 160-83. For a detailed study of the *voyage*, see Heinemann, "Network."

[43] Milman Parry, "Studies in the Epic Technique of Oral Verse-Making: I. Homer and Homeric Style," *Harvard Studies in Classical Philology* 41 (1930): 80.

[44] A useful summary of past and recent definitions may be found in Marjorie Windelberg and D. Gary Miller, "How (Not) to Define the Epic Formula," *Olifant* 8 (1980-81): 29-50.

[45] Joseph J. Duggan, *The Song of Roland: Formulaic Style and Poetic Craft* (Berkeley, Los Angeles, London: University of California Press) 23.

[46] This concept of "formula system" should be distinguished from that of Milman Parry. Parry's object of research was the global definition of formulaic properties, while the present study is concerned rather with the specific formulas comprising certain motifs.

The first hemistichs of these two lines differ as follows: in the first example, the knights in question don their own shields, while in the second, several attendants arm a single knight. This variation generates the syntactic variation of the possessive adjective "lor" and the indirect object pronoun "li." Nevertheless, the two hemistichs may be seen as surface manifestations of the same formula, related constituents of the "suspension" system. Similarly, the second hemistichs differ in the type of article used, the number of shields, and the choice of a final adjective. Both, however, name the shield(s), employ the preceding adjective "fort," and end the hemistich with a participial adjective indicating the ornamentation of the shield. Thus, the two lines contain opening and closing hemistichs belonging to the same formula systems.

This broad definition of the formula would not be appropriate for a determination of the formulaic density of an epic poem. Such an analysis must be based on a rigorous metrical, syntactic, morphological, and semantic comparison of hemistichs both within and between texts; until concordances have been established for large numbers of *chansons de geste*, these studies will remain unsatisfactory. The present study will thus not attempt to determine the percentage of "formulas" in each half of *Hervis de Mes*.[47] Rather, we shall examine transformation and convention at the level of motifs and their components. Once again, special attention will be given to Part One, for it is this half of the text that presents significant modifications in traditional composition.

A detailed outline of motifs in *Hervis de Mes* is provided in Appendix C.

Part One

The introduction of "romanesque" subject matter does not effect a shift to typically "romanesque" style in Part One of *Hervis*. Medieval verse romance springs from a written tradition and generally adopts the rhetorical devices of this learned and literate her-

---

[47] Marguerite Rossi, *Huon de Bordeaux et l'évolution du genre épique au XIIIe siecle*, Nouvelle Bibliothèque du Moyen Age 2 (Paris: Champion, 1975) 174. For a lengthy debate on studies of formulaic density, see the articles by William Calin and Joseph Duggan in *Olifant* 8 (1980-81): 227-316.

itage.⁴⁸ Like other *chansons de geste*, *Hervis de Mes* as a whole is composed rather in the manner of orally improvised texts, by the juxtaposition of recurring motifs and formulas. Nevertheless, the "romanesque" portion of the text does present several modifications of traditional formulaic style; these changes include the transformation of conventional motifs and the fabrication of new formal units. The former category, our first object of analysis, may be divided into three different modes of transformation: combination, fragmentation, and displacement.

Combination in this instance involves the fusion of two traditionally separate motifs into a single unit. The phenomenon occurs in Manuscript **E** of *Hervis de Mes*, during the struggle between Hervis and the bandits led by the giant Hinbaut: Hinbaut's nephew Clarembaut attacks Hervis with a lance, but the latter responds with a sword, even though there is no evidence that he has shattered his lance (vv. 4186-93, 4193a-f, 4194-4201).⁴⁹ In conventional epic battles, the motifs of lance- and sword-combat are generally distinct phases; most often, the former occupies the first stage of battle and the latter occurs after the lances have been broken (cf. vv. 9499-9510). In this passage, however, a traditional sword-combat formula makes its intrusion in the midst of a typical lance-combat progression. Clarembaut begins the encounter with a *défi*, and then proceeds to spur his horse.⁵⁰ The series is interrupted by the first stage of sword-combat, as Hervis draws his weapon:

> 'De mort novelle orendroit te deffi!'
> Le destrier lait aler, l'arabi,
> Et Hervis traist le branc d'acier fourbi.
>
> (vv. 4191-93)

Clarembaut, however, continues to enact the conventional scene of lance-combat: he strikes Hervis and damages the latter's shield, but the hero's armor remains intact; in the process, Clarembaut breaks

---

⁴⁸ Jauss, *Toward* 84.
⁴⁹ Mss. **NT** do not specify Clarembaut's weapon.
⁵⁰ Rychner outlines the traditional motif of lance-combat in seven stages (p. 141); I have added the *défi*, which generally precedes and spurs the struggle. It should also be noted that this passage represents a typical variation on Rychner's model, namely the failure of the evil or unfortunate adversary. My references to the less stereotypical sword-combat are generally based on other instances of the motif in *Hervis de Mes*.

his lance. These stages typify the fate of the evil adversary in accounts of lance-combat.

Upon completion of this motif, the poet relates the remaining phases of sword-combat: Hervis holds his sword, strikes the adversary, splits his helmet and head in two, and unhorses the dead Clarembaut. Each character thus participates in his own form of combat, and the stock phrases used to represent each type are interwoven and juxtaposed in the same poetic framework.

This conspicuous departure from canonical modes of representation is perhaps linked to the unconventional nature of the hero's adversary; the stylistic device of assigning different motifs to the two characters functions to signal the great discrepancy between the worthy Hervis and the wicked giant bandit. Furthermore, the modified motif emphasizes the unorthodox nature of this pre-epic battle: Hervis, the noble merchant, has neither been dubbed nor accorded the title of duke. As we have seen, his status before the *adoubement* remains mixed; the combination of two distinct battle motifs therefore complements the mixture of two social heritages within Hervis.

The fragmentation of traditional motif components is a more common modification, and one that has been noted in other thirteenth-century epics.[51] Instances in *Hervis de Mes* often spring from the heroine's unusual prominence in the narrative. Witness the following example of the *repas* motif from the episode of the Spanish embassy to Tyre; innovations in the traditional motif are marked with [>].

> Li roys les fait servir et honourer,
> Grans fu la joie el palais principel,
> Bïatris ont la pucele amené, [...]
> A la grant table s'asistrent a disner,
> \> De sa biauté furent tuit trespensé,
> \> Le mangier laissent pour son cors regarder,
> Aprés mangier font les nappes oster.
> (vv. 748-750, 756-59)

The *repas* motif is one of the more flexible formulaic units in Old French epic poetry. Typical elements, such as the entrance into

---

[51] e.g. *Huon de Bordeaux*. See Rossi, *Huon* 167.

the palace, the pleasure of the diners, the enumeration of abundant food and drink, and the removal of tablecloths, may appear in varying order or may be eliminated from any single occurrence. However, the interruption of a meal by the contemplation of a lady's transcendent beauty is an irregular modification of the motif, generated by the introduction of romanesque content. Marguerite Rossi observes a similar phenomenon in *Huon de Bordeaux*, in which the *repas* motif is dissociated and transformed by the intervention of *merveilleux* elements.[52] This technique generally functions to give narrative emphasis to the anomalous elements: the rather banal *repas* sequence provides a conventional framework from which the audience measures variation. In this instance, the interpolated formulas in line 757 also foreshadow Hervis's later reaction to Biatris, which is expressed in a similar line containing one identical and one related formula: "De sa biauté par fut toz esbahis" (v. 1253). This line echoes the ambassadors' interrupted meal and further accentuates the beauty of the heroine. In this instance, then, the conventions of epic form furnish a backdrop for the emergence and salience of typical romance content.

A similar formal modification occurs during Hervis's first experience in battle, when he must defend Biatris against the three lecherous would-be kidnappers (vv. 1577-1635). During the initial sword-combat, the traditional motif is broken by the intrusion of a female voice:

> Detint le cop du bon branc aceré.
> Et Bïatrix commencha a crïer:
> 'Hé dignes dix, le damoisel gardés,
> Que il ne soit ochis ne affolés!'
> Hervis escrie li damoisiax membrés:
> 'Bele, n'ai garde, la merci damedé.'
> Lors trait le branc, du fuerre l'a geté.
> (vv. 1587-93)

This exchange stresses the heroine's function as guardian angel. Like Enide, Biatris intervenes vocally in the hero's adventure to protect her own interests and those of her champion; like Erec, Hervis claims control over his own adventure, refusing temporarily

---

[52] Rossi, *Huon* 167-68.

to acknowledge the value of his lady's *parole*. Once again, the fragmentation of stock epic components draws attention to romanesque innovations in the narrative.

A third example of fragmented motifs does not involve the introduction of romance matter, but rather the infusion of the "merveilleux chrétien." When God intervenes in Hervis's behalf during the struggle against the giant Hinbaut, the miracle occurs in the midst of a typical lance-combat:

> A ces paroles laist le destrier aler.
> Hinbaus i vint comme foudre doré,
> Hervi ne prise I denier monnaé.
> > La fist miracles li roys de maïsté, [...]
> Feri li rais du soleil qui luist cler, [...]
> Et Hervi faut del roit espiel quarré,
> Hervis le fiert de si grant poësté
> Que nulz haubers ne le puet contrester...
>   (vv. 4162-65, 4172, 4175-77)[53]

This instance of fragmentation rejuvenates the conventional lance-combat motif, not only by adding an impressive miracle to the series, but also by associating the miraculous event with a typical phase of combat. The sun, like a knightly opponent, *strikes* the unfortunate giant in the eyes ("Feri"); this military metaphor prepares the hero's powerful blow ("fiert") and thereby associates Hervis with the strength of God and the sun. The intervening lines therefore revitalize the formula "X le fiert" and indeed all of the following stages of the lance motif. Fragmentation can also function, then, to enrich the poetic force of conventional epic motifs and formulas.

The third mode of transformation to be considered is the displacement of traditional motifs and formulas onto new units of content. The most striking example of this technique is the modification of the *planctus*, a stylized discourse typically pronounced over

---

[53] This passage may be contrasted with the Baligant episode in the Oxford *Roland*. During the sword combat between Baligant and Charlemagne, the angel Gabriel speaks to the emperor and changes the course of the duel; however, the jongleur recounts the divine intervention only after Baligant's first blow has been struck and reacted to. *La Chanson de Roland*, ed. Gérard Moignet (Paris: Bordas, 1985) vv. 3602-12.

the body of a fallen hero or a hero who is presumed to be dead. This motif has been expertly catalogued by scholars of the earlier *chanson de geste*.[54] In a scene from Part One of *Hervis de Mes*, however, the general framework of the *planctus* is adapted to King Uistasse's lament over his daughter's abduction (vv. 1039-64). The passage incorporates the following stages of the motif:[55]

1) *Narrative link*: "Li rois l'entent" (v. 1046).

2) *External signs of mourning*: "a terre chiet pasmés" (v. 1046).

3) *Apostrophe*: "'He roys d'Espaingne, tant fais a redouter!'" (v. 1053).

4) *Misfortune of the survivors*: "'Mar fut li cors Bïatrix engenrez / Par li perdrai mes riches eritez'" (v. 1051-52).

5) *Pledge of vengeance*: "'Haï Baudris, dix te puist vergonder! ... Tu en pendrais, tes garedons iert tez'" (vv. 1061, 1064).

Alterations of the basic pattern are evident: the king does not address his apostrophe to his missing daughter, nor does he exhibit signs of grief at losing her. His regrets are centered on the anticipated revenge of the Spanish King and the loss of Tyre. In this passage, then, the romanesque episode of the abduction assumes epic value by the use of an epic motif and, curiously, by the displacement of personal regret onto the plane of feudal rights and agreements.

Thus, the transformation of conventional forms serves diverse purposes in this thirteenth-century *chanson de geste*. New types of subject matter may be highlighted by modifications of conventional formulaic molds; conversely, these molds may be used to assimilate new *matière* into the texture of the *chanson de geste*. Indeed, these two processes operate jointly in each transformation, for changes in the canon tend to emphasize novelty while altering the scope of generic variation.[56]

The creation of new motifs also fulfills the functions outlined above. The most significant and elaborate instance of motif fabrication may be observed in the fair episodes, whose parallel structure we examined in the previous section. As we observed, these episodes are divided into symmetrical sub-episodes which exhibit a form of dispersed parallelism on the level of laisse structure. An

---

[54] See Zumthor, "Planctus" and Duggan, *Roland* (162-63).

[55] References to traditional components of this motif are based on Duggan's reconstitution, *Roland* p. 163.

[56] Jauss calls this a "change of horizons." See *Toward* 25.

analysis of the "micro-composition" of these sub-episodes reveals that formal parallels are not limited to narrative and assonantal similarity. Each sub-episode constitutes a veritable motif, complete with more or less fixed narrative details represented by characteristic formulas or members of the same formula system.

Like conventional motifs, these fabricated units are not all stereotyped to the same degree. The following discussion will consider first of all one of the more stable stylized units of the Provins-Lagny fairs, the initial quarrel between Hervis and his paternal uncles. Constitutive narrative details and their associated formulas are outlined below.

1. *General degree of expenses*: "Tant despendi" (v. 360, 1213); This phase presents identical first hemistichs.

2. *Spender named*: "li damoisiaus gentis" (v. 360); "li damoisiaus de pris" (v. 1213); these second hemistichs display lexical substitution of epithets.

3. *Numerical account of expenses*: "Plus de M mars" (v. 363); "Mil mars despent" (v. 1214). These hemistichs diverge according to the presence or absence of the repeated verb *despendre* as well as the amount of money spent.

4. *Type of money*: "que d'argent et d'or fin" (v. 363); "que d'argent que d'or fin" (1214). These second hemistichs differ only in the equivalent conjunctions "et" and "que."

5. *Uncles' emotive reaction*: "Si oncle en furent corresoz et mari" (vv. 364, 1215). This phase presents identical full-line formulas.

6. *Introductory speech formula*: "Il le castïent" (vv. 365, 1216).

7. *Ineffectiveness of chastisement*: "mais pour noient l'on dit" (vv. 365, 1216). Identity of formulas in the sixth and seventh stages results in a full-line formula.

8. *Epithet of address*: "'Biax sire niés'" (vv. 366, 1217).

9. *Oath*: "'pour diu qui ne menti'" (vv. 366, 1217). Here, as in the four following stages, the identical first and second hemistichs produce a full-line formula.

10. *Expenses questioned*: "'Pour coi despens'" (vv. 367, 1218).

11. *Type of money*: "'et l'argent et l'or fin'" (vv. 367, 1218).

12. *Source of money*: "'Que te carga li tiens peres Thieris'" (vv. 368, 1219)

13. *Original purpose of money*: "'Pour accater et dou vair et dou gris'" (vv. 370. 1220); "'Des dras de Flandres, des joiaus de Paris'" (vv. 372, 1221).

14. *Projected consequence*: "'Batus seras'" (vv. 373, 1222)

15. *Anticipated timing of consequence*: "'saiches au revenir'" (v. 373); "'par deu a revenir'" (v. 1222)

16. *Silencing of the "vilains"*: "'Taisiez, vilain!'" (vv. 374, 1123). The concluding hemistich, "ce lor a dit Hervis," is also identical.

17. *Insult*: "'Peletier estes'"(vv. 375, 1124). The concluding hemistich, which provides emphasis, is identical: "'si com il m'est avis.'"

18. *Declaration of economic independence*: "'J'accaterai mon bon et mon plaisir'" (vv. 377, 1228)

19. *Uncles' perception*: "Si oncle l'oënt" (vv. 379, 1229)

20. *Uncles' reaction*: "s'en sont grain et mari" (v. 379); "s'en sont grief et marri" (v. 1229). Only the first adjective has been changed, and even then the substituted word contains identical consonants in the first two positions.

21. *Cowardice of uncles*: "Mais ne l'oserent" (v. 380); "Il ne l'oserent" (v. 1230). In the second instance, the optional subject pronoun is substituted for the conjunction.

22. *Uncles' desired behavior*: "ne toucier ne ferir" (v. 380); "ne batre ne ferir" (v. 1230). Lexical variation of the first infinitive produces a more forceful expression in the second instance.

23. *Uncles' calculation*: "pour quel sevent" (v. 381); "Car trop le sevent" (v. 1231)

24. *Hervis's superiority*: "grant et gros et fournis" (v. 381); "de corage hardi" (v. 1231). The first formula underlines the hero's physical size, while the second highlights his valor.

This lengthy fabricated motif thus presents minimal formulaic variation. The predominance of full-line formulas renders the unit even more stable than the standard lance-combat motif. This is due in part to the extreme assonantal stability of *Hervis*, which decreases the necessity for second-hemistich variation. Furthermore, the motif is highly specialized, fabricated – to the best of our knowledge – for two particular episodes in a particular poem. Certain formulas, such as "que d'argent que d'or fin," are multi-purpose hemistichs which are employed elsewhere in the text; it is the consistent joining of such formulas with another identical hemistich or member of the same formula system that creates a specialized motif.

The motif of the host's praise is a more elastic formulaic unit, which, unlike the previous example, occurs in two different assonantal frameworks. Three common stages of the motif are as follows:

1. *Epithet of address*: "[Oïl] biau sire" (v.420); "Damoisiax sire" (v. 1521). The epithets display lexical and syntactic variation.

2. *Hyperbolic praise*: "Onques plus large" (v. 421); "Nul si large oste" (v. 1523). The negation presents syntactic variation between the adverb "onques" and the indefinite adjective "nul." Forms of the comparative diverge as well: "plus" vs. "si" specifies the role of Hervis: "oste." Finally, the second example includes the modified noun in the first hemistich: "oste."

3. *Experience of the host*: "home de vos ne vi" (v. 421); "je n'oï en mon aé" (v. 1523). This detail presents significant syntactic and lexical variation. The first example begins with the noun modified in the previous hemistich, and the *comparant* "vos" is expressed; the host's form of perception (seeing) is conveyed without a subject pronoun. The second example begins with the host's perception (hearing [of]), includes the optional subject pronoun, and adds the emphatic qualifier "en mon aé."

Aside from these variations in hemistich composition, the motif of the host's praise contains more flexibility in the number and nature of narrative details. In the first occurrence of the motif, for example, the host's remarks are generated by Hervis's question "Iestes paiez?" (v. 419); in the second example, the motif is triggered by Hervis's offer of twenty pounds sterling in exchange for armor (v. 1509). Nevertheless, most details remain constant, and the formulas expressing those details generally possess at least one fixed element.

The sub-episodes of the Provins-Lagny fair sequence thus constitute specialized formal units constructed on the same principles as traditional motifs. These fabricated segments may well be the products of written composition: since the motifs are unique to *Hervis de Mes*, it is unlikely that they could have been improvised with such precision. Nevertheless, it is clear that the *Hervis* poet sought to imitate the composition of earlier, orally-composed texts in his elaboration of these episodes.

This technique may be contrasted with that of the *Enfances Vivien*, in which the hero also attends multiple fairs. In this roughly contemporary epic, the fair episodes do contain several repetitions and refrains, but they do not display a systematic fabrication of specialized motifs.[57] In *Hervis de Mes*, the style of improvised songs is adapted more rigorously to new narrative content. Indeed, the phenomenon is not limited to the fair episodes, but also occurs in passages depicting the debts of various characters (vv. 50, 2152, 2873, 2885) and the predicament of the noble wife who has married below her station (vv. 545, 1902). The effects of this adaptation are similar to those generated by the transformation of existing motifs. Familiar modes of composition assimilate the new story material within conventional parameters of the *chanson*; these familiar techniques also serve as a backdrop for the conspicuous appearance of new matter.

PART Two

Once again, the second part of *Hervis de Mes* is characterized by a more conservative use of epic composition. The rupture in style is partly connected, of course, to the increase in typical epic themes. Numerous battle scenes permit the more frequent use of ready-made motifs gleaned from familiar *chansons de geste*. For instance, ninety-seven per cent of the occurrences of the general battle motif appear in Part Two; this part also accounts for eighty per cent of the "hero(es) in the *mêlée*" and lance-combat segments.[58]

Such motifs often occur in densely formulaic passages that systematically distribute the most stylized battle motifs of the epic tradition. The battle between Messins and Tyrians, for example, begins with two consecutive occurrences of the armament motif, followed by a canonical evocation of general battle; a typical lance-combat ensues, followed by a rescue, a typical sword-combat, and various portrayals of the "hero(es) in the mêlée." Before a brief pause in the battle sequence, the general battle and the "hero(es) in the mêlée" are evoked once again (vv. 8369-8445).

This is not to say that Part Two presents merely a mechanical reproduction of stock motifs and formulas, for motifs are often distributed symmetrically in the course of several short laisses to enhance the strophic structure of the *chanson*. Furthermore, like early

---

[57] Alfred Nordfelt, ed., *Les Enfances Vivien* (Upsala: Librairie de l'université; Paris: Librairie Emmile Bouillon, 1895) vv. 844-1359.

[58] See Appendix C.

chansons de geste, this text introduces subtle variations of traditional forms in order to highlight the special conflicts and themes that characterize *Hervis de Mes*. For example, the flexible motif of lineage, which permeates the entire *geste des Loherains*, is adapted to the particular heritage of Hervis in Part Two.[59] Whereas *Garin le Loherain* generally employs the motif to contrast the good Loherain lineage with the evil Bordelais line, *Hervis de Mes* opposes the "good" interpretation of Hervis's lineage (grandson of Duke Pierre) with the "bad" interpretation of his status (son of a bourgeois):

> (Pierre): 'Fix est ma fille Aelis au vis cler.
> Voir de Braibant la rice duceé
> – Dont sui drois oirs, seignour, bien le savés –
> Doné li ai la terre et le regné.'
> (vv. 6826-29)

> (Anseÿs): 'Niés est le duc de Mes la fort cité,
> Et la ducoize Aelis au vis cler
> Vostre cousine qui tant a de bonté
> Voir le porta IX mois en ses costés.
> Mais saichiez bien, vilain l'ait engenrés,
> Fix d'un prevost est voir si m'aït des.'
> (vv. 6912-17)

Formulaic components of the motif within *Hervis de Mes* therefore present similar syntactic and semantic frameworks: (X is the son/grandson of Y). The lexical substitution of "vilain" for "Aelis" or "duc" in the Y position determines the validity of the speaker's assertion and thus his or her status as ally or adversary. This variation on the typical Loherain motif justifies the noble status of the lineage as a whole and also emphasizes the particular situation of the first Loherain hero.

The lineage motif is also an indicator of formal bipartition within *Hervis de Mes* itself. The motif appears several times in Part One as well, but it is usually connected with the heritage of Biatris:

> (Hervis): 'Fille est de roi et de grant parenté,
> Je ne cuit dame en la crestïenté
> De tel linage ne de tel parenté.'
> (vv. 4654-56)

---

[59] On the lineage motif in *Garin le Loherain*, see Gittleman 150-52.

Such statements are repeatedly used in Part One to reveal Biatris's hitherto secret identity and to justify the hero's amorous quest. In Part Two, the substitution of *Hervis* for *Biatris* in the same motif is symptomatic of the change in subject matter: the epic struggle for feudal rights replaces the questionable purchase of a foreign princess.

* * *

Bipartition in subject matter is thus closely related to the formal rupture between Parts One and Two of *Hervis de Mes*. Rather than adopting learned, romanesque modes of composition, however, the first part of the text manifests an effort to integrate new content into the traditional framework of the *chanson*. Significant modifications of this framework are evident both in laisse structure and formulaic style; however, variation and stability are transcended by a new synthesis of romanesque *matière* and epic form. Part Two, on the other hand, largely abandons this synthesis in favor of formal and thematic convention. This poetic process is consonant with the ideological developments noted in the previous chapter: mixed heritage is transcended in Part One and eliminated in Part Two. In *Hervis de Mes*, then, conservative formal practices correspond rather closely to conservative ideological functions.

CHAPTER TWO

NARRATION AND PERFORMANCE

Studies on the form of "romanesque" epics have tended to neglect an important dimension of textual organization, namely the principles governing narration in such works.[1] Yet the narrating instance provides valuable indices for the understanding of a text's performance, reception, and social function, all of which were subject to transformation in the thirteenth-century *chanson de geste*. In her transgeneric study of thirteenth-century prologues, Emmanuèle Baumgartner documents the later epic narrator's "glissement" in the direction of romance discursive practices.[2] Indeed, generic slippage may be discerned not only in certain preambles, but in the overall relationship between the narrator and his material. Before considering the extent and significance of such shifts in *Hervis de Mes*, let us recall the principal characteristics of epic and romance narrators as they manifest themselves in twelfth-century vernacular texts.

Narration in Early Epic and Romance

The structuralist critics of the 1960's and 1970's devised elaborate typologies to describe the numerous forms of narration found in the texts of literature and the mass media. Many of these paradigms have been deemed insufficient for the study of medieval narratives. Genette's distinctions between intra/extradiegetic and

---

[1] Notable exceptions include the following studies of the *jongleur*'s voice in the late *chanson de geste*: Marguerite Rossi, *Huon de Bordeaux et l'évolution du genre épique au XIIIe siècle*, Nouvelle Bibliothèque du Moyen Age 2 (Paris: Champion, 1975) 128 & 604; and especially Emmanuèle Baumgartner, "Texte de prologue et statut du texte," *Essor et fortune* 2 (465-74).
[2] Baumgartner 473.

homo/heterodiegetic, for example, do not elucidate the divergent narrators of medieval romance and *chansons de geste*, nearly all of whom are extra-heterodiegetic (i.e., non-characters operating outside the fiction).[3] Nonetheless, certain structural classifications retain their validity and usefulness for the description of medieval narrators. The distinctions between narrative *mood*, *time* and *voice* are particularly valuable tools, and may be described as follows:

Mood indicates the regulation of narrative information, the degree of a narrator's presence in the communication of a story. The first modal sub-category, distance, recalls Plato's distinctions between *mimesis* (the illusion of direct discourse by a character), and *diegesis* (the mediation of events by a narrator). Although all fictional occurrences are mediated, direct discourse is perceived as closer to the receiver of the tale; "narrativized" events or discourses are perceived as more distant.[4] The second sub-category of mood, perspective, concerns the narrator's point of view, his or her knowledge and revelations about events and characters; this level of narration also involves the degree of penetration into characters' thoughts and motivations.[5]

The narrator's regulation of time pertains to the relationship between the *temps du récit* and the *temps de l'histoire*. Although this dimension includes three angles – order, duration, and frequency – only the first will occupy us here.[6] The narrator may of course choose to relate events in the order of their fictional occurrence. Frequently, however, a text contains narrative anachronisms: ulterior events may be recounted in advance (prolepse) or anterior events may be related at a later point in the fictional chronology (analepse).[7]

Finally, voice may be defined as the linguistic marks of the presence of an enunciating subject; this voice may be fragmented into

---

[3] See John L. Grigsby, "The Ontology of the Narrator in Medieval French Romance," *The Nature of Medieval Narrative*, ed. Minnette Grunmann-Gaudet and Robin F. Jones (Lexington: French Forum, 1980) 165. For Genette's paradigm, see *Figures III* 238-53.

[4] Genette, *Figures III* 183-193; Tzvetan Todorov, *Qu'est-ce que le structuralisme?*, Collection Poétique 2 (Paris: Seuil, 1968) 50-51.

[5] Genette, *Figures III* 203-19; Todorov 50, 56-62. Todorov, following J. Pouillon, refers to *perspective* as "vision." See also Todorov, "Les catégories du récit littéraire," *Communications* 8 (1966): 141-42.

[6] See the previous chapter for references to frequency. The present chapter will focus on order because this dimension demonstrates a rather clear division between the *chanson de geste* and romance.

[7] Genette, *Figures III* 75-82.

various personae, including those of the historical author, the person relating a tale, the judge or interpreter of this tale, and the more communal voice of proverbial expression.[8]

Early epic and verse romance do share some common aspects of narration. Points of contact include the frequent use of direct discourse and, above all, traces of the reciter or performer in narrative voice. Paul Zumthor has convincingly demonstrated that the texts of all medieval genres were performed orally through the twelfth century, and to a somewhat lesser degree in the thirteenth and fourteenth centuries; the pervasive function of the human voice is reflected in various textual indices of vocality. These indices, such as the abundant use of the couple *dire-ouïr* to designate the discursive situation, may occasionally represent narrative artifice or stem from the inertia of vocabulary; nonetheless, their original function has left indelible marks on the reception process: "L'emploi du couple *dire-ouïr* a pour fonction manifeste de promouvoir (fût-ce fictivement) le texte au statut de locuteur et de désigner sa communication comme une situation de discours *in praesentia*."[9]

The actual discursive situations of epic and romance, however, were originally quite different. During the improvisation or recitation of an oral *chanson de geste*, the functions of poet, reciter, narrator, and text were perceived directly and simultaneously by the audience. During the recitation of a written romance, poet, narrator, and reciter were perceived as separate entities with interrelated functions; the poet could exploit the narrator to comment upon the text, and the reciter could contribute the physiological commentary of gestures and voice inflection.[10] These divergent modes of performance were consonant with the rather distinct styles of narration characterizing early French *chansons de geste* and romances.

First of all, the two genres manifest certain particularities of narrative mood, especially in the nature of perspective. Both types of narrators do tend to project a nearly omniscient vision of charac-

---

[8] See Genette, *Figures III* 225-26; Douglas Kelly, "Chrétien de Troyes: The Narrator and His Art," *The Romances of Chrétien de Troyes: A Symposium*, ed. Douglas Kelly (Lexington: French Forum, 1985) 15.

[9] Paul Zumthor, *La Lettre et la voix: De la "littérature" médiévale*, Collection Poétique (Paris: Seuil, 1987) 42; see also 22-37.

[10] Franz H. Bäuml, "The Unmaking of the Hero: Some Critical Implications of the Transition from Oral to Written Epic," *The Epic in Medieval Society: Aesthetic and Moral Values*, ed. Harald Scholler (Tubingen: Max Niemeyer, 1977) 90-91.

ters and events; their narrative authority stems principally from the oral or written sources to which they frequently refer. The epic narrator, however, does not habitually intervene to reveal the inner thoughts and motivations of the characters. Presumably, these factors were clear to the audiences of the *chanson de geste*, who shared the general world-view of the narrator and thus interpreted emotion and motivation on the basis of the characters' outward actions or words. On the contrary, the romance narrator penetrates the minds and hearts of the protagonists with much greater frequency in order to elucidate the hidden significance of their actions. This is often accomplished by a narrativized account that renders the narrator's mediation fairly conspicuous. In addition, romance also exploits the resources of the interior monologue, thereby revealing internal conflicts in direct fashion and reducing narrative distance. The passage from exterior to interior monologue has been viewed as a major aesthetic departure in the development of romance.[11]

A second distinction between epic and romance narration lies in the narrators' regulation of information on the story's outcome. H. R. Jauss distinguishes between the "how-suspense" of epic and the "if-suspense" of romance.[12] The epic narrator frequently pauses to announce events that will come to pass in the near or distant future; audience anticipation lies in the way these events will occur and in the jongleur's art of storytelling. The jongleur's perspective, like that of God in Boethius's *De consolatione Philosophiae*, is that of an eternal present, in which past, present, and future are simultaneously perceived and evoked.[13] Romance narrators, on the other hand, are much more inclined to sustain suspense; narrative interest is thus diverted in some measure to the nature of the story's outcome.

Finally, epic and romance present marked differences in the nature and function of narrative voice. In the *chanson de geste*, the narrator generally takes on the persona of the jongleur or per-

---

[11] Zumthor, *Voix* 236.

[12] Hans-Robert Jauss, *Toward an Aesthetic of Reception*, trans. Timothy Bahti, Theory and History of Literature 2 (Minneapolis: University of Minnesota Press, 1982) 84. Zumthor notes, however, that the romance *Eracle* contains instances of *annonces*. This particular work seems in many ways to represent the inverse of *Hervis de Mes*, i.e. a romance incorporating typically epic strategies into its repertoire. See Zumthor, *Voix* 228.

[13] On epic time as eternal present, see François Suard, *Guillaume d'Orange: Etude du roman en prose* (Paris: Champion, 1979) 167-71.

former, whose discourse facilitates and conditions the intended performance. Occasionally, the jongleur mentions the poet in the third person, but the author-narrator remains otherwise effaced. The voice of the jongleur tends to generate an emotional unity among performer, text, and audience. This is accomplished by emotionally-charged epithets evoking the bonds of a community ("dulce France", "nostre emperere magnes"); exclamations evoking participation in the hero's fate ("Deus! quel dulur que li Franceis nel sevent!" [14]), and a continual dialogue between the first person (narrator and virtual performer) and second person plural (narratee and virtual audience).

It is true that some early *chansons de geste* display a certain "univocity", in that the jongleur does not refer to himself in the first person; epithets used by both characters and narrator further reinforce the unity of their voices.[15] In most cases, however, the teller remains distinct from his tale by occasional reference to his own function; an ongoing metadiscourse, in which the jongleur designates himself as "je" or "nous", distinguishes the narrating instance from that which is narrated. This distinction was likely maintained during the performance of *chansons de geste*, in which the referent of this implicit or explicit "je/nous" was an actual voice. Scholars have postulated that different performers may have taken on different roles in the recitation of epic poetry – or, inversely, that a single jongleur incarnated several characters by modulations in voice and differentiated gestures.[16]

Finally, it must be noted that the early epic narrator rarely interrupts the story to interpret or comment upon the action. He occasionally injects commonplaces or proverbial expressions, but these interventions reflect a collective voice. Generally, aside from performance-related prologues and interpolations, the jongleur "retreats behind material, so that the occurrences seem to narrate themselves."[17] The narrator's attitude toward characters and events is certainly perceived in the choice of epithets and other formulas, but

---

[14] *La Chanson de Roland*, ed. Gérard Moignet (Paris: Bordas, 1985) v. 716.

[15] See Peter Dembowski, "Monologue, Author's Monologue, and Related Problems in the Romances of Chrétien de Troyes," *Approaches to Medieval Romance*, Yale French Studies 51 (1974): 103. This is true of the Oxford *Roland*, for example, but not of *Garin le Loherain*.

[16] See Zumthor, *Voix* 263.

[17] Jauss, *Toward* 83.

the jongleur's voice is not given to explanatory digression. The primary functions of this voice thus remain the relatively transparent narration of events and the establishment of a dialogue between narrator, text, and audience.

In verse romance, on the other hand, the voice of the narrator is more conspicuous, and it is fragmented into various roles. The presence of the historical author and his or her writer-persona is often manifest in explanatory prologues and epilogues, which may evoke the circumstances of a work's production as well as the author's conception of romance composition.[18] In the course of the story, interpolations of the narrator-commentator serve to elucidate mysteries of the *matière*. On occasion, the narrator's assertions may be at variance with the characters' actions, thereby posing an ironic distance between text and enunciating subject. Hence the narrator of courtly romance is perceived more as a mediating instance between story and reader or audience.[19]

The romance narrator's self-proclaimed function is often described by verbs such as *parler*, *dire*, and *conter*, all of which reflect the dimension of the potential reciter. Like the jongleur, the romance narrator-reciter initiates contact with the receiver by means of a first person – second person dialogue; nevertheless, the mediation of the commentator prevents the emotional unity established in the *chanson de geste*. The function of the romance narrator is rather to initiate the audience into the latent meanings which must be extracted from the matter.

* * *

In light of the formal and thematic bipartition we have observed on other levels of the text, the narrating function in *Hervis de Mes* exhibits a remarkable unity, employing narrative strategies typical of the earlier *chanson de geste*. Nonetheless, certain discrepancies reveal the traces of different conceptions of narration. Part One

---

[18] On this function of the narrator in Chrétien de Troyes's romances, see Kelly, "Chrétien" 13-23.

[19] Jauss, *Toward* 83-84. Jauss states, however, that *matière* and *sens* are separate in romance. In fact, at least in the verse romances of Chrétien de Troyes, these two levels are joined. By means of amplification, the narrator may elucidate the mysteries of the *matière*, but these explanations "make of the *matière* and *san* a meaningful amalgam." See Kelly, "Chrétien" 30.

cannot be said to possess a romance narrator; indeed, we shall see that in one respect, it is more "epic" than the second half of the text. However, its narrating subject occasionally expands the scope of epic narration in the direction of romance; conversely, Part Two intensifies the conventional strategies of the *chanson de geste*.

* * *

Mood

Daniel Poirion has noted the rather extensive use of direct discourse in *Hervis*.[20] This phenomenon is characteristic of the work as a whole, as 48 % of the text is given over to direct speech (5059 lines); the figure is significantly higher than that of traditional epics such as the Oxford *Roland*, whose proportion of direct discourse is 39 % (1560 lines). Nonetheless, Parts One and Two of *Hervis* differ perceptibly in the degree and nature of this "mimetic" material. In Part One, direct speech occupies over half of the text (51 %, 2893 lines); Part Two reduces the use of the technique to a more nearly conventional level (44 %, 2166 lines). Moreover, the form and effects of direct discourse in each part are consonant with the dual narrative and ideological systems present in the work.

The art of dialogue, for example, is generally used in Part One to represent conflicting ideas and values in direct form; the style of these passages does not always imitate the lyric *élan* of traditional epic dialogue, but rather approaches the aesthetic of certain *romans d'aventure*. As Poirion notes, "On allait vers la conversation, s'éloignant de l'incantation."[21] The validity of this judgment is evident in numerous scenes, particularly those opposing the frugal Thieri and his profligate son. Before Hervis's departure for the fair in Provins, for instance, Thieri admonishes his son:

---

[20] Daniel Poirion, Préface, *Hervis de Metz: Roman du moyen âge adapté par Philippe Walter*, Editions Serpenoises (Nancy: Presses universitaires de Nancy, 1984) 8.

[21] Poirion 8 (see also p. 9). He refers in this quote to *Hervis de Mes* as a whole, but the description is much more applicable to Part One than to Part Two. While percentages of direct discourse cannot properly be used as generic indicators, it is noteworthy that high levels of direct speech are characteristic of the thirteenth-century romance of adventure. See Zumthor on *Eracle* in *Voix* 235-236.

> 'Fix, soies sages pour diu que je t'en pri!
> Quant tu verras a la foire a Provins,
> Trop n'i despendre, biax fix, je le te pri!'
> 'Bien vous enten, peres,' ce dist Hervis.
>
> (vv. 332-35)

Only a few lines later, Hervis's conversation with his *oste* belies his dutiful reply:

> 'Biax tresdous ostes,' ce dist l'enfes Hervis,
> 'I mengier rice me faites establir,
> Des marcheans me mandés IIII XX!'
>
> (vv. 344-46)

Such passages provide comic effect and dramatize the contrasts between representatives of the profligate nobility and the tight-fisted bourgeoisie. At the same time, within the constraints of the assonanced decasyllabic line, the dialogue imitates the admonition-response-transgression pattern of an actual domestic conversation.

Some of the dialogues in Part Two correspond to the conversational tone of the above example. More often, however, the nature of direct speech in this part recalls instead the aesthetic of the earlier *chanson de geste*. This modification is due in part to the more traditional nature of Part Two's subject matter. Battle cries and *défis* punctuate the narration of combat:

> 'Rois orguillous, dix te puist vergonder!
> Je te desfi dou roi de maïsté!'
> . . .
> Escotois broce, chival laissent aler,
> Tresc'ai Hervi ne se sont arresté.
> En haut escrïent: 'Lecieres, n'en irés!'
>
> (vv. 9686-87, 9705-7)

Such forms of discourse are perceived less as plausible conversation than as ancillary weaponry. Just as in the *Roland*, these eruptions of direct speech are brutal and stark: ". . . fruit d'une violence, la parole, comme l'Epée, tranche, jette sa clarté sur le monde, puis retombe."[22]

---

[22] Zumthor, *Voix* 234.

Therefore, although both parts of the text favor the direct narration of speech, this dialogue changes form and function with modifications of subject matter. In Part One, direct passages exemplify typical behavior patterns but nonetheless exhibit greater mimetic tendencies; in Part Two, dialogue tends to revert back to the symbolic function it fulfills in earlier epic poetry.

Direct speech is also present to a lesser degree in the monologue. Generally, these passages conform to monologues of the epic tradition, i.e. prayers and laments (cf. vv. 1166-69, 1712-15). However, Part One does include two monologues that expand the parameters of the *chanson de geste* in the direction of romance technique. First of all, this portion of the text offers one brief interior monologue. After Hervis's return from Tyre, Thieri begs Biatris to reconcile him with his son; this request is followed by the direct expression of the heroine's thoughts:

> Lors ce pansait la dame a vis cler:
> 'Qui que met guerre, ceu est pechiez mortez,
> Antre lou fil et lou peire autretel,
> Ne pesant piere ne puet on lons porter.'
> (vv. 4925-28)

This single example obviously does not revolutionize the structure of the *chanson*; indeed, the content of the monologue reflects an impersonal, almost proverbial form of expression. It is significant, however, that no such passage appears in Part Two, which avoids the verb *penser* as a means of introducing the characters' utterances.

Moreover, another monologue pronounced by Biatris in Part One does recall the more penetrating analysis of romance. Although the discourse is presented in the form of a prayer and framed by indications of exterior speech, the lady is alone in her chambers and reflecting on love. Privately, she objects to the marriage arranged by her father and would prefer the attentions of a younger man; her monologue reveals the precise modalities of this preference:

> 'Dix,' dist la dame, 'qui te laissas pener,
> Li roys mes peres certes a fol penser
> Qu'au roy d'Espaigne me cuide marïer.

> Vix est et frailles, et s'ait ses jours usez,
> Quatre-vins ans a il moult bien d'aé,
> Ne croit en diu nes qu'en I chien tué.
> J'amaisse mix I legier baceler,
> Preu et hardi pour ses armes porter;
> S'il n'eüst terre, jeu en eüsse assés!'
>
> (vv. 861-869)

This passage is distinctive in that traditionally epic modes of reasoning are largely replaced by those of a romance heroine. In a *chanson de geste*, prayers concerning a suitor's religion are commonplace: Christian heroines yearn for the conversion of pagan men and Saracen heroines pray that they themselves might convert.[23] However, it has already been made abundantly clear to both heroine and audience that the King of Spain is willing, even eager, to convert himself and his subjects to Christianity for the sake of the fair Biatris (vv. 680-82, 728, 769-71). The objection to his religion is thus undermined and supplemented by a stylized analysis of the yearnings of this potential *mal mariée*. The antithesis *vix-frailles / baceler-legier-hardi* creates an imaginary triangle that will be realized in subsequent episodes. Such schemas often project the desires of romance heroines, whose monologues (interior or exterior) reveal typical configurations of love conflict. Witness the following lament pronounced by the heroine of Marie de France's *Yonec*:

> 'Lasse,' fait ele, 'mar fui nee! [. . .]
> Cist *viel gelus*, de quei se crient,
> Quë en si grant prisun me tient?
> Mut par est *fous* e *esbaïz*. [. . .]
> Malëeit seient mi parent
> Et li autre communalment
> Ki a cest gelus me donerent! [. . .]
> Mut ai sovent oï cunter
> Que l'em suleit jadis trover
> Aventures en cest païs, [. . .]
> E dames truvoënt *amanz*
> Beaus e *curteis*, [pruz] e *vaillanz*.[24]

---

[23] See, for example, *La Prise d'Orenge*, ed. Blanche Katz (Morningside Heights: King's Crown Press, 1947) vv. 1545-51, Orable's prayer.

[24] Marie de France, *Lais*, ed. Alfred Ewert (Oxford: Blackwell, 1960) vv. 67, 71-73, 81-83, 91-93, 97-98.

Just like Biatris's monologue, this discourse reflects a configuration of desire that will be fulfilled by subsequent developments in the narrative. While such passages do not approach the psychological analyses of the modern novel, they do reveal certain patterns of character motivation in direct, self-analytical form. The earlier *chanson de geste* generally does not allow this sort of access to the impulses governing love conflict. Once again, therefore, the introduction of romance matter in Part One stimulates the use of romance narrative technique.

Generic bipartition is also evident in narrative perspective, the degree of knowledge and penetration exhibited by the narrator with regard to events and characters. It is true that in the text as a whole, the narrator manifests near-omniscience; the only supposed gaps in his knowledge concern the non-essential details of the characters' journeys: "De lor journees ne sai conte tenir" (v. 338, cf. vv. 483, 775, 2952, 3177, 4566, 4698, 7473, 7745, 8956, 9000, 9441). The locution *ne sai* is replaced on two occasions by *ne welt* (vv. 7619, 9441), indicating that the characters' travels generally hold no narrative pertinence; lack of knowledge is thus related in these instances to lack of desire or necessity. In every other respect, the narrator knows more than any individual character; indeed, he occasionally exploits this knowledge by sharing information that is unavailable to certain actors within the fiction. Numerous instances of disguise throughout the text, for example, serve either to mock the unsuspecting victims (adversaries) or to create sympathy for them (protagonist); in both cases, this strategy common to epic and romance establishes complicity between narrator and narratee, between performer and audience.[25]

Although the narrator's degree of knowledge is fairly uniform in *Hervis*, the two parts of the text do diverge with respect to the degree of penetration into characters' thoughts. Just as Part One introduced the more penetrating interior monologue and romanesque lament, it contains many more narrativized incursions into the minds and motivations of the characters. Generally, these indications are rather sparse and reveal negative motivation, i.e. why cer-

---

[25] Instances of disguise in *Hervis de Mes* are quite numerous. For a detailed discussion of this topic, see Catherine Jones, "Identity and Disguise in a Late French Epic: *Hervis de Mes*," *Essays in Medieval Studies*, Proceedings of the Illinois Medieval Association 4 (1987): 107-17.

tain characters *didn't* do certain things. Their reasons are usually framed by the negative of the verb *oser*. For example, after the fair in Provins, the narrator explains why Hervis's paternal uncles refrain from punishing the young hero:

> Si oncle l'oënt, s'en sont grain et mari;
> Mais *ne l'oserent* ne toucier ne ferir,
> Pour chou quel sevent grant et gros et fourni.
> (vv. 379-81)

This intervention serves to contrast the robust young Hervis with his cowardly bourgeois relatives. A different kind of weakness is attributed to Thieri in a later episode, as Hervis is departing for the tournament in Senlis. Thieri, who has obstinately refused to forgive his son, is moved by Hervis's departure but does not yet have the courage to disavow his previous oaths:

> Or *se repent* de Hervi le membré
> C'ansi s'en va tous seus hors du regné;
> Mais li prevos *ne s'ose* parjurer.
> (vv. 1942-44)

These passages remain exceptional in Part One, and they certainly do not provide lengthy, profound analyses of the characters' emotions. Yet they do furnish an indication of bipartite narrative perspective: the narrator offers thirteen brief insights of thoughts or motivation in Part One, and only two such passages in Part Two (vv. 379-80, 809-13, 951, 1423, 1809-12, 1942-44, 2051-52, 2193, 3240, 3361-63, 3451-52, 3517, 4903-06, Part One; vv. 7891-93, 8313-14, Part Two).[26] Indeed, the second part of the text portrays inner sentiment almost exclusively in the tradition of the early *chanson de geste*, i.e. by means of the characters' outward actions: "Il se pasma" (v. 7485); "Voit le la dame, coulour prist a muër" (v. 7925).

It is noteworthy that the later manuscripts **N** and **T** exhibit increased depth of narrative perspective in Part Two. For example, while Biatris is waiting for Hervis to ambush the Tyrian/Spanish embassy and rescue her, she insists on resting in the vicinity of

---

[26] This list excludes the frequent use of the epic formula "le sens cuide derver," which is generally accompanied by an outward demonstration of anger or grief such as fainting.

Hervis's hiding-place in order to attract his attention to her whereabouts. Manuscript **E** furnishes only the external manifestation of the heroine's motivation:

> Or escoutés de la dame a vis cler,
> Coment elle ait *esploitiet* et *ourei*,
> Les III rois a maintenant apellés,
> 'Seignour,' dist ele, 'vers moi en entendés!
> Un petitet wel mon cors repozer...'
> (vv. 8298-8303)[27]

Manuscripts **N** and **T**, however, add an account of Biatris's thought process; the following citation reproduces the version found in **T**:

> Or escoutés, comment a *pourpensé*!
> Ele *doutoit* que ne fussent passé,
> Que dus Hervis nes eust avizés,
> Les III rois a maintenant apellés...
> (vv. 8298-8301)

A similar phenomenon occurs in a later scene, in which the young Bégon finds himself unarmed in battle. While manuscript **E** portrays only his actions (disarming a dead Navarois), **N** and **T** reveal the boy's inner concern. The following citation provides the reading found in manuscript **T**:

> Il *s'apensa*, pour chou k'iert desarmés,
> Se il estoit el grant estour entrés,
> Que moult errant l'averoit on tué.
> (vv. 10167-69)

Hence, Part One and both parts of the late manuscripts display a significantly greater tendency to make thought and motivation more explicit: the narrator occasionally takes on the role of informant by employing the indirect or summarized mental discourse typical of romance narration. In these passages, the narrating presence is perceived as a mediating factor between character and potential audience. In the second half of the text, the narrator of **E**

---

[27] Ms. **E** omits line 8300 of Stengel's edition.

consistently maintains the role of portrayer by limiting information to that which may be gathered from external representation. As the narrator's mediating function dwindles, events and characters take on the (illusory) transparency typical of epic narration: the story seems to narrate itself.

The two parts of *Hervis* may therefore be distinguished by the narrator's expression, choice, and regulation of narrative information. Part One characteristically weaves a number of romance techniques into its narrative fabric, while Part Two displays the generic conservatism we have found on other levels.

Time

The distinguishing characteristics of Part One do not always align it with the narrative strategies of romance. Indeed, in one respect, the first half of the text accentuates the conventions of the *chanson de geste*. This process concerns the narrator's disclosure of future events within the poem or in the *geste* as a whole. Part One contains a total of nineteen anticipations or *annonces*, fourteen of which are homodiegetic: (vv. 252-55, 488-89*, 609-15*, 630-633*, 775-76*, 802*, 838*, 853-55*, 914-15*, 1447*, 2152-54*, 2290-2300, 2366-67*, 2399-2403, 2862-63, 3419-21*, 3983-84*, 5106-07, 5277-80*).[28] Thus, the narrator frequently evokes the outcome of particular episodes, allowing only for the "how-suspense" typical of epic poetry. Such anticipations may be in the past tense, emphasizing the narrator's perspective as conveyer of the *passé du savoir*;[29] or in the future, creating the illusion that the *temps du récit* is unfolding simultaneously with the *temps de l'histoire*.

These proleptic passages include anticipations of events that usually lend themselves to the "if-suspense" of romance narration. For example, before Hervis arrives at the fair in Lagny, and before the narrator has introduced Biatris into the story, we learn the nature of their future encounter and their ultimate relationship:

---

[28] Genette distinguishes between heterodiegetic (outside the primary story line) and homodiegetic (within the story line) elements. For our purposes, we may consider as heterodiegetic those *annonces* which evoke future events in the cycle; homodiegetic *annonces* reveal ulterior events within *Hervis de Mes*. (The latter passages are marked with an asterisk in the verses cited.) See *Figures III* 89-121.

[29] Jauss, *Toward* 84.

> Dix, quel accat li damoisiaus i fist! [...]
> Qu'il accata la bele Bïatris:
> Cele fu mere a Loherenc Garin
> Et le quen Begue dou castel de Belin. [...]
> Huimais dirons, seignour, de Bïatris,
> Comme ses cors fut tolus et ravis.
>
> (vv. 609, 613-15, 629-30)

Before the fact, then, we learn of the abduction and the purchase of the heroine; we may easily conjecture that the couple will marry, since we are told that Biatris will give birth to the celebrated children of Hervis. What remains to be told is the *way* in which the heroine will be kidnapped, purchased, and married to the hero. Indeed, the "how" of these events holds just as much narrative interest as the "if." In the course of a public performance, such anticipations functioned in part to attract and hold the attention of the ambulatory crowd: "... [le jongleur] annonce ce qu'il chantera, pour piquer la curiosité du public, le retenir par l'attente d'événements sensationnels."[30] Part Two, on the other hand, makes little use of this epic procedure; the narrator anticipates the outcome of story events only twice.[31] In the first example, we learn that the Spanish King's ambassadors will not succeed in escorting Biatris to Spain; instead, they will do battle with Hervis and his knights (vv. 8323-27). In the second, we learn only that the bourgeois of Metz will never again see Hervis after he rescues his wife (vv. 9240-41): this example provides a hint that the Messin townspeople may die in a siege. Other major events, such as the Loherain victories in Brabant and Metz, are recounted without explicit anticipation. Although the occasional mention of Hervis's future exploits in *Garin le Loherain* provides the reasonably secure expectation of a happy ending, Part Two generally sustains the "if-suspense" associated with romance.

While it is not surprising that the narrator's regulation of temporal order should differ in the two parts of *Hervis*, the nature of the divergence is atypical: in this instance, disjunction reverses the generic associations commonly exhibited by Parts One and Two.

---

[30] Jean Rychner, *La Chanson de geste: Essai sur l'art épique des jongleurs*, Société de publications romanes et françaises 53 (Geneva: Droz, 1955) 54.

[31] This excludes a false anticipation, in which the narrator tells us that Bïatris will never see her children again (v. 7285).

Indeed, the strong dose of epic anticipation in Part One serves to balance its romance innovations by situating them in the all-encompassing time frame of the *chanson de geste*.

VOICE

The dimension of narrative voice is one of the most homogeneous factors in this work. Throughout the poem, the conventional jongleur's voice functions as a cohesive force to draw together narrator, text and narratee. These textual marks serve as indices of the work's actual performance in the Middle Ages, attesting to the poet's desire for an emotional bond between performer, text, and audience.

Hervis de Mes does not exhibit the "univocity" that has been attributed to such works as the Oxford *Roland*. Nevertheless, narrator and characters alike share the use of certain formulas that tend to assimilate their voices. The most notable instance is the epithet "Mes la mirable cité," which is employed throughout the text by narrator, protagonists, and adversaries alike (vv. 8, 240, 2030, 6519, 6366, 7003, et al.). This epithet functions much in the same way as "dulce France." Metz stands at the center of Loherain legend just as Carolingian France plays a crucial role in the *cycle du roi*; in the more localized *geste des Loherains*, too, such geographical formulas reverberate throughout the text in the form of a communal refrain. The epithet "mirable cité" projects the city into the realm of myth; at the same time, it carries the potential of emotional ties between performer, characters, and local audiences.

The jongleur also interjects periodic exclamations evoking his involvement in the hero's adventures and exploits. For instance, when Hervis vows to purchase whatever he pleases at the fair in Lagny, the narrator expresses and elicits admiration: "Dix, quel accat li damoisiaus i fist!" (v. 609). In Part Two, when the hero is in the midst of a bitter single combat against King Oudart of Scotland, the jongleur's voice participates in Hervis's misfortune: "Dix, quel damage en vint au duc membré!" (v. 9649). When Floire engineers the plot to kidnap his sister, the narrator curses the scheme as if he himself were its victim: "Dix, con se ment li fors rois couronnés! / Mal dou mangier qu'il ait fait apresté!" (vv. 7212-13). Such interventions thus punctuate both romanesque adventure and epic exploit, evoking and eliciting emotional participation in Hervis's fate.[32]

Participation is also present in the multiple indices of performance. An ongoing metadiscourse reflecting the jongleur's role as reciter (singer?) and the audience's role as listeners permeates the entire text of all three manuscripts. The lexical and grammatical indices present in the jongleur's narrative articulations are far too numerous to dismiss as empty formulas; rather, they posit the discursive situation as a dialogue and they facilitate the process of oral performance. The textual manifestations of this dialogue are as follows:

In both parts, the narrator designates his own function by means of the verb *chanter*:

> Des Loherens vos voromes *chanter*.
> Quant leus en iert, bien en vorrons *chanter*.
> (vv. 3, 6872)

No empirical evidence allows us to assume that *Hervis de Mes* was actually sung in the Middle Ages, although contemporaries of the *Hervis* poet do distinguish the *chanson de geste* from other kinds of narrative texts by a specific use of vocal art. The oft-cited writings of Jehan Bodel and Jehan de Grouchy offer strong evidence of the continued musical performance of the *chanson de geste* in the thirteenth century.[33] These contemporary accounts also suggest, however, that the melody of the *chanson de geste* was linked to changes in laisse.[34] Given the tremendous length of the strophe in *Hervis de Mes*, it would be presumptuous to postulate sung performances of this work. What does seem quite evident is that the text was at least orally recited in the Middle Ages. Indeed, the jongleur refers to his function much more frequently by means of the verbs *parler* (56 occurrences); *dire* (16 occurrences); and *conter* (16 occurrences). These verbs are most often in the infinitive, and are accompanied by modals indicating the narrator's duty (*devomes*) and especially his will/desire (*vorromes*). The insistent repetition of the latter verb,

---

[32] This rhetorical device is also present in romance, but to a much lesser degree. *Hervis de Mes* offers 36 interventions of this sort.

[33] See Zumthor, *Voix* 39.

[34] Rychner 69.

which appears 51 times in conjunction with verbs of "telling", represents more than a mere transitional formula. Paul Zumthor has described the forces underlying vocal acts of all sorts in the Middle Ages; the *parole* of poetry (as well as that of law and theology) arises from a primal desire:

> Un vouloir y fermente et en fait lever les oeuvres: volonté de dépasser la contingence du vécu, de freiner la dispersion aléatoire des paroles, de transcender l'accidentel en en dégageant l'historicité propre, sur quoi se construit et par quoi se soutiennent la puissance morale, la conscience d'une collectivité et sa capacité d'action.[35]

This "vouloir" thus lurks beneath the surface of a rather cliché narrative articulation; the desire to speak initiates a poetic/vocal act which, as we shall see, will ultimately function to solidify the community around a specific structure of power.

The participation of the potential receiver is also clearly present in the text. The receiver's role is indicated by the verbs *oïr* (43 occurrences); *escouter* (10 occurrences); and *entendre* (6 occurrences). These verbs are often in the imperative, accompanied by the apostrophic "Seignour." The true dialogue between performer and audience, however, is reflected in the play of pronouns and verbal inflections. The indirect object pronoun *vos* almost always appears as a complement to the first-person verb in narrative articulations (e.g. "vos voromes parler", 29 occurrences). Occasionally, the first-person subject pronoun is expressed, which indicates strong emphasis in Old French (e.g. "je vous di", v. 616). This constant juxtaposition of narrator and narratee generates potential partnership to be realized in performance: the jongleur continually evokes his own function and elicits the attention of his listeners, whose role is likened to that of interlocutor in a conversation.

One aspect of later epic narrative voice is absent from *Hervis de Mes*. In *Huon de Bordeaux* and other *chansons*, the jongleur intervenes to request payment for his song; such indications of monetary exchange are not a part of the jongleur's persona in *Hervis*.[36] This

---

[35] Zumthor, *Voix* 100.
[36] Pierre Ruelle, ed., *Huon de Bordeaux*, Travaux de la Faculté de Philosophie et Lettres 20 (Paris: Presses universitaires de France; Bruxelles: Université Libre de

pragmatic dimension is implicit, however, in images of the jongleur, which appear in numerous passages (vv. 189-93, 569, 2462-78, 4612-20, 5168-70, 5503, 7099, 7929, 9065-67). The presence of such performers at feasts and other special occasions is a common motif in both romance and *chanson de geste*. However, the *Hervis* poet consistently emphasizes the jongleurs' compensation:

> Grant fut li joie ou palais principel,
> Adons vïele doucement li jonglers.
> Hervis li donne I· hermin engoulé,
> Et li jougleres l'a forment mercïé.
> (vv. 4617-20)

> Cantent et notent, vïelent cil jongler,
> Et li prevos fait bien toz loër.
> Tous li plus povres ot blïaut de cendel.
> (vv. 9065-67)

Even the bourgeois Thieri abandons his greedy ways when the jongleur is present in the story. While the narrator does not explicitly promote the largess from which such characters benefit, the repetition of this motif creates another link between text and audience: Hervis and his reformed father are to the fictional jongleurs what the audience is to the actual performer. The partnership between performer and audience thus implies material as well as poetic exchange.

Despite the overall consistency of narrative voice, traces of fragmentation may be discerned in two principal areas. The first distinction concerns the articulation of the bond between narrator and narratee, between performer and virtual audience. The two halves of *Hervis de Mes* display different strategies for marking *séances*, or dividing the text into segments which correspond to the actual sittings of a performance. Basing their judgments on the practice of modern Yugoslavian bards, scholars have postulated that 1000 to 2000 lines might have been recited or sung – with several pauses – in a *séance* of two hours; between pauses, a jongleur probably per-

---

Bruxelles, 1960) Laisse XLII. Marguerite Rossi maintains that such passages are narrative artifices (*Huon* 128). For a contrasting opinion, see Joseph J. Duggan, "Le mode de composition des chansons de geste: Analyse statistique, jugement esthétique, modèles de transmission," *Olifant* 8 (1981): 299-302.

formed 150 to 600 lines.[37] Few *chansons de geste* contain explicit textual signs of performance distribution: Nico van den Boogaard demonstrates that the fourteenth-century *Tristan de Nanteuil* is exceptional in its consistent use of specific performance articulations.[38] Part One of *Hervis de Mes*, however, manifests a similar attention to overt textual division; these indices of *séance* suggest a deliberate framing of textual segments in view of potential recitation.

The first half of *Hervis de Mes* features its own system of articulation aimed at establishing contact between reciter and audience. Segments of 175 to 594 lines are consistently framed by at least two of the following devices: change of laisse; anticipation of future story events; recall of story events already recounted; transition indicating a beginning; transition indicating the telling function of the jongleur and/or the listening function of the audience. The resulting divisions indicate possible performance segments from lines 1 through 5533, i.e. until the pivotal episode of the dubbing ceremony: vv. 1-245; 246-630; 631-805; 806-1195; 1196-1395; 1396-1773; 1774-2281; 2282-2873; 2874-3147; 3148-3584; 3585-3985; 3986-4560; 4561-4964; 4965-5533.

The vast majority of these segments are divided at the laisse. Although strophic breaks do not correlate precisely with narrative blocks, the segments in question consistently appear within several lines of a story division, i.e. an episode or sub-episode. It is this coincidence of narrative, strophic, and performance articulation which distinguishes Part One of *Hervis de Mes* from the epic tradition as a whole and particularly from Part Two of the same work: the systematic distribution of textual material into performable segments suggests a deliberate effort on the part of the poet or redactor, a conscious attempt to organize the text in view of potential recitation.

The jongleur's transitions do continue to punctuate narrative and narration in Part Two. The compositional technique of interlace favors the constant use of formulas such as "Or vous lairons (de)... / (De)... vos vorromes parler." Due to this change in com-

---

[37] See Rychner 49; also Nico Van den Boogaard, "Le caractère oral de la chanson de geste tardive," *Langue et littérature françaises du Moyen Age: Etudes réunies par R.E.V. Stuip* (Assen: Van Gorcum, 1978) 30-33.
[38] Van den Boogaard 30-33.

position, the second part of *Hervis* contains a far greater proportion of verbs indicating the jongleur's function, and a smaller proportion of verbs indicating the listeners' function. This modification of the narrator's metadiscourse is balanced by the increased use of the pronoun *vos*, which serves to maintain contact with the potential audience. These transitions are not, however, accompanied by adjacent articulatory strategies such as anticipation, recall, and change of strophe. (Anticipation and recall do play a role in the composition of Part Two, but these passages do not necessarily accompany narrative transition.) Indeed, it is the *multiplicity* of signals that has disappeared. While a performer might choose any number of transitions to articulate his recital, that range of choices is not emphatically indicated in the text; supplementary performance aids would have to be supplied by the reciter. Thus narrative voice in Part Two regulates to a lesser degree the initiation and maintenance of contact between performer, text, and audience: these functions are treated rather as a given of the epic tradition.

Secondly, although the narration of events generally proceeds without mediation by an overtly instructive presence, suggestions of the narrator's attitude toward his tale may be gleaned from the play of epithets and other designative formulas between the voices of character and narrator. The configuration of this interplay mirrors the changing pattern we have discerned in the form and sequence of events:

In Part One, before the hero is dubbed, the narrator frequently designates him as "li damoisiaus Hervis," "li damoisiaus de pris," "Hervis li membrés," or "li gentis et li ber." The words "damoisel" and "gentis" evoke the hero's youth and nobility, while "de pris," "ber", and "membrés" attest to his worth, strength, and valiance. Although these epithets most often represent a straightforward depiction of the hero's birth and character, they occasionally betray an ironic stance. At the fair in Lagny, for example, the lofty epithet "le gentil et le ber" introduces a rather mundane commercial operation, i.e. the weighing of silver:

> Or vous devons de Bïatrix conter
> Et de Hervi *le gentil et le ber*.
> Vint a Ligni, *l'avoir fist delivrer*,
> Trestot l'a fait *a balance peser*.
>
> (vv. 1448-51)

The juxtaposition of noble epithet and merchant pursuit creates a meaningful dissonance between narration and context, highlighting the problematic nature of the hero's heritage. Such incongruities are typical of the later epic tradition, which often appropriates the distancing techniques of the romance narrator. Many scholars associate this strategy with the transition from oral to written text; as the reciter became distinct from the poet, the narrating subject of the *chanson de geste* was increasingly able to assume a critical posture. This would suggest once again that *Hervis*, like many of its contemporaries, was composed in writing to be recited to an audience.[39]

The narrational conflict between merchant and noble identities escalates when Hervis displays his wares at the fair in Tyre. Whereas the narrator continues to designate Hervis as "damoisel," the Tyrians, who believe the hero to be a Norman merchant, address him as "'Marceans freres'" (vv. 3565, 3688, 3715, 3727, 3758) or "'Marceans dous amis'" (v. 3567); indeed, although the audience knows that Hervis is not entirely the person he pretends to be, he demonstrates remarkable skill as a tradesman in this episode. As a rule, however, the nouns "damoisel" and "marceant" were mutually exclusive; the interplay between narrator and character thus highlights once again the protagonist's crisis of lineage. The conflict is seemingly resolved when, at the end of the successful business transaction, Baudri of Tyre calls Hervis "Marceans frere, damoisiax dous amis" (v. 3791). This designation unites the formulas of narrator and characters into a single decasyllabic line; the two identities of Hervis, the noble merchant, can be temporarily assimilated.

In Part Two, the narrator's epithets generally reflect the hero's accession to the duchy of Lorraine: Hervis has become "li dus de Mes." As we have seen, his enemies habitually designate him as "'Fix de vilain'" (vv. 6376, 6600, 7346, 8698, 8822, 9499) or "'Fix d'un prevost'" (vv. 6917). These formulas are and remain mutually exclusive for both narrator and characters: no assimilation takes place. The hero's victory causes his former enemies to join the narrator's voice in recognizing Hervis's matrilineal nobility. At the end of the story, King Anseÿs of Cologne humbly addresses the con-

---

[39] For an *état-présent* of research in this area, see D.H. Green, "Orality and Reading: The State of Research in Medieval Studies," *Speculum* 65.2 (April 1990) 267-80. See also Bäuml 93.

quering hero as "'Nobiles dus'" (v. 10,325), thereby effacing the discursive conflict.

The interplay of epithets and other formulas designating the hero thus conforms to the pattern we observed in the narrative as a whole: dual lineage is possible in Part One, but subverted and replaced by matrilineal nobility in Part Two. The lesson to be drawn from Hervis's story is not explained or even elucidated by overt narrative intervention, even in the more romanesque portion of the text. In Part One, however, the narrator occasionally stands at a greater critical distance from his material, implicitly inviting the audience to do the same; his voice is open to question and may enter into an implied dialogue with that of the characters. In Part Two, the narrator's choice of epithets consistently serves as an assertion of truth to which other appellations may be compared; in this respect, his voice is more faithful to the conventions of epic poetry.

In fact, although narrative voice creates a certain emotional unity throughout *Hervis de Mes*, Part Two magnifies the socio-poetic function of the *chanson de geste*, gradually uniting the textual and real communities with the cohesive voice of the narrator. This is accomplished by the use of a well-known epic strategy involving the transformation of a single modifier: on two occasions, the narrator rejects his common nominal phrase *li bourgois* in favor of the possessive *nos bourgois*. Both of the passages occur during the siege of Metz, when "la commune" must contribute to the defense of the city. Since the bourgeois lack the noble prowess of their aristocratic enemies, they suffer enormous losses ("Mais li bourgois ne se porent tenir / Quar trop i vint dou barnage de pris," vv. 9992-93). In the first example, Garin retaliates in behalf of the Messins:

> Sor l'escu va ferir Aÿmer;
> Nes de Navarre, riches dus fu clamés,
> De *nos* bourgois avoit moult vergondés.
>
> (vv. 10053-55)

Like the noble young hero, the narrator participates in the fate of the Messin community, uniting their cause in the first-person plural *nos*. Moreover, this *nos* embraces and engages the potential audience, who thereby becomes implicated in the civic cause common to narrator and characters.

This strategy by no means creates a bond of equality between noble and bourgeois. Rather, the passage in question reflects the feudal obligation requiring the noble to protect weaker members of the social hierarchy who cannot be expected to protect themselves. Indeed, the narrator's use of *nos* has protective connotations which align his voice with the traditional function of the noble. Narrative voice thus confirms and contributes to the social conservatism of Part Two, reflecting the desires and aspirations of the declining feudal class. This conservatism informs the emotional and poetic bond uniting the multiple components of textual community, i.e. the narrator's voice, the Messins' plight, Garin's valiance, and the sympathies of the potential audience.

In the second example, the remaining bourgeois enter Metz in triumph after the remarkable exploits of Garin and Bégon:

> Et *no* bourgois dedens Mes sont entré;
> Et la ducoise ne se volt arrester.
> Uns messaigiers li a dit et conté:
> 'Vo dui fil, dame, qui tant ont de bonté
> An la baitaille se sont molt bien provez.'
>
> (vv. 10206-10)

As they shared in the common defense of Metz, the bourgeois citizens now share in the victory of their benefactors. Once again, the jongleur's use of the first person plural possessive integrates his voice into the community and elicits the participation of the potential audience. This use of the all-encompassing "nos" is completely absent from the narration of Part One. It is in Part Two that *Hervis de Mes* assumes the epic social function to its fullest: "la parole épique fonde ou cimente la communauté, dans le temps même qu'elle se prononce et s'entend..."[40]

* * *

Although the actual performances of a medieval text can only be glimpsed through the filter of textual analysis, the study of narration identifies the potential mode and effects of these lost representations. *Hervis de Mes* reveals in many ways a dual conception of

---

[40] Zumthor, *Voix* 175.

narration: Part One broadens the scope of epic discourse by appropriating romance strategies of dialogue, monologue, perspective and irony; it also displays a distinct style of temporal ordering and performance articulation. All of these factors point to the conscious, written orchestration of a thirteenth-century *chanson* whose utterances are occasionally mediated by a separate authorial presence. Although it too necessarily bears the stamp of written intervention, the latter half of the text remains closer to the immediacy of an orally-composed poem.

At the same time, the pervasive resonance of the jongleur's voice attenuates the fragmented generic structure of the work: the integrative powers latent in the jongleur's vocal art lend coherence to the multiplicity of textual systems. As the text unfolds, this voice increasingly binds text and audience into a common allegiance and a common past. Paul Zumthor postulates that the performer's actual voice often conferred unity upon multiple, fragmented medieval texts: "C'est en performance en effet que se fixe, pour le temps d'une audition, le point d'intégration de tous les éléments qui constituent 'l'oeuvre.'"[41] In this particular work, unification operates on two levels: the jongleur's voice binds text, narrator, and receiver as well as disparate formal and thematic structures within the text itself. While the hero's dual lineage may have caused a diverse public to identify now with the merchant, now with the noble, the function of social identification ultimately fades before the epic goal of social community. Indeed, this phenomenon has survived the metamorphoses of time and reception, prompting one modern French reader to exclaim:

> Surprenante légende!... Dans le récit, Hervis et le duc Pierre ont un ennemi juré. Il s'appelle... le roi de Cologne et subit une humiliation exemplaire! En somme, la légende d'Hervis de Mes prouverait cette autre évidence: au treizième siècle déjà, Metz avait choisi la France![42]

---

[41] Zumthor, *Voix* 182.
[42] Philippe Walter, Postface, *Hervis de Metz: Roman du moyen âge adapté par Philippe Walter*, Editions Serpenoise (Nancy: Presses universitaires de Nancy, 1984) 201.

CONCLUSION

Like many epics of the thirteenth century, *Hervis de Mes* appropriates some of the narrative and poetic resources of romance, but restricts their scope to a limited portion of the text. This poem's binary structure is manifest on many levels: the romanesque subject matter of Part One is accompanied by the occasional use of romance narrating strategies as well as the transformation of strophic and formulaic style. Conversely, the narrative content of Part Two resembles more closely the thematic conventions and ideological foundations of the early *chanson de geste*; this shift in content coincides with a partial return to the formal properties of the earlier *chanson de geste*.

The fundamental duality of *Hervis de Mes* does not correspond to an epic/romance dichotomy in every respect. Indeed, Part One offers many examples of typical epic motifs, lyric devices, and narrational strategies. The maintenance of the epic laisse and consistent efforts to link *Hervis de Mes* with the Loherain tradition indicate that romance generic functions play a secondary and dependent role in this self-proclaimed *chanson*. Similarly, Part Two does not always exemplify the conventions of epic poetry, particularly in its portrayal of love and its deployment of the interlace techniques associated with prose romance. Nonetheless, the analysis of *tresse* and *chanson* reveals that the overwhelming majority of generic innovations occur in the first half of the text, while the second part manifests a distinct generic conservatism.

The bipartite form of *Hervis de Mes* does suggest that a redactor may have combined diverse legends or songs into a single *chanson*; indeed, the formal ruptures of the Senlis episode bear witness to a process of amalgamation. However, the question of origin is perhaps less vital than the effects produced by a dual poetic and narrative system. In *Hervis de Mes*, the representation of social order reproduces the text's relation to the epic genre: Part One admits and assimilates the growing influence of bourgeois figures and values just as it incorporates the narrative strategies of a competing genre; Part Two reestablishes the near-exclusive dominion of both noble lineage and conventional generic traits. The bipartite generic pattern of *Hervis* thus constitutes a metaphor of its underlying ideological implications.

The implications of later epic "binarism" go beyond the mere assertion of fragmentation and difference: it is the cumulative effect of textual progression that reveals the work's function in the poetic and social context of its time. Although the social order could initially be expanded to include the values of the marketplace, and the epic framework could initially accommodate the properties of romance, the subsequent purge of both lineage and genre strives to alleviate the influence of merchant and romance. In this sense, *Hervis de Mes* interacts with its generic and social context by attempting to eliminate competing poetic and ideological systems. However, the relative success of such an attempt within the poem is mitigated by the fact that these competing systems continued to manifest themselves in the epics of subsequent generations.

In its transgression and reorientation of lineal and poetic boundaries, *Hervis de Mes* attests to the remarkable range of thematic and formal possibilities mobilized by the later *chanson de geste*. The poem's blend of innovation and convention exemplifies the process of genre expansion: duplicating certain generic functions and transforming others, *Hervis* and its contemporaries redefined the parameters of the Old French epic. Far from signalling the decline of the *chanson de geste*, this diversification rejuvenated a genre whose popularity would endure for the next two centuries.

APPENDIX A

ARTICULATIONS OF THE NARRATIVE

I) PART ONE (vv. 1-5652)

A) *Hervis* (1-615)

   1) Prologue (1-7)
   2) Antecedents of characters (8-43)
      a) Duke Pierre (8-21)
      b) Thieri (22-43)
   3) *Conseil* of Duke Pierre (44-185)
   4) Marriage of Aelis and Thieri (186-194)
   5) Departure of Pierre (195-245)
   6) Birth and early childhood of Hervis (246-269)
   7) Preparations for fair at Provins (270-339)
      a) Father/son quarrel: dubbing vs. fair (270-323)
      b) Departure of Hervis and paternal uncles (324-339)
   8) Fair at Provins (340-383)
      a) Separate lodging, extravagant meals (340-363)
      b) Quarrel with paternal uncles (364-383)
   9) Purchase of hunting animals (384-457)
   10) Return to Metz / Repercussions of fair (458-570)
       a) Quarrel with paternal uncles (458-480)
       b) Voyage (481-484)
       c) Quarrel Hervis/Thieri (485-537)
       d) Reconciliation effected by Aelis (538-565)
       e) Celebration (566-570)
   11) Preparations for fair at Lagny (571-615)

B) *Biatris* (616-1197)

   1) Antecedents of characters (616-637)
      a) Biatris (616-624)
      b) Spanish King (625-637)

APPENDIX A 163

2) *Conseil* of Spanish King (638-695)
3) Spanish embassy to Tyre (696-776)
4) Wedding preparations of Spanish King (777-806)
5) Departure of Biatris's parents (807-855)
    a) Silent conflict father/daughter (807-813)
    b) Biatris entrusted to Baudri (814-855)
6) Kidnapping of Biatris (856-1197)
    a) Biatris in garden (856-915)
    b) Kidnapping (916-951)
    c) Search led by Baudri (952-1008)
    d) Dream of Biatris's mother (1009-1035)
    e) Return of Biatris's parents / punishment of Baudri (1036-1118)
    f) Kidnappers' decision to sell Biatris (1119-1197)

C) *Union of Hervis and Biatris* (1198-2301)

1) Fair at Lagny (1198-1233)
    a) Separate lodging, extravagant meals (1198-1214)
    b) Quarrel with paternal uncles (1215-1233)
2) Purchase of Biatris (1234-1394)
3) Attack of the three "demoisel" (1395-1724)
    a) Plot of the three "demoisel" (1395-1466)
    b) Hervis warned by Biatris (1467-1505)
    c) Hervis armed by host (1506-1543)
    d) Battle and victory of Hervis (1544-1677)
    e) Fruitless pursuit by families of "demoisel" (1678-1724)
4) Voyage to Metz (1725-1816)
    a) Food procured from *bouvier* (1725-1771)
    b) Quarrel with paternal uncles (1772-1815)
5) Return to Metz / Repercussions (1817-1973)
    a) Quarrel Hervis/Thieri (1817-1904)
    b) Exile of Hervis and Biatris (1905-1973)
6) Generosity of Baudri and wife (1974-2173)
7) Forced marriage of Hervis and Biatris (2174-2284)
8) Birth of Garin (2285-2301)

D) *Preliminary Adventures of Hervis* (2302-2903)

1) Tournament at Senlis (2302-2777)
    a) Preparation, departure (2302-2429)
    b) Voyage (2430-2431)
    c) Arrival of Hervis and Gerart in Senlis (2432-2478)
    d) Host's tale (2479-2525)

           e) Preparations for tournament (2526-2560)
           f)   Battle (2561-2630)
           g) Capture of Count of Flanders (2631-2656)
           h) Gerart and his horse rescued by Hervis (2657-2744)
           i)   Loherains' search for mysterious warrior (2745-2770)
           j)   Largess and departure of Hervis (2771-2777)
     2) Further adventures (2778-2783)
     3) Loherains in Metz (2784-2822)
     4) Further adventures and expenditures (2823-2835)
     5) Births of Bégon and a daughter (2836-2863)
     6) Further adventures (2864-2869)
     7) Ruin of Baudri (2870-2903)

E) *Expedition to Tyre* (2904-4698)

     1) Biatris's plan (2904-3148)
           a) Predicament (2904-2925)
           b) Instructions to Hervis (2926-3111)
           c) Preparations for Tyre / Hervis's departure (3112-3148)
     2) Voyage, arrival of Hervis (3149-3299)
     3) Extravagant meals and lease of *estal* (3300-81)
     4) Revelation of Biatris's identity (3382-3418)
     5) Sale of the *drap* (3419-3795)
           a) display (3419-3462)
           b) arrival of Floire (3463-3497)
           c) Bargaining with Floire (3498-3574)
           d) Uistasse and Queen informed (3575-3654)
           e) Bargaining with Uistasse (3655-3766)
           f)   Property returned to Baudri (3767-3795)
     6) Uistasse's attempt to imprison Hervis (3796-3886)
     7) Spies recruited by Floire (3887-3938)
     8) Departure of Hervis with guards (3939-3984)
     9) Voyage (3985-3988)
   10) Hervis vs. Hinbaut and thirty bandits (3989-4563)
           a) Description of Hinbaut (3989-4001)
           b) Plight of the monks and abbots (4002-4035)
           c) Desertion of the 20 cowardly bourgeois / loyalty of the 20 valets (4036-4140)
           d) Battle (4141-4164)
           e) Miracle and victory of Hervis over Himbaut (4165-4185)
           f)   Victory over Clarembaut and most bandits (4186-4249)
           g) Conversion of Thieri the bandit (4250-4264)
           h) Massacre of the 20 cowardly bourgeois (4265-4310)
           i)   Treasure appropriated by Hervis (4311-4327)

APPENDIX A   165

        j)   Liberation of clerics (4328-4457)
        k) New attack by bandits, victory of Hervis (4458-4551)
        l)   Arrival of Floire's spies (4552-4563)
   11) Voyage to Metz, stop at Neufchatel (4564-4698)
        a)   Meal Hervis/Floire's spies (4564-4625)
        b) Homage paid to Hervis (4626-4698)

F) *Reunions and Celebrations* (4699-5653)

   1) Return to Metz / Repercussions of Tyre (4699-5036)
        a)   Hunger of family / arrival of Thieri II (4699-4839)
        b) Encounter Thieri I / Baudri (4840-4856)
        c)   Encounter Hervis/Thieri I (4857-4902)
        d) Reconciliation Thieri/Biatris (4903-4932)
        e)   Reunion Hervis/family (4933-4963)
        f)   Reconciliation Hervis/Thieri, by Biatris (4964-5036)
   2) Belated wedding feast (5037-5284)
        a)   Formal introductions Hervis/Count of Bar (5037-5124)
        b) Public apology by Thieri (5125-5165)
        c)   Meal (5166-5183)
        d) Hervis recognized (exploits at Senlis) (5184-5284)
   3) Return of Duke Pierre (5285-5506)
        a)   Introductions (5285-5324)
        b) Feast (5325-5506)
   4) Arrival / departure of Floire's spies (5507-5532)
   5) Dubbing of Hervis (5533-5653)
        a)   Preparations and *Veille* (5533-5549)
        b) Dubbing and presentation of sword (Florence) (5550-5582)
        c)   Gift of horse (Rufin) (5583-5615)
        d) *Quintainne* (5616-5653)

II) PART TWO (vv. 5654-10,572)

A) *War in Brabant* (5654-6963)

   1) Announcement of duke of Brabant's death / siege of Brabant by Anseÿs of Cologne (5654-5706)
   2) Hervis invested with Metz, Lorraine (5707-5753)
   3) Siege of Louvain by Anseÿs (5754-5779)
   4) Preparations of Loherains (5780-5831)
   5) Siege of Louvain, announcement of Loherains' imminent arrival (5832-5883)
   6) Floire's plan to kidnap Biatris (5884-5966)]
   7) Arrival of Loherains in Brabant (5967-6017)

8) Battle, Loherains vs. Clèves (6018-6229)
9) Return of Loherains to camp, booty (6230-6272)
10) Siege of Louvain by Anseÿs (6273-6288)
11) Anseÿs's refusal to surrender (6289-6411)
12) Preparations for battle: Loherains, Brabançons, Anseÿs (6412-6585)
13) Battle (6586-6807)
   a) Hervis vs. a Frisian (6586-6630)
   b) *Chanson* about battle (6631-6639)
   c) General battle (6640-6733)
   d) Hervis vs. King of Frisia (6734-6764)
   e) Retreat of Frisians and Anseÿs (6765-6807)
14) Homage to Hervis and celebration (6808-6850)
15) Preparations for siege of Cologne (6851-6870, 6955-63)
16) Preparations of Anseÿs and Frisians (6871-6954)

B) *Kidnapping and Rescue of Biatris* (6964-9119)

1) Floire's arrival in Metz, deal with Thieri (6964-7094)
2) Meal at the house of Floire (7095-7119)
3) Encounter Floire/Garin (7120-7163)
4) Floire's scheme (7164-7227)
5) Premonitory dream of Biatris (7228-7287)
6) Kidnapping (7288-7366)
7) Search (7367-7456)
8) In Brabant, preparations for rescue (7457-7598)
9) Anseÿs apprised of kidnapping (7599-7616)
10) Biatris in Tyre, reunion with family (7617-7743)
11) Spanish embassy sent to Tyre (7744-7804)
12) Arrival of Thieri II in Tyre (7805-7849)
13) Arrival of Spanish embassy, feast (7850-7926)
14) Ruse of Biatris (7927-8087)
15) Rescue of Biatris (8088-8894)
   a) Biatris's ruse reported to Hervis (8088-8177)
   b) Departure of Biatris, her family, Spanish embassy (8178-8239)
   c) Dismissal of Biatris's family (8240-8290)
   d) Ambush and battle (8291-8445)
   e) Dream of Biatris (8446-8474)
   f) Retreat of Spaniards (8475-8577)
   g) Treasure ("dowry") to Hervis (8578-8606)
   h) Battle Hervis/Floire, wounding of Floire (8607-8807)
   i) Escape of Hervis and Biatris (8808-8894)
16) Repercussions: threats of Spanish King (8895-8996)
17) Return of Hervis and Biatris to Metz (8997-9119)

APPENDIX A 167

      a) Celebration (8997-9039)
      b) Reconciliation Hervis/Baudri, by Biatris (9040-9119)

C) *Wars in Brabant and Metz* (9120-10,572)
   1) Siege of Louvain by Anseÿs (9120-9241)
      a) Announcement in Metz (9120-9177)
      b) Assembly of knights, departure of Hervis (9178-9241)
   2) Siege of Metz by Spaniards, Biatris's family (9242-9272)
   3) Battle in Louvain (9273-9807)
      a) Siege of Louvain (9273-9318)
      b) Arrival of Hervis (9319-9355)
      c) Anseÿs's refusal to surrender (9356-9443)
      d) Preparations for battle on both sides (9444-9492)
      e) Duel Hervis/Oudart, capture of Oudart (9493-9751)
      f) General battle (9752-9807)
   4) Defense of Metz by Garin and Bégon (9808-10,227)
      a) Siege of Metz (9808-9864)
      b) Gerart captured by Spanish (9865-9946)
      c) Arming of the bourgeois, rescue of Gerart (9947-10,009)
      d) Dubbing of Garin (10,010-10,049)
      e) Garin in battle (10,050-10,076)
      f) Bégon prepares for battle (10,077-10,125)
      g) Garin, Bégon, and Thieri I in battle (10,126-10,177)
      h) Capture of Bégon and Thieri I (10,178-10,227)
   5) Peace in Brabant (10,228-10,366)
      a) Anseÿs persuaded to surrender (10,228-10,340)
      b) Peace agreements (10,341-10,366)
   6) Peace in Metz (10,367-10,531)
      a) Plight of the *gent menue* (10,367-10,393)
      b) Spanish King persuaded to surrender (10,394-10,498)
      c) Meeting Biatris/Spanish King (10,499-10,531)
   7) Return of Hervis, celebration (10,532-10,562)
   8) Epilogue (10,563-10,572)

APPENDIX B

THE LAISSE (Edition Stengel)

Laisse	Assonance	Lines	Lines/Laisse
I	[e]	1-97	97
II	[i]	98-109	12
III	[e]	110-168	59
IV	[i]	169-180	12
V	[e]	181-245	65
VI	[i]	246-257	12
VII	[e]	258-292	35
VIII	[i]	293-565	273
IX	[e]	566-583	18
X	[i]	584-630	47
XI	[e]	631-805	175
XII	[i]	806-838	33
XIII	[e]	839-1194	356
XIV	[i]	1195-1284	90
XV	[e]	1285-1304	20
XVI	[i]	1305-1363	59
XVII	[e]	1364-1378	15
XVIII	[i]	1379-1395	17
XIX	[e]	1396-1773	378
XX	[i]	1774-1907	134
XXI	[e]	1908-2281	374
XXII	[i]	2282-2300	19
XXIII	[e]	2301-2604	304
XXIV	[i]	2605-2619	15
XXV	[e]	2620-2657	38
XXVI	[i]	2658-2675	18
XXVII	[e]	2676-2744	69
XXVIII	[i]	2745-2777	33
XXIX	[e]	2778-2874	97

APPENDIX B

Laisse	Assonance	Lines	Lines/Laisse
XXX	[i]	2875-3147	273
XXXI	[e]	3148-3179	32
XXXII	[i]	3180-3190	11
XXXIII	[e]	3191-3236	46
XXXIV	[i]	3237-3392	156
XXXV	[e]	3393-3552	160
XXXVI	[i]	3553-3584	32
XXXVII	[e]	3585-3726	142
XXXVIII	[i]	3727-3831	105
XXXIX	[e]	3832-4185	354
XL	[i]	4186-4224	39
XLI	[e]	4225-4559	335
XLII	[i]	4560-4574	15
XLIII	[e]	4575-6017	1443
XLIV	[i]	6018-6027	10
XLV	[e]	6028-6133	106
XLVI	[u]fem.	6134-6141	8
XLVII	[a]fem.	6142-6146	5
XLVIII	[e]	6147-6180	34
XLIX	[i]	6181-6190	10
L	[e]	6191-6368	178
LI	[i]	6369-6378	10
LII	[e]	6379-6471	93
LIII	[i]	6472-6494	23
LIV	[e]	6495-6630	136
LV	[a]	6631-6639	9
LVI	[e]	6640-6673	34
LVII	[i]	6674-6697	24
LVIII	[e]fem.	6698-6711	14
LIX	[u]	6712-6717	6
LX	[ie]	6718-6729	12
LXI	[e]	6730-7529	800
LXII	[i]	7530-7545	16
LXIII	[e]	7546-8142	597
LXIV	[i]	8143-8166	24
LXV	[e]	8167-8314	148
LXVI	[i]	8315-8356	42
LXVII	[e]	8357-8427	71
LXVIII	[a] (-al)	8428-8434	7
LXIX	[e]fem.	8435-8441	7
LXX	[e]	8442-9492	1051

Laisse	Assonance	Lines	Lines/Laisse
LXXI	[i]	9493-9501	9
LXXII	[e]	9502-9522	21
LXXIII	[i]	9523-9534	12
LXXIV	[e]	9535-9541	7
LXXV	[a]fem.	9542-9547	6
LXXVI	[e]	9548-9748	201
LXXVII	[i]	9749-9780	32
LXXVIII	[e]	9781-9989	209
LXXIX	[i]	9990-10,001	12
LXXX	[e]	10,002-10,07	73
LXXI	[i]	10,075-10,09	24
LXXXII	[e]	10,099-10,57	474

Results

Average number of lines per laisse: 128.926
First half: 139.9 / Second half: 116.8

* * *

Number of laisses containing 10 lines or less: 12 (100 % in second half)
Number of laisses containing 15 lines or less: 24 (67 % in second half)
Number of laisses containing 20 lines or less: 29 (59 % in second half)
Number of laisses containing 50 lines or less: 47 (55 % in second half)

* * *

Number of laisses containing 100 lines or more: 25 (60 % in first half)
Number of laisses containing 200 lines or more: 15 (60 % in first half)
Number of laisses containing 300 lines or more: 11 (64 % in first half)
Number of laisses containing 500 lines or more: 4 (75 % in *second* half) * *
  All are bordered on both sides by laisses of 24 lines or less.

* * *

APPENDIX B

ASSONANCES

Number of laisses with assonance [e]: 39 (8845 lines, 83.6% of poem)

[i]: 34 (1653 lines, 15.6% of poem)

[e]fem.: 2 (21 lines)

[a]: 2 (16 lines)

[ie]: 1 (12 lines)

[a]fem.: 2 (11 lines)

[u]fem.: 1 (8 lines)

[u]: 1 (6 lines)

APPENDIX C

MOTIFS (Edition Stengel)

(The following index is by no means exhaustive. However, it does take into account some of the motifs fashioned exclusively for *Hervis de Mes* as well as many of the traditional categories found in earlier epic. Since most scholarly references to motifs are in French, I have here retained the use of French titles for each category. Asterisks mark motifs catalogued by Rychner for several early *chansons de geste*. Numerical references indicate the first verse in each passage.)

ACCUEIL: 487, 715, 5350, 4815, 4853, 4934, 6998, 7649, 9007, 10550
* ADOUBEMENT: 5535, 10011
* ARMEMENT: 1435, 1529, 2546, 4088, 4132, 6061, 8368, 8378, 8636, 8660, 9444, 9455, 9958
* ASSAUT AUX ARMES DE JET: 5868, 6273
* BATAILLE EVOQUEE EN TERMES GENERAUX: 2561, 4213, 4225, 6179, 6628, 6640, 6674, 6678, 6705, 6712, 6768, 8383, 8405, 8428, 8432, 8442, 8475, 8528, 8753, 9705, 9745, 9752, 9773, 9781, 9979, 9998, 10075, 10129
* COMBAT SINGULIER A LA LANCE: 4175, 4186, 6118, 6594, 6736, 8391, 8510, 8701, 9499, 9970, 10052
* COMBAT SINGULIER A L'EPEE: 1576, 1619, 4193, 4512, 6124, 8722, 8730, 9510, 9640, 9755
CONCEPTION: 248, 2283, 2838, 2860
DEGUISEMENT, PELERIN: 3920, 7814

DETTES: 50, 2152, 2873, 2885
DON/PARDON: 4967, 8243, 9083
EMBUSCADE: 1443, 6077, 9488
ENFANCE DU HEROS: 257
EXPLOITS FUTURS DU HEROS: 2400, 5096, 10563
FUITE DE L'ENNEMI: 6186, 6778, 8550, 8771, 9778, 9784
* HEROS DANS LA MELEE: 2596, 4215, 4226, 6171, 6181, 6647, 6676, 6700, 6707, 6730, 6764, 8410, 8423, 8429, 8437, 8443, 8479, 8531, 8762, 9715, 10126, 10149, 10178, 10189
* HISTOIRE DES ARMES ET DES CHEVAUX: 5335, 5562, 5594
LIGNAGE, HEROS & HEROINE: 3395, 4448, 4654, 4680, 4836, 4880, 4950, 5058, 5145, 5418, 6095, 6826, 6912, 7346, 7520, 8685, 8817, 9302, 9610, 10441
MEDECIN: 561, 6226, 6765, 8885, 9743
* MESSAGES, AMBASSADES: 485, 683, 702, 965, 1039, 1112, 1817,

2077, 2306, 5286, 5654, 5840, 5890, 6022, 6204, 6293, 6412, 6540, 6971, 7458, 7599, 7621, 7706, 7789, 7851, 8088, 8607, 8895, 8938, 9276, 9319, 9356, 9861, 10136, 10228, 10271, 10534, 10537
MESSE: 4695, 5164, 5483, 6235, 6845, 7199, 7875, 9035, 10555
* MOBILISATION DES TROUPES: 5780, 6516, 6948, 6958, 9178
NOCES: 188, 2264
PAIX: 10341, 10499
PLAINTE DE LA MAL MARIEE: 545, 1902
* PLANCTUS: 1046, 1706
* PLEURS, TRISTESSES, PAMOISONS: (numerous instances)
POURSUITE DE L'ENNEMI: 8555, 9785
POURSUITE MANQUEE: 998, 1720, 7431
RASSEMBLEMENT DES TROUPES: 5754, 6075, 6556, 6565, 9478
* REPAS: 568, 748, 2456, 2750, 2788, 4580, 4610, 4686, 5167, 5488, 6260, 6838, 7095, 7876, 9039, 10556
"RESCOUSSE": 2616, 2640, 6749, 8403, 8526
RESSEMBLANCE: 2505, 2810, 4424, 5197

* SONGE: 1015, 7257, 8446
VOYAGE: (numerous instances, often combined with MESSAGES)

* * *

THEME DE LA FOIRE:

INSTRUCTIONS: 299, 589
DECLARATION SECRETE: 320, 604
LOGEMENT SEPARE: 341, 1203
(FOIRE et al.), "MANGIER RICE": 345, 1206, 3328, 7095
PREMIERE DISPUTE AVEC ONCLES: 366, 1215
TRANSACTION: 384, 1364
LARGESSE DU HEROS: 417, 1519
SECONDE DISPUTE AVEC ONCLES: 458, 1775
DEPENSES DU HEROS RACONTEES: 500, 1820
COLERE DU PERE: 458, 1774
FOIRE TYRIENNE, PERCEPTION DU DRAP: 3482, 3673
FOIRE TYRIENNE, ORIGINES DU DRAP: 3499, 3689
FOIRE TYRIENNE, PRIX DISCUTE: 3520, 3704

WORKS CONSULTED

I) Primary Sources

Aiol. Ed. Jacques Normand and Gaston Raynaud. Société des anciens textes français 7. Paris: Didot, 1877.

Anseÿs de Mes According to Ms. N (Bibliothèque de l'Arsenal 3143): Text, published for the first time in its entirety, with an Introduction. Ed. Herman J. Green. Paris: Les Presses modernes, 1939.

Aucassin et Nicolette. Ed. Mario Roques. 2nd ed. Classiques français du moyen âge 41. Paris: Champion, 1982.

Bodel, Jehan. *Saisnes*. Ed. Annette Brasseur. 2 vols. Textes littéraires français 369. Geneva: Droz, 1989.

La Chanson de Guillaume. Ed. Duncan McMillan. Société des anciens textes français 87. Paris: Picard, 1949-50.

La Chanson de Roland. Ed. Gérard Moignet. Collection "Pour connaître." Paris: Bordas, 1985.

Le Charroi de Nîmes: Chanson de geste du XIIe siècle. Ed. Duncan McMillan. Paris: Klincksieck, 1972.

Chrétien de Troyes. *Le Chevalier de la Charrete*. Ed. Mario Roques. Classiques français du moyen âge 86. Paris: Champion, 1981.

———. *Erec et Enide*. Ed. Mario Roques. Classiques français du moyen âge 80. Paris: Champion, 1981.

———. *Le Roman de Perceval ou le Conte du Graal*. Ed. William Roach. Textes littéraires français 71. Geneva: Droz; Paris: Minard, 1959.

———. *Yvain (Le Chevalier au lion)*. Ed. Wendelin Foerster. Manchester: Manchester University Press, 1942.

Le Conte de Floire et Blanchefleur. Ed. Jean-Luc Leclanche. Classiques français du moyen âge 105. Paris: Champion, 1980.

Les Rédactions en vers du Couronnement de Louis. Ed. Yvan G. Lepage. Textes littéraires français 261. Geneva: Droz, 1978.

De Pange, Maurice Comte. *La Chanson de geste de Garin le Loherain, mise en prose par Philippe de Vigneulles de Metz: Table des chapitres avec reproduction des miniatures d'après le manuscrit appartenant à Monsieur le Comte d'Hunolstein*. Paris: H. Leclerc, 1901.

Les Enfances Vivien. Ed. Alfred Nordfelt. Upsala: Librairie de l'Université; Paris: Librairie Emile Bouillon, 1895.

Floovant. Ed. Frédéric Hewitt. 1938. Geneva: Slatkine Reprints, 1973.

Garin le Loheren, according to Manuscript A, with Text, Introduction and Linguistic Study. Ed. Josephine E. Vallerie. Diss. Columbia University, 1947. Ann Arbor: Edwards Bros., 1947.

Garin le Lorrain: Chanson de geste du XIIe siècle. Trans. Bernard Guidot. Nancy: Presses Universitaires de Nancy, Editions serpenoise, 1986.
Gerbert: Chanson de geste du XIIIe siècle. Trans. Bernard Guidot. Nancy: Presses Universitaires de Nancy, 1988.
Gerbert de Mez: Chanson de geste du XIIe siècle. Ed. Pauline Taylor. Bibliothèque de la Faculté de Philosophie et de Lettres de Namur 11. Namur, Lille, Louvain: Nauwelaerts, 1952.
Guillaume le Clerc. *The Romance of Fergus.* Ed. Wilson Frescoln. Philadelphia: William H. Allen, 1983.
Hervis de Metz: Roman du moyen âge adapté par Philippe Walter. Trans. Philippe Walter. Metz: Editions Serpenoise; Nancy: Presses universitaires de Nancy, 1984.
Hervis von Metz: Vorgedicht der Lothringer Geste nach allen Handschriften zum erstenmal vollständig herausgegeben. Ed. Edmund Stengel. Gesellschaft für romanische Literatur 1. Dresden: Niemeyer, 1903.
Huon de Bordeaux. Ed. Pierre Ruelle. Travaux de la Faculté de Philosophie et Lettres 20. Paris: Presses universitaires de France; Bruxelles: Université Libre de Bruxelles, 1960.
Marie de France. *Lais.* Ed. Alfred Ewert. Oxford: Basil Blackwell, 1976.
La Mort de Garin le Loherain: Poème du XIIe siècle, publié pour la première fois, d'après douze manuscrits. Ed. Edélestand Du Méril. Romans des douze pairs de France 10. 1846. Geneva: Slatkine Reprints, 1969.
Pamfilova, X. "Fragments de manuscrits de chansons de geste." *Romania* 57 (1931): 504-547. Ms. **Em** of *Hervis de Mes* 539-46.
Philippe de Vigneulles. *La Chronique de Philippe de Vigneulles.* Ed. Charles Bruneau. 4 vols. Metz: Société d'histoire et d'archéologie de la Lorraine, 1927.
La Queste del Saint Graal. Ed. Albert Pauphilet. Classiques français du moyen âge 33. Paris: Champion, 1978.
Raoul de Cambrai. Eds. Paul Meyer and Auguste Longnon. Société des anciens textes français 17. Paris: Picard, 1882.
Renart, Jean. *L'Escoufle: Roman d'aventure.* Ed. Franklin Sweetser. Textes littéraires français. Geneva: Droz, 1974.
Renaut de Beaujeu. *Le Bel Inconnu: Roman d'aventure.* Ed. G. Perrie Williams. Classiques français du moyen âge 38. Paris: Champion, 1983.
Richars li biaus: Roman du XIIIe siècle. Ed. Anthony J. Holden. Classiques français du moyen âge 106. Paris: Champion, 1983.
Le Roman d'Alexandre. Eds. E.C. Armstrong, D.L. Buffum, Bateman Edwards, L.F.H. Lowe. Elliott Monographs 37. Princeton: Princeton University Press; Paris: Presses Universitaires de France, 1949.
Li Romans de Garin le Loherain, publié pour la première fois et précédé de l'examen du système de M. Fauriel sur les romans carlovingiens. Ed. Alexis-Paulin Paris. Romans des douze pairs de France 2, 3. Paris: Techener, 1833-35.
Schädel, B. "Bruchstück der Chanson de Hervis." *Jahrbuch für romanische und englische Sprache und Literatur* ns 3 15 (1876): 445-50. Ms. **Da** of *Hervis de Mes* 448-50.
Stengel, Edmund. *Mitteilungen aus französischen Handschriften der Turiner Universitäts-Bibliothek.* Halle: Lippert, 1873.
Villehardouin, Geoffroi de. *La Conquête de Constantinople.* Ed. and trans. Edmond Faral. 2 vols. Classiques français du moyen âge 18. Paris: Belles Lettres, 1938.
Villon, François. *The Poems of François Villon.* Ed. and trans. Galway Kinnell. Boston: Houghton Mifflin, 1977.
Yon or la Venjance Fromondin: A Thirteenth-Century Chanson de Geste of the Loherain Cycle. New York: Publications of the Institute of French Studies, Columbia University, 1935.

II) Secondary Sources

Adler, Alfred. "*Hervis de Mes* and the *Geste des Lorrains*." *Romanic Review* 38 (1947): 289-96.

———. "*Hervis de Mes* and the Matrilineal Nobility of Champagne." *Romanic Review* 37 (1946): 150-61.

———. *Rückzug in epischer Parade: Studien zu Les quatre fils Aymon, La Chevalerie Ogier, Garin le Lorrain, Raoul de Cambrai, Aliscans, Huon de Bordeaux*. Analecta Romanica 11. Frankfurt am Main: Klosterman, 1963.

Altman, Charles. "Medieval Narrative vs. Modern Assumptions: Revising Inadequate Typology." *Diacritics* 4 (1974): 12-19.

Baumgartner, Emmanuèle. "Texte de prologue et statut du texte." *Essor et fortune de la chanson de geste dans l'Europe et l'Orient latin*. Actes du IXe congrès de la Société Rencesvals. Vol. 2. Modena: Mucchi, 1984.

Barthes, Roland. *S/Z*. Paris: Seuil, 1970.

Bédier, Joseph. *Les Légendes épiques: Recherches sur la formation des chansons de geste*. 4 vols. 2nd ed. Paris: Champion, 1914-21.

Bélanger, Joseph L. *Damedieus: The Religious Context of the French Epic. The Loherain Cycle viewed against Other Early French Epics*. Geneva: Droz, 1975.

Benary, Walther. "*Hervis von Metz* und die Sage vom dankbaren Toten." *Zeitschrift für romanische Philologie* 37 (1913): 57-92, 128-44.

Bloch, R. Howard. *Etymologies and Genealogies: A Literary Anthropology of the French Middle Ages*. Chicago and London: University of Chicago Press, 1983.

Bonnardot, François. "Essai de classement des manuscrits des Loherains, suivi d'un nouveau fragment de *Girbert de Metz*." *Romania* 3 (1874): 195-262.

Boogaard, Nico van den. "Le caractère oral de la chanson de geste tardive." *Langue et littérature françaises du moyen âge: Etudes réunies par R.E.V. Stuip*. Assen: Van Gorcum, 1978.

Boutet, Dominique. *Jehan de Lanson: Technique et esthétique de la chanson de geste au XIIIe siècle*. Paris: PENS, 1988.

Bowman, Russell Keith. *The Connections of the Geste des Loherains with other French Epics and Mediaeval Genres*. Diss. Columbia University 1940. New York: Columbia University Press, 1940.

Braet, Herman. *Le Songe dans la chanson de geste au XIIe siècle*. Romanica Gandensia 15. Ghent: University of Ghent, 1975.

Buschinger, Danielle. "L'image du marchand dans les romans de Tristan en France et en Allemagne." *Tristania* 10 (1984-85): 43-51.

Calin, William. *The Epic Quest: Studies in Four Old French "Chansons de geste"*. Baltimore: Johns Hopkins Press, 1966.

———. "Rapport introductif." *Essor et fortune de la chanson de geste dans l'Europe et l'Orient latin*. Actes du IXe congrès international de la Société Rencesvals. Vol. 2. Modena: Mucchi, 1984. 407-24.

———. "Textes médiévaux et tradition: la chanson de geste est-elle une épopée?" *Romance Epic: Essays on a Medieval Literary Genre*. Ed. Hans-Erich Keller. Studies in Medieval Culture 24. Kalamazoo: Medieval Institute Publications, 1987. 11-19.

Calin, William and Joseph J. Duggan. "Un Débat sur l'épopée vivante." *Olifant* 8 (1980-81).

Combarieu (du Grès), Micheline de. "Image et représentation du 'vilain' dans les chansons de geste (et dans quelques autres textes médiévaux)." *Exclus et systèmes d'exclusion dans la littérature et la civilisation médiévales. Senefiance 5*. Edition CUER MA. Paris: Champion, 1978. 9-26.

Combarieu (du Grès), Micheline de. *L'idéal humain et l'expérience morale chez les héros des chansons de geste des origines à 1250.* 2 vols. Etudes littéraires 3. Aix-en-Provence: Publications de l'Université de Provence; Diffusion Paris: Champion, 1979.

Comfort, W. W. "The Essential Difference Between a *Chanson de Geste* and a *Roman d'Aventure.*" *PMLA* 19 (1904): 64-74.

Cook, Robert Francis. "'Méchants romans et Epopée française: Pour une philologie profonde." *Esprit Créateur* 23 (1983): 64-74.

———. "Unity and Esthetics of the Late *Chansons de geste.*" *Olifant* 11 (1986): 103-114.

Crist, Larry S. "Deep Structures in the *Chansons de geste*: Hypotheses for a Taxonomy." *Olifant* 3 (1975): 3-35.

Culler, Jonathan. *Structuralist Poetics: Structuralism, Linguistics, and the Study of Literature.* New York: Cornell University Press, 1975.

Dembowski, Peter. "Monologue, Author's Monologue and Related Problems in the Romances of Chrétien de Troyes." *Approaches to Medieval Romance.* Yale French Studies 51 (1974): 102-114.

Dorfman, Eugene. *The Narreme in the Medieval Romance Epic: An Introduction to Narrative Structures.* University of Toronto Romance Series 13. Toronto: University of Toronto Press, 1969.

Doutrepont, Georges. *Les Mises en prose des Epopées et des romans chevaleresques du XIVe au XVIe siècles.* Brussels: Palais des académies, 1939.

Duggan, Joseph J. "Die zwei 'Epochen' der Chansons de geste." *Epochenschwellen und Epochenstrukturen im Diskurs der Literatur- und Sprachhistorie.* Hans Ulrich Gumbrecht et al., eds. Frankfurt: Suhrkamp, 1985. 389-408.

———. "Medieval Epic as Popular Historiography: Appropriation of Historical Knowledge in the Vernacular Epic." *La Littérature historiographique des origines à 1500.* Grundriss der romanischen Literaturen des Mittelalters 11/1. Heidelberg: Carl Winter, 1986. 285-312.

———. *The Song of Roland: Formulaic Style and Poetic Craft.* Berkeley, Los Angeles, London: University of California Press, 1973.

Eckhardt, Alexandre. "Franco-Hungarica." *Mélanges d'histoire littéraire générale et comparée offerts à Fernand Baldensperger.* 2 vols. Paris: Champion, 1930. 1: 215-24.

Farnsworth, W.O. *Uncle and Nephew in the Old French Chansons de geste.* New York: Columbia University Press, 1913.

Fernández, María Luisa Donaire. "*Enfances Renier*: l'entrelacement, une technique du roman." *Essor et fortune de la chanson de geste dans l'Europe et l'Orient latin.* Actes du IXe congrès de la Société Rencesvals. Vol. 2. Modena: Mucchi, 1984. 489-508.

Ferrante, Joan M. *Woman as Image in Medieval Literature.* New York: Columbia University Press, 1975.

Fleischman, Suzanne. "A Linguistic Perspective on the *Laisses Similaires*: Orality and the Pragmatics of Narrative Discourse." *Romance Philology* 43 (1989): 70-89.

Foulet, Alfred, and Mary Blakely Speer. *On Editing Old French Texts.* Lawrence: The Regents Press of Kansas, 1979.

Frappier, Jean. *Les Chansons de geste du cycle de Guillaume d'Orange.* 3 vols. Paris: Société d'édition d'enseignement supérieur, 1955-83.

———. *Chrétien de Troyes: L'homme et l'oeuvre.* Paris: Hatier, 1957.

———. "Réflexions sur les rapports des *chansons de geste* et de l'histoire." *Zeitschrift für romanische Philologie* 63 (1957): 1-19.

———. "Structure et sens du *Tristan*: version commune, version courtoise." *Cahiers de civilisation médiévale* 6 (1963): 255-80.

Gautier, Léon. *Les Epopées françaises: Etudes sur les origines et l'histoire de la littérature nationale.* 3 vols. Paris: Victor Palmé, 1865-68.

Geertz, Clifford. *The Interpretation of Cultures.* New York: Basic Books, 1973.

Genette, Gérard. *Figures II.* Collection "Tel Quel." Paris: Seuil, 1969.

———. *Figures III.* Collection Poétique. Paris: Seuil, 1972.

———. *Palimpsestes: La Littérature au second degré.* Collection Poétique. Paris: Seuil, 1982.

Gittleman, Anne Iker. *Le Style épique dans Garin le Loherain.* Publications romanes et françaises 94. Geneva: Droz, 1967.

Godefroy, Frédéric Eugène. *Dictionnaire de l'ancienne langue française.* 10 vols. Paris: F. Vieweg, 1881-1969.

Green, D.H. "Orality and Reading: The State of Research in Medieval Studies." *Speculum* 65 (1990): 267-80.

Grigsby, John L. "The Ontology of the Narrator in Medieval French Romance." *The Nature of Medieval Narrative.* Eds. Minnette Grunmann-Gaudet and Robin F. Jones. Lexington: French Forum, 1980.

Grisward, Joël. "Essai sur *Garin le Loherain*: Structure et sens du prologue." *Romania* 88 (1967): 289-322.

———. Review of *Rückzug in epischer Parade* by Alfred Adler. *Cahiers de civilisation médiévale* 7.4 (1964): 497-504.

Grunmann-Gaudet, Minnette. "From Epic to Romance: The Paralysis of the Hero in the *Prise d'Orange*." *Olifant* 7 (1979): 22-30.

Guidot, Bernard. "Continuité et rupture: L'univers épique de *Garin le Lorrain* et *Gerbert*." *Olifant* 13 (1988): 123-40.

———. "La partialité du trouvère est-elle discrètement infléchie dans *Garin le Loherain?*" *Au Carrefour des routes d'Europe: La Chanson de geste.* Actes du Xe Congrès International Rencesvals. Vol. 1. Aix-en-Provence: CUERMA, 1987. 601-27.

———. *Recherches sur la chanson de geste au XIIIe siècle d'après certaines oeuvres du Cycle de Guillaume d'Orange.* 2 vols. Aix-en-Provence: Université de Provence, 1986.

Heinemann, Edward A. "'Composite Laisse' and Echo as Organizing Principles: The Case of Laisse 1 of the *Charroi de Nîmes*." *Romance Philology* 37 (1983): 127-38.

———. "Composition stylisée et technique littéraire dans la *Chanson de Roland*." *Romania* 94 (1973): 1-28.

———. "Network of Narrative Details: The Motif of the Journey in the *Chanson de geste*." *The Epic in Medieval Society.* Ed. Harald Scholler. Tubingen: Max Niemeyer, 1977. 178-92.

Hub, Heinrich. *La Chanson de Hervis de Metz.* Heilbronn, 1879.

Huet, Gédéon. "Le Retour merveilleux du mari." *Revue des traditions populaires* 32 (1917): 97-109, 145-63.

Iser, Wolfgang. *The Act of Reading: A Theory of Aesthetic Response.* Baltimore and London: Johns Hopkins Press, 1978.

Jauss, Hans-Robert. "The Alterity and Modernity of Medieval Literature." *New Literary History* 10 (1978-79): 181-227.

———. "Chanson de geste et roman courtois." *Chanson de geste und höfischer Roman.* Heidelberger Kolloquium 1961. Studia Romanica 4. Heidelberg: Carl Winter, 1963.

———. *Toward an Aesthetic of Reception.* Trans. Timothy Bahti. Theory and History of Literature 2. Minneapolis: University of Minnesota Press, 1982.

Jones, Catherine M. "Dispersed Parallelism in *Hervis de Mes*." *Olifant* 13 (1988): 29-40.

Jones, Catherine M. "Identity and Disguise in a Late French Epic: *Hervis de Mes.*" *Essays in Medieval Studies.* Proceedings of the Illinois Medieval Association 4. 107-17.

———. "Recasting *Raoul de Cambrai*: The Loherain Version." *Olifant* 14 (1989): 1-18.

———. "'La Tresse': Interlace in the *chanson de geste.*" *French Forum* 15.3 (1990): 261-75.

Jordan, Leo. "Die Quelle des *Hervis von Metz.*" *Archiv für das Studium der neueren Sprachen und Literaturen* 114 (1905): 432-40.

Keller, Hans-Erich. "Changes in Old French Epic Poetry and Changes in the Taste of its Audience." *The Epic in Medieval Society.* Ed. Harald Scholler. Tubingen: Max Niemeyer, 1977. 150-77.

Kelly, Douglas. "Chrétien de Troyes: The Narrator and His Art." *The Romances of Chrétien de Troyes: A Symposium.* Ed. Douglas Kelly. Lexington: French Forum, 1985.

———. "Topical Invention in Medieval French Literature." *Medieval Eloquence: Studies in the Theory and Practice of Medieval Rhetoric.* Ed. James J. Murphy. Berkeley: University of California Press, 1978.

Ker, William P. *Epic and Romance: Essays on Medieval Literature.* 1897. New York: Dover Publications, 1957.

Kibler, William W. "La Chanson d'aventures." *Essor et fortune de la chanson de geste dans l'Europe et l'Orient latin.* Actes du IXe congrès international de la Société Rencesvals. Vol. 2. Modena: Mucchi, 1984. 501-15.

———. "Relectures de l'épopée." *Au Carrefour des routes d'Europe: la chanson de geste.* Actes du Xe congrès de la Société Rencesvals. Vol. 1. Aix-en-Provence: CUER MA, 1987. 103-40.

Köhler, Erich. *L'Aventure chevaleresque: Idéal et réalité dans le roman courtois.* Trans. Eliane Kaufholz. Paris: Gallimard, 1970.

———. "Quelques Observations d'ordre historico-sociologique sur les rapports entre la chanson de geste et le roman courtois." *Chanson de geste und höfischer Roman.* Heidelberger Kolloquium 1961. Heidelberg: Carl Winter, 1963.

Kristeva, Julia. "L'engendrement de la formule." *Recherches pour une sémanalyse.* Collection Tel Quel. Paris: Seuil, 1969.

———. *Le Texte du roman: Approche sémiologique d'une structure discursive transformationnelle.* Le Hague: Mouton, 1970.

Lacy, Norris J. "Spatial Form in Medieval Romance." *Yale French Studies* 51 (1974): 160-69.

———. "Spatial Form in the *Mort Artu.*" *Symposium* 31 (1977): 337-45.

Le Goff, Jacques. *La Civilisation de l'Occident médiéval.* Paris: Gallimard, 1984.

Lévi-Strauss, Claude. *Anthropologie Structurale.* 2 vols. Paris: Plon, 1958, 1973.

Lot, Ferdinand. "L'élément historique de *Garin le Loherain.*" *Etudes d'histoire du Moyen Age dédiées à Gabriel Monod.* Paris: Cerf, 1896. 201-20.

———. *Etude sur le Lancelot en prose.* 2nd ed. Paris: Champion, 1918.

Lyons, Faith. *Les Eléments descriptifs dans les romans d'aventure au XIIIe siècle.* Geneva: Droz, 1965.

Madelénat, Daniel. *L'Epopée.* Littératures modernes. Paris: PUF, 1986.

MacInnes, John W. "Gloriette: The Function of the Tower and the Name in the *Prise d'Orange.*" *Olifant* 10 (1982-83): 24-40.

Maddox, Donald. "Les Figures romanesques du discours épique et la confluence générique." *Essor et fortune de la chanson de geste dans l'Europe et l'Orient latin.* Actes du IXe congrès international de la Société Rencesvals. Vol. 2. Modena: Mucchi, 1984. 517-27.

Martin, Jean-Pierre. "Sur le jeu des motifs dans *Garin le Loheren*: Une Narration plurilinéaire." *Revue des langues romanes* 91 (1987): 81-90.

Matarasso, Pauline. *Recherches historiques et littéraires sur "Raoul de Cambrai."* Paris: Nizet, 1962.

Ménard, Philippe. "'Berte au grant pié, Bietris, Alis' ou la résurgence de la culture épique dans la 'Ballade des dames du temps jadis.'" *Romania* 102 (1981): 114-29.

Nichols, Stephen G., Jr. "Deeper into History." *Esprit créateur* 23 (1983): 91-102.

———. "Poetic Reality and Historical Illusion in the Old French Epic." *French Review* 43 (1969-70): 23-33.

———. *Romanesque Signs: Early Medieval Narrative and Iconography*. New Haven and London: Yale University Press, 1983.

———. "The Spirit of Truth: Epic Modes in Medieval Literature." *New Literary History* 1 (1969-70): 365-86.

Noiriel, Gérard. "La Chevalerie dans la geste des Lorrains." *Annales de l'Est* 28 (1976): 167-96.

Obergfell, Sandra C. "The Problem of Didacticism in the Romance Epic: *Aiol*." *Olifant* 6 (1978): 21-33.

Paquette, Jean Marcel. "Epopée et roman: Continuité ou discontinuité?" *Etudes littéraires* 4 (1971): 9-38.

Paris, Gaston. "La légende de Pépin le Bref." *Mélanges Julien Havet*. Paris: Leroux, 1895. 603-22.

Paris, Paulin. "Etudes sur les Chansons de geste et sur *Garin le Loherain*." *Le Correspondant* 58 (1863): 721-50.

———. "Trouvères, chansons de geste." *Histoire littéraire de la France*. 41 vols. to date, 1733-. Vol. 22. Paris: Didot, 1852. 587-643.

———. "Trouvères – Les Lorrains." *Histoire littéraire de la France*. Vol. 22. Paris: Didot, 1852. 755.

Parmly, Ruth. *The Geographical References in Garin le Loherain*. New York: Publications of the Institute of French Studies, Columbia University, 1935.

Parry, Milman. "Studies in the Epic Technique of Oral Verse-Making. I. Homer and Homeric Style." *Harvard Studies in Classical Philology* 41 (1930): 73-147.

Pickens, Rupert T. "Comedy, History, and Jongleur Art in the *Couronnement de Louis*." *Olifant* 11 (1986): 205-18.

Poirion, Daniel. "Chanson de geste ou épopée? Remarques sur la définition d'un genre." *Travaux de Linguistique et de Littérature*. Strasbourg: Centre de Philologie et de Litteratures Romanes, 1972. 7-20.

———. "Literary Meaning in the Middle Ages: From a Sociology of Genres to an Anthropology of Works." *New Literary History* 10 (1978-79): 401-08.

———. Préface, *Hervis de Metz: Roman du moyen age adapté par Philippe Walter*. Metz: Editions Serpenoise; Nancy: Presses universitaires de Nancy, 1984. 5-9.

Pollmann, Leo. "Von der Chanson de geste zum höfischen Roman in Frankreich." *Germanisch-Romanische Monatsschrift* ns 16 (1966): 1-14.

Prost, Auguste. *Etudes sur l'histoire de Metz: Les Légendes*. Metz: 1865.

———. "Die Beziehungen zwischen den Chansons de Geste *Hervis de Mes* und *Garin le Loherain*." *Ausgaben und Abhandlungen* 3 (1881): 121-70.

Riquer, Martin de. "Epopée jongleresque à écouter et épopée romanesque à lire." *Technique littéraire des chansons de geste*. Actes du Colloque de Liège 1957. Paris: Belles lettres, 1959. 75-84.

Rossi, Marguerite. *Huon de Bordeaux et l'évolution du genre épique au XIIIe siècle*. Nouvelle Bibliothèque du Moyen Age 2. Paris: Champion, 1975.

———. "Les séquences narratives stéréotypées: Un aspect de la technique épique." *Mélanges de langue et de littérature françaises du Moyen Age offerts à Pierre Jonin*. Paris: Champion, 1979. 593-607.

Rychner, Jean. *La Chanson de geste: Essai sur l'art épique des jongleurs.* Société de publications romanes et françaises 53. Geneva: Droz, 1955.
Ryding, William. *Structure in Medieval Narrative.* Paris and Le Hague: Mouton, 1971.
Schilperoort, Gijsbert. *Le commerçant dans la littérature française du moyen âge: Caractère, vie, position sociale.* Groningen, Den Haag, Batavia: J.B. Wolters, 1933.
Schurfranz, Barbara D. "Strophic Structure versus Alternative Divisions in the *Prise d'Orange.*" *Romance Philology* 33 (1979): 247-64.
Suard, François. *Guillaume d'Orange: Etude du roman en prose.* Paris: Champion, 1979.
Subrenat, Jean. *Etude sur Gaydon, chanson de geste du XIIIe siècle.* Aix-en-Provence: Université de Provence, 1974.
Tobler, Adolf and Erhard Lommatzsch. *Altfranzösisches Wörterbuch.* 10 vols. to date. Berlin: Weidmann, 1925-.
Todorov, Tzvetan. *Littérature et signification.* Langue et Langage. Paris: Larousse, 1962.
―――. *Mikhail Bakhtin: The Dialogical Principle.* Trans. Wlad Godzich. Theory and History of Literature 13. Minneapolis: University of Minnesota Press, 1984.
―――. *Qu'est-ce que le structuralisme?* Collection Poétique. Paris: Seuil, 1968.
Uitti, Karl D. *Story, Myth, and Celebration in Old French Narrative Poetry 1050-1250.* Princeton: Princeton University Press, 1973.
Vance, Eugene. *Mervelous Signals: Poetics and Sign Theory in the Middle Ages.* Lincoln and London: University of Nebraska Press, 1986.
―――. *Reading the Song of Roland.* Landmarks in Literature. Englewood Cliffs: Prentice-Hall, 1970.
Van Emden, W.G. "Contribution à l'étude de l'évolution sémantique du mot 'geste' en ancien français." *Romania* 96 (1975): 105-22.
Van Nuffel, P. "Problèmes de sémiotique interprétative: L'épopée." *Lettres romanes* 27 (1973): 150-62.
Vansina, Jan. *De la Tradition orale: Essai de méthode historique.* Tervuren: Musée royale de l'Afrique Centrale, 1961.
Vietor, Wilhelm. *Die Handschriften der Geste des Loherains.* Halle: Niemeyer, 1876.
Vinaver, Eugène. *A la Recherche d'une poétique médiévale.* Paris: Nizet, 1970.
―――. *The Rise of Romance.* Oxford: Clarendon Press, 1971.
Von Wartburg, Walther. *Französisches etymologisches Wörterbuch.* 25 vols to date. Bonn: F. Klopp, 1928-.
Walter, Philippe. "Géographie et géopolitique dans la légende d'*Hervis de Metz.*" *Olifant* 13 (1988): 141-63.
―――. "*Hervis de Metz*: le griffon et la 'fée'." *Vox romanica* 45 (1986): 157-67.
Windelberg, Marjorie and D. Gary Miller. "How (Not) to Define the Epic Formula." *Olifant* 8 (1980): 29-50.
Woledge, Brian. *Bibliographie des romans et nouvelles en prose française antérieurs à 1500.* Geneva: Droz, 1954.
Woods, Ellen Rose. *Aye d'Avignon: A Study of Genre and Society.* Histoire des idées et critique littéraire 172. Geneva: Droz, 1978.
Zumthor, Paul. *Essai de poétique médiévale.* Collection Poétique. Paris: Seuil, 1972.
―――. *La Lettre et la voix: De la "littérature" médiévale.* Collection Poétique. Paris: Seuil, 1987.
―――. "Y a-t-il une 'littérature' médiévale?" *Poétique* 66 (1986): 131-39.

INDEX

Adler, Alfred, 21, 85
Aelis, 21, 77-78, 92
Aiol, 83n
Altman, Charles, 22, 71n
Ami et Amile, 73
Anseÿs de Cologne, 35, 38, 40, 60-61, 76-78, 156
Anseÿs de Mes, 14
Aucassin et Nicolette, 71n, 73
Aye d'Avignon, 33, 40

Barthes, Roland, 79n
Baumgartner, Emmanuèle, 20n, 135
Béroul, 47
Biatris, 46-56, 74, 85-86, 87, 112, 115, 126, 148; abduction of, 31, 42, 66, 76, 91, 149; and embroidered cloth, 43-44, 79, 108; and matrilineal nobility, 21, 54; monologues of, 143-45; narrative perspective of, 146-47; as object of dispute, 46, 77; purchase of, 103; sources of, 37
Bloch, R. Howard, 21, 79, 80
Bodel, Jehan, 34, 36, 151
Boethius, 138
Boogard, Nico van den, 154
Buschinger, Danielle, 80

Calin, William, 34n
Chanson de geste: and history, 34-35; kinship patterns in, 56-58. *See also Chanson de geste* vs. romance
Chanson de geste vs. romance, 18-20; diegetic world of, 61-67; love in, 46-56; *merveilleux* in, 59-60; narration in, 135-40; narrative events in, 40-46; narrative repertory of, 33-34; "realism" in, 65; secondary characters in, 56-61; women in, 46-56

Chanson de Guillaume, 18, 47, 55
Chanson de Roland: mentioned, 18, 22, 35, 39, 44, 46, 53, 56, 58, 59, 60, 61, 67, 70, 74, 93, 97, 99, 101, 105, 113, 119, 120, 127, 141, 142, 150
Chanson de toile, 37
Chanson des Saisnes, 34
Charroi de Nîmes, 41
Chrétien de Troyes, 42; *Chevalier de la charrete*, 52, 54; *Chevalier au lion*, 42-43, 51; *Erec et Enide*, 47, 126; *Perceval*, 73
Combarieu du Grès, Micheline de, 52
Comfort, William, 47
Cook, Robert F., 22
Couronnement de Louis, 59, 60, 70, 71 and n, 72, 75, 82, 101, 105, 113

Duggan, Joseph, 103n

Eckhardt, Alexander, 35
Enfances Vivien, 16, 83n, 131
Epic. *See Chanson de geste* and *Chanson de geste* vs. romance
Escoufle, 44, 47, 48, 53, 82

Fairs, 58, 84-87, 111-16, 128-32, 146, 148, 150
Fergus, 16, 57
Fernández, María L. D., 71
Ferrante, Joan, 48n
Fin'amors, 47, 51, 53
Floire, King of Hungary, 31, 61, 66, 89-90, 114, 150
Floire et Blancheflor, 42
Floovant, 33
Formula: definition of, 122-23
Formulaic style, 95, 121-23
Frappier, Jean, 47

Garin le Loherain: as historical figure, 36
Garin le Loherain: assonance in, 110; conflict in, 41, 92-93; as early epic, 16, 18, 40, 59, 67; Hervis in, 15, 48-49, 149; and history, 35; lines per laisse in, 101, 119; motifs in, 133; place in cycle, 13-14, 27-28; structural alternation in, 72n, 75; truth assertions in, 37; women in, 47
Gautier d'Arras, 65
Gautier, Léon, 16
Genette, Gérard, 103, 135
Genre: theories of, 17-18, 33-34
Gerbert de Mez, 14, 15-16n, 110
Geste des Loherains: branches, 13-15; feudal conflict in, 46, 93, 133; geographical precision of, 62, 150; and history, 35
Gormont et Isembart, 46
Grateful Dead, legend of, 84-86, 89
Grisward, Joël, 19n, 21
Grouchy, Jehan de, 151

Heinemann, Edward A., 121
Hervis de Mes: historical antecedent of, 35
Hervis de Mes: assonance in, 110, 130; diegetic world of, 61-67; formulaic style in, 121-34; genre and lineage in, 21-22, 68-69, 160-61; and ideology, 21, 80-94, 158-59, 160-61; kinship patterns in, 56-58; laisses in, 100-21; love in, 46-56; manuscripts of, 27-29; matter of, 37-40; medieval reception of, 16-17; *merveilleux* in, 43-45, 59-60, 127; narration in, 140-59; narrative events in, 40-46; narrative structure of, 68-80; place in cycle, 15; prologue of, 20, 95; secondary characters in, 56-61; and social reality, 22-23, 93; sources of, 35; summary of, 23-27; temporal structure of, 43; truth assertions in, 37-38
Hinbaut the giant, 43, 60, 63-64, 66, 67, 124, 127
Hub, Heinrich, 29, 116
Huon de Bordeaux, 33, 40, 64, 126, 152

Interlace, 70-73, 79-80

Jauss, Hans-Robert, 17-19, 33, 34n, 42, 61, 98n, 138

Jongleur, 31-32, 51, 76, 95, 106-7, 121, 138-40, 150-59
Jordan, Leo, 86

Kelly, Douglas, 36n
Ker, W. P., 16
Köhler, Erich, 63-64

Lacy, Norris J., 70n, 74
Laisses: bifurcated, 99, 106; "compression" in, 105-10, 118; "dispersed" parallelism in, 110-18; *enchaînement* of, 99, 102-4, 119; lines per, 101, 118, 168-71; parallel, 99, 104, 108, 109, 113, 116; similar, 99; structure of, 95, 98-100
Lévi-Strauss, Claude, 93n
Loherain cycle. *See Geste des Loherains*
Lot, Ferdinand, 35, 38, 70-71

Madelénat, Daniel, 18
Marie de France: "*Laüstic,*" 44; "*Yonec,*" 144
Martin, Jean-Pierre, 72n
Matrilineal nobility, 21
Ménard, Philippe, 16-17, 49
Metz, 46, 62, 150, 157-58
Motifs, 121; "compression" of, 124-25; displacement of, 127-28; fabricated, 128-32; fragmentation of, 125, 127; list of, 172-73

Nichols, Stephen G., 61
Noiriel, Gérard, 45

Paris, Paulin, 68
Pickens, Rupert, 113
Pierre, duke of Metz, 40-41, 45, 67, 81, 83-84, 88, 102
Plato, 136
Poirion, Daniel, 53, 100, 141
Prise d'Orange, 47, 88-89
Prost, Auguste, 21, 28

Queste del Saint Graal, 54, 71, 72

Raoul de Cambrai, 39, 59
Renart, Jean, 44, 65
Resemblance, 87-88, 92
Rhode, August, 15n
Roman de la Rose, 80
Romance. *See Chanson de geste* vs. romance

Rossi, Marguerite, 18, 111n, 126
Rychner, Jean, 69, 97, 99, 105, 120, 121
Ryding, William, 71n

Somnium, 91
Stengel, Edmund, 19, 65n, 110
Structuralist theory, 70, 135-37

Testament, 16-17
Thieri, father of Hervis, 57, 81-84, 86-87, 90, 102, 108, 141-42, 146
Todorov, Tzvetan, 70
Tournament of Senlis, 58, 88, 116-18, 160
Tresse, as metatextual term, 31-32, 76, 79-80

Tristan, 47

Vance, Eugene, 51
Van Nuffel, P., 93
Venjance Fromondin, la, 14
Vigneulles, Philippe de, 17, 28, 36, 38, 49
Villon, François, 16-17

Walter, Philippe, 21, 28, 37, 62

Yon. See *Venjance Fromondin, la*

Zumthor, Paul, 22, 23, 63, 137, 152, 159

NORTH CAROLINA STUDIES IN THE ROMANCE LANGUAGES AND LITERATURES

I.S.B.N. Prefix 0-8078-

Recent Titles

"LA QUERELLE DE LA ROSE": Letters and Documents, by Joseph L. Baird and John R. Kane. 1978. (No. 199). -9199-1.
TWO AGAINST TIME. A Study of the Very Present Worlds of Paul Claudel and Charles Péguy, by Joy Nachod Humes. 1978. (No. 200). -9200-9.
TECHNIQUES OF IRONY IN ANATOLE FRANCE. Essay on Les Sept Femmes de la Barbe-Bleue, by Diane Wolfe Levy. 1978. (No. 201). -9201-7.
THE PERIPHRASTIC FUTURES FORMED BY THE ROMANCE REFLEXES OF "VADO (AD)" PLUS INFINITIVE, by James Joseph Champion. 1978. (No. 202). -9202-S.
THE EVOLUTION OF THE LATIN /b/-/u/ MERGER: A Quantitative and Comparative Analysis of the B-V Alternation in Latin inscriptions, by Joseph Louis Barbarino. 1978. (No. 203). -9203-3.
METAPHORIC NARRATION: THE STRUCTURE AND FUNCTION OF METAPHORS IN "A LA RECHERCHE DU TEMPS PERDU", by Inge Karalus Crosman. 1978. (No. 204). -9204-1.
LE VAIN SIECLE GUERPIR. A Literary Approach to Sainthood through Old French Hagiography of the Twelfth Century, by Phyllis Johnson and Brigitte Cazelles. 1979. (No. 205). -9205-X.
THE POETRY OF CHANGE: A STUDY OF THE SURREALIST WORKS OF BENJAMIN PÉRET, by Julia Field Costich. 1979. (No. 206). -9206-8.
NARRATIVE PERSPECTIVE IN THE POST-CIVIL WAR NOVELS OF FRANCISCO AYALA "MUERTES DE PERRO" AND "EL FONDO DEL VASO", by Maryellen Bieder. 1979. (No. 207). -9207-6.
RABELAIS: HOMO LOGOS, by Alice Fiola Berry. 1979. (No. 208). -9208-4.
"DUEÑAS" AND DONCELLAS": A STUDY OF THE DOÑA RODRÍGUEZ EPISODE IN "DON QUIJOTE", by Conchita Herdman Marianella. 1979. (No. 209). -9209-2.
PIERRE BOAISTUAU'S "HISTOIRES TRAGIQUES": A STUDY OF NARRATIVE FORM AND TRAGIC VISION, by Richard A. Carr. 1979. (No. 210). -9210-6.
REALITY AND EXPRESSION IN THE POETRY OF CARLOS PELLICER, by George Melnykovich. 1979. (No. 211). -9211-4.
MEDIEVAL MAN, HIS UNDERSTANDING OF HIMSELF, HIS SOCIETY, AND THE WORLD, by Urban T. Holmes, Jr. 1980. (No. 212). -9212-2.
MÉMOIRES SUR LA LIBRAIRIE ET SUR LA LIBERTÉ DE LA PRESSE, introduction and notes by Graham E. Rodmell. 1979. (No. 213). -9213-0.
THE FICTIONS OF THE SELF. THE EARLY WORKS OF MAURICE BARRES, by Gordon Shenton. 1979. (No. 214). -9214-9.
CECCO ANGIOLIERI. A STUDY, by Gifford P. Orwen. 1979. (No. 215). -9215-7.
THE INSTRUCTIONS OF SAINT LOUIS: A CRITICAL TEXT, by David O'Connell. 1979. (No. 216). -9216-5.
ARTFUL ELOQUENCE, JEAN LEMAIRE DE BELGES AND THE RHETORICAL TRADITION, by Michael F. O. Jenkins. 1980. (No. 217). -9217-3.
A CONCORDANCE TO MARIVAUX'S COMEDIES IN PROSE, edited by Donald C. Spinelli. 1979. (No. 218). 4 volumes, -9218-1 (set), -9219-X (v. 1), -9220-3 (v. 2); -9221-1 (v. 3); -9222-X (v. 4).
ABYSMAL GAMES IN THE NOVELS OF SAMUEL BECKETT, by Angela B. Moorjani. 1982. (No. 219). -9223-8.
GERMAIN NOUVEAU DIT HUMILIS: ÉTUDE BIOGRAPHIQUE, par Alexandre L. Amprimoz. 1983. (No. 220). -9224-6.
THE "VIE DE SAINT ALEXIS" IN THE TWELFTH AND THIRTEENTH CENTURIES: AN EDITION AND COMMENTARY, by Alison Goddard Elliot. 1983. (No. 221). -9225-4.

When ordering please cite the *ISBN Prefix* plus the last four digits for each title.

Send orders to: University of North Carolina Press
P.O. Box 2288
CB# 6215
Chapel Hill, NC 27515-2288
U.S.A.

NORTH CAROLINA STUDIES IN THE ROMANCE LANGUAGES AND LITERATURES

I.S.B.N. Prefix 0-8078-

Recent Titles

THE BROKEN ANGEL: MYTH AND METHOD IN VALÉRY, by Ursula Franklin. 1984. (No. 222). -9226-2.
READING VOLTAIRE'S CONTES: A SEMIOTICS OF PHILOSOPHICAL NARRATION, by Carol Sherman. 1985. (No. 223). -9227-0.
THE STATUS OF THE READING SUBJECT IN THE "LIBRO DE BUEN AMOR", by Marina Scordilis Brownlee. 1985. (No. 224). -9228-9.
MARTORELL'S TIRANT LO BLANCH: A PROGRAM FOR MILITARY AND SOCIAL REFORM IN FIFTEENTH-CENTURY CHRISTENDOM, by Edward T. Aylward. 1985. (No. 225). -9229-7.
NOVEL LIVES: THE FICTIONAL AUTOBIOGRAPHIES OF GUILLERMO CABRERA INFANTE AND MARIO VARGAS LLOSA, by Rosemary Geisdorfer Feal. 1986. (No. 226). -9230-0.
SOCIAL REALISM IN THE ARGENTINE NARRATIVE, by David William Foster. 1986. (No. 227). -9231-9.
HALF-TOLD TALES: DILEMMAS OF MEANING IN THREE FRENCH NOVELS, by Philip Stewart. 1987. (No. 228). -9232-7.
POLITIQUES DE L'ECRITURE BATAILLE/DERRIDA: le sens du sacré dans la pensée française du surréalisme à nos jours, par Jean-Michel Heimonet. 1987. (No. 229). -9233-5.
GOD, THE QUEST, THE HERO: THEMATIC STRUCTURES IN BECKETT'S FICTION, by Laura Barge. 1988. (No. 230). -9235-1.
THE NAME GAME. WRITING/FADING WRITER IN "DE DONDE SON LOS CANTANTES", by Oscar Montero. 1988. (No. 231). -9236-X.
GIL VICENTE AND THE DEVELOPMENT OF THE COMEDIA, by René Pedro Garay. 1988. (No. 232). -9234-3.
HACIA UNA POÉTICA DEL RELATO DIDÁCTICO: OCHO ESTUDIOS SOBRE "EL CONDE LUCANOR", por Aníbal A. Biglieri. 1989. (No. 233). -9237-8.
A POETICS OF ART CRITICISM: THE CASE OF BAUDELAIRE, by Timothy Raser. 1989. (No. 234). -9238-6.
UMA CONCORDÂNCIA DO ROMANCE "GRANDE SERTÃO: VEREDAS" DE JOÃO GUIMARÃES ROSA, by Myriam Ramsey and Paul Dixon. 1989. (No. 235). Microfiche, -9239-4.
CYCLOPEAN SONG: MELANCHOLY AND AESTHETICISM IN GÓNGORA S "FÁBULA DE POLIFEMO Y GALATEA", by Kathleen Hunt Dolan. 1990. (No. 236). -9240-8.
THE "SYNTHESIS" NOVEL IN LATIN AMERICA. A STUDY ON JOÃO GUIMARÃES ROSA'S "GRANDE SERTÃO: VEREDAS", by Eduardo de Faria Coutinho. 1991. (No. 237). -9241-6.
IMPERMANENT STRUCTURES. SEMIOTIC READINGS OF NELSON RODRIGUES' "VESTIDO DE NOIVA", "ÁLBUM DE FAMÍLIA", AND "ANJO NEGRO", by Fred M. Clark. 1991. (No. 238). -9242-4.
"EL ÁNGEL DEL HOGAR". GALDÓS AND THE IDEOLOGY OF DOMESTICITY IN SPAIN, by Bridget A. Aldaraca. 1991. (No. 239). -9243-2.
IN THE PRESENCE OF MYSTERY: MODERNIST FICTION AND THE OCCULT, by Howard M. Fraser. 1992. (No. 240). -9244-0.
THE NOBLE MERCHANT: PROBLEMS OF GENRE AND LINEAGE IN "HERVIS DE MES", by Catherine M. Jones. 1993. (No. 241). -9245-9.
JORGE LUIS BORGES AND HIS PREDECESSORS OR NOTES TOWARDS A MATERIALIST HISTORY OF LINGUISTIC IDEALISM, by Malcolm K. Read. 1993. (No. 242). -9246-7.
DISCOVERING THE COMIC IN "DON QUIXOTE", by Laura J. Gorfkle. 1993. (No. 243). -9247-5.
THE ARCHITECTURE OF IMAGERY IN ALBERTO MORAVIA'S FICTION, by Janice M. Kozma. 1993. (No. 244). -9248-3.
THE "LIBRO DE ALEXANDRE". MEDIEVAL EPIC AND SILVER LATIN, by Charles F. Fraker. 1993. (No. 245). -9249-1.

When ordering please cite the *ISBN Prefix* plus the last four digits for each title.

Send orders to: University of North Carolina Press
                    P.O. Box 2288
                    CB# 6215
                    Chapel Hill, NC 27515-2288
                    U.S.A.

The Department of Romance Studies Digital Arts and Collaboration Lab at the University of North Carolina at Chapel Hill is proud to support the digitization of the North Carolina Studies in the Romance Languages and Literatures series.

www.ingramcontent.com/pod-product-compliance
Lightning Source LLC
Chambersburg PA
CBHW030655230426
43665CB00011B/1102